Anxiety: Hidden Causes

Also by Sharon Heller

*Too Loud, Too Bright, Too Fast, Too Tight: What to do if you
are sensory defensive in an overstimulating world*

*The Vital Touch: How intimate contact with your baby leads
to healthier, happier development*

Anxiety: Hidden Causes

Why your anxiety may not be "all in your head" but from something physical

Sharon Heller, Ph.D.

Symmetry
Delray Beach, Florida

This book is for information only and does not substitute for the qualified advice of a medical professional. Readers should use their own judgment or consult a holistic medical expert or their personal physician for specific care to their individual problems. The author and publisher have exhaustively researched all sources to ensure the accuracy and completeness of the information contained in this book. We assume no responsibilities for errors, inaccuracies, omissions, or inconsistency herein. Any slights of people or organizations are unintentional.

Book cover by Antonio Nogueira (www.antonio.bz)
Cover painting by artist Sharon Heller, www.anya.artspan.com

Printed in the United States of America
1st printing – January 2011

www.sharonheller.net

To my grandfather Benjamin Heller (1894-1962).

When as a child I was forced to swim against a tide of misunderstanding and denial of self, my wise, deep-thinking, grandfather fostered my independent thinking and encouraged me to always express and be true to self. Mining my inner jewels has been and continues to be my life's journey.

Acknowledgements

I wish to express my gratitude to the many anxiety sufferers who shared their stories. Special thanks to occupational therapists Moya Kinnealey and Lucy Jane Miller for their help and guidance in my quest to better understand sensory processing, and to my lifelong friend Donna Harris for her heartfelt involvement and support.

Contents at a Glance

Contents

Part II: Neurological Compromise & Anxiety

Part III: Toxicity & Anxiety

Author Bio

Sharon Heller, Ph.D. is a developmental psychologist, college professor, and author of four popular psychology books, including *Too Loud, Too Bright, Too Fast, Too Tight, What to do if you are sensory defensive in an overstimulating world* (HarperCollins, 2002). She received her master's degree from the University of Chicago and her doctorate from Loyola University of Chicago. She lives in Delray Beach, Florida.

Introduction

★

Anxiety Isn't All in Your Head

Cynthia is terrified of heights. While walking up or downstairs, taking an escalator or walking along a catwalk, she feels vertigo, loss of balance and terror.

Darlene has panic attacks. Suddenly, a wave of panic overcomes her – her heart races, her pulse throbs, the world spins, and she can hardly catch her breath. She feels as if she's dying and losing her mind.

Ronald is afraid of leaving his house. When he does venture out, he often suffers a panic attack. The attacks come out of nowhere – sitting in church, shopping at the supermarket, standing in line at the bank, or driving down the street.

Abdul is constantly tense and nervous. He startles at the slightest noise, jumps at a stranger brushing past him, winces at bright lights and, as the day goes by, feels progressively fatigued and depleted. He worries constantly that he won't make it through the day and meet his family and work obligations.

According to DSM-IV-R of the American Psychiatric Association all these sufferers have an anxiety disorder:

➢ Cynthia is **phobic**. She has an intense, irrational fear that realistically poses no real danger but causes her to panic.
➢ Darlene has **panic disorder**. She feels sudden inexplicable disabling terror, accompanied by racing heart, labored breathing, sweating, dizziness, and other symptoms evoked by the flight/fight response.

➤ Ronald suffers **panic disorder with agoraphobia**. He fears harm if he leaves the safety of his home and often has a panic attack when he does.

➤ Abdul has **generalized anxiety disorder (GAD)**. He feels chronic and exaggerated tension, irritability, restlessness, concentration problems and worry and apprehension over matters most consider routine. As his worries build up, he has an anxiety attack.

In fact, *none have mental illness.*

➤ **Inner ear dysfunction** (which controls balance) triggers Cynthia's height phobia.

➤ **Mitral valve prolapse** (a cardiac disorder) triggers Darlene's panic attack.

➤ **Type two diabetes** (high blood sugar) triggers Ronald's panic.

➤ **Sensory defensiveness** (hypersensitivity to ordinary sensation) triggers Abdul's generalized anxiety.

Anxiety disorders are the number one mental health diagnosis in the United States.

➤ **At** some point in their lifetime, one fourth of the population or some 65 million people will become incapacitated by anxiety, panic, or abnormal fears.

➤ **Some** 13 percent of the general population has reported at least one phobic reaction, the most common anxiety disorder.

➤ **Fifteen** percent will experience panic attack symptoms during their lifetime, a horrifying experience.

➤ **Almost** half of the people who suffer repeated panic attacks develop major depression and 20 percent will attempt suicide.

➤ **Two** and a half million Americans develop obsessive, compulsive disorder, a complicated form of anxiety disorder characterized by uncontrollable, persistent or irrational thoughts and rituals.

Yet, an untold number of anxiety sufferers *may not have any mental illness*. If you are reading this book, there's a good chance you may be one or know someone who is.

ANXIETY SYMPTOMS

PHYSICAL

Muscle Tension
♦ Headache
♦ Lower back pain
♦ Neck, face, jaw pain
♦ Body aches and pains
♦ Trembling, twitching, shaky
♦ Restlessness

Hyperventilation
♦ Dizziness
♦ Faintness
♦ Palpitations

Hyperarousal (flight/fight)
♦ Sweating or cold clammy
  hands
♦ Lightheadedness or dizziness
♦ Pounding heart
♦ Dilated pupils
♦ Upset stomach
♦ Sinking feel in stomach
♦ Dry mouth
♦ Frequent urination,
  defecation
♦ Lump in the throat
♦ Fast pulse
♦ Quick respiration
♦ Hot or cold spells

Arousability
♦ Sleep difficulties
♦ Nightmares
♦ Fatigue
♦ Restlessness

PHYSICAL CONT.

Sensory
♦ Hypersensitivity to light,
  noise, touch, odors, movement

PSYCHOLOGICAL

Feelings
♦ Fear
♦ Irritability
♦ Apprehensive about
  future
♦ Panic

Thinking
♦ Distractibility
♦ Racing thoughts
♦ Poor concentration
♦ Memory problems

Behavior
♦ Hypervigilance
♦ Exaggerated startle
♦ Incessant& rapid speech
♦ Worried expression
♦ Fidgeting
♦ Pacing
♦ Strained facial
  expressions
♦ Furrowed brows
♦ Deep sighs
♦ Trembling
♦ Impotence or frigidity
♦ Sexual acting out
♦ Abusive substances
♦ Obsessions & compulsions

The anxiety symptoms on page three are not specific to anxiety disorders. Any anxiety symptom can indicate a biological problem.

- ➢ **Sugar imbalance** to heart problems to vitamin deficiencies can produce symptoms identical to a panic attack.
- ➢ **Head injuries**, brain tumors, strep throat, and encephalitis can create obsessive-compulsive behavior.
- ➢ **Environmental pollutants** and allergens can produce panic like symptoms.
- ➢ **Sensory defensiveness** (hypersensitivity to sensation) produces generalized anxiety, panic, OCD, and even depersonalization (see my book *Too Loud, Too Bright, Too Fast, Too Tight, What to do if you're sensory defensive in an overstimulating world,* HarperCollins, 2002).
- ➢ **Inner Ear Dysfunction** creates panic attack and space related phobias like fear of heights, flying and enclosed spaces.
- ➢ **Fear of failure**, which appears entirely mental in origin, may emanate from undiagnosed sensorimotor and neurological deficits that impede competency (see my book *Uptight & Off Center,* Symmetry, 2011*)*.

Potential Causes of Psychiatric Symptoms	
◆ Food	◆ Environmental toxicity
◆ Illness	◆ Poor posture
◆ Infection	◆ Neurological problems
◆ Poor sleep	◆ Hyperventilation
◆ Internal toxicity	◆ Psyche

Rampant Misdiagnosis

As demonstrated, most physical distress can fall under anxiety's dismal umbrella yet not one anxiety symptom can be linked *exclusively* to an anxiety disorder. Nevertheless, most people assume that jitteriness, worry, or panic falls within the psyche's realm -- that it results from stress, sensitivity, low self-esteem, a learned fear, poor coping, dependency, negative thinking, or weak character, and as such can be voluntarily controlled. Consequently, if you cannot control your anxiety, you feel weak, damaged, neurotic, and even a bad person. Such self-blame gets easily reinforced by frustrated and generally well-meaning family and friends who advise: "Chill out" or "Don't let everything get to you."

Professional Misinterpretation

Professionals too tend to make the same short-sighted assumption that anxiety is primarily psychological and under voluntary control. Experts in their field often have little information about areas outside of their specialty. Specialists of the mind, like psychiatrists, psychologists, counselors, social workers and mental health workers see behavior primarily from a psychopathology lens. They may be largely unaware that something physical, neurological, structural, sensory, or environmental can produce symptoms that mimic anxiety or panic. Confusing symptoms with cause, they will diagnose patients as anxious or depressed and quickly dispense a tranquilizer or anti-depressant pill and suggest psychotherapy.

Physician Misinterpretation

Primary care physicians, the ones generally in the front line of patient complaints, see the world primarily through an allopathic lens of medical illness. If the cause of something is vague and doesn't show up on standard tests like routine blood work, they tend to assume the patient to be stressed, neurotic, or a hypochondriac and dish out anti-anxiety drugs like candy, and particularly with women. One study found that women seen in the ER for chest pain and palpitations are far more likely then men diagnosed with anxiety and sent home with a prescription for a tranquilizer than to be evaluated for heart disease.

Consequences of Misdiagnosis

Such misdiagnosis and mistreatment of anxiety symptoms can have dire consequences.

Unnecessary Therapy: You may be struggling in psychotherapy that is expensive, time consuming, unnecessary, and completely misses the mark.

Lost Time: Years may go by as drugs, psychotherapy and, often, an endless pursuit of self-help techniques and stress reduction strategies fail to pay off.

Left in the Dark: Invalidated, confused, frustrated and *still anxious*, you feel at a loss. How do you dismantle hurdles if you don't know what they are! Unable to cope successfully with ordinary situations, you may watch your career and personal life fall apart without knowing how to stop the downfall. Despairing of getting better, you become depressed as well as anxious.

Undiagnosed Serious Condition: Worst of all, a serious organic condition such as hypoglycemia, hyperthyroidism, or a brain tumor can progress undetected and worsen.

Pass the Valium

Prevalence of psychiatrists and other medical practitioners who diagnose anxiety disorder for complaints ranging from headaches, backaches, nervousness, insomnia, or panic attacks made Valium the most popular psychiatric drug of the 1970's, and one of the most profitable drugs of all time; in 1988, it was the number-one prescribed medication in the US with $400 million in worldwide sales. Today it has been replaced by Xanax as the premier anti-anxiety medication.

Case Study

Consider Maya. For years, she looked like someone in the war zone: her face was wan and tight, her leg shook as she sat hunched and cross-legged, her eyes darted when you talked to her, and her hands trembled as she endlessly puffed away at a cigarette.

Everything had always seemed to make Maya's heart flutter and her body shake. As a child, she refused to go to children's parties for the bursting balloons. She was excused from going to church as she would frequently faint or become sick during the service. She refused to hang out with the other kids at malls as the barrage of advertisement, noise, and crowds overexcited and upset her.

By adolescence, panic attacks struck without warning and frequently. Out of nowhere, her heart would race, her body would tremble and the room would spin. The first one struck at 15 when she was sitting alone in her room reading. She screamed, "I'm dying!" and her mother rushed her to the emergency room.

Therapeutic Revolving Door

Her life felt a living hell and she contemplated suicide more than once. By her 20's, a psychiatrist diagnosed her with panic disorder and, to help her relax, put her on the tranquilizer Valium. The medication helped somewhat and she became dependent on it, relying on it through her 30's. She then switched to Xanax and soon became dependent on that drug.

From her twenties through her forties, she was continually in and out of individual and group therapy. One psychologist felt her anxiety resulted from maternal rejection and fear of abandonment. This rang true. Maya's conception was accidental and her mother repeatedly told Maya that she had not wanted her; Maya always feared her mother would leave her. Another psychologist identified her anxiety as stemming from a fear of strangers. This rang true also. Her father abandoned the family when she was three. Maya's mother had to work long hours and Maya was cared for by a string of babysitters. Frightened of being left alone with strangers, she would cry and cling to her mother's leg as her mother fled out the door.

Falling Apart

In spite of therapy and drugs, she barely functioned. At work, her heart beat so wildly she could hardly focus on what her clients said. Constantly anxious, shaky, ill-tempered, fatigued, and jumpy during sex, she had little to give a relationship and at age 37 her eight-year marriage had broken up.

Self-Medicating

Maya coped by self-medicating with stimulants, like cocaine and nicotine. And though these substances generally increase panic, they helped drown out Maya's constant excitability. Masturbation helped as a diversion, though sexual intercourse felt overwhelming.

An Answer!

Finally, in her 40's, a physician suspected that Maya's resting pulse of 110, sweats, tremors, fine silky hair, inability to gain weight, and red, itchy eyes indicated hyperthyroidism. Indeed. A thyroid stimulating hormone test revealed elevated thyroid levels. He prescribed Lopressor, a beta blocker to bring her heart rate down. Panic attacks ceased and Maya finally felt normal.

Paying Dearly

The misdiagnosis of Maya's panic as a psychiatric condition and subsequent delay of proper medical treatment cost her dearly. After a year on antithyroid drugs, her thyroid was killed with radioactive iodine treatments. As this immediately creates hypothyroidism, she must be on thyroid replacement therapy for the rest of her life. Panic free, however, she takes no psychotropic medication.

Prevalence of Misdiagnosis

Stories like Maya's are more common than suspected. Dr. Mark Gold, a biopsychiatrist at the University of Florida in Gainesville estimates that over fifty medical conditions can cause prominent anxiety symptoms! One research study found that out of 100 patients at a psychiatric center diagnosed by psychiatrists as suffering mental problems, 46 percent suffered medical problems that caused or contributed to their psychiatric symptoms. When properly diagnosed and treated, 61 percent showed a dramatic clearing of psychiatric symptoms. Had the misdiagnosis not been caught, the authors concluded that all these patients would have been committed to state mental institutions. After reviewing studies such as the above, Joan Rittenhouse of the National Institute of Mental Health concluded that up to 81% of all psychiatric patients, both inpatient and out-patient, probably have misdiagnosed physical disorders, including potentially lethal misdiagnosed cancers. She noted an increase in lawsuits against therapists who failed to investigate a possible physical disorder among patients that they had been seeing for more than a year.

And this research does not include conditions such as minor head trauma, nutritional problems, or sensory processing disorders, which may afflict as much as 30% of the population. Sensory processing problems occur when there is a glitch in the brain between sensory reception and motor output, distorting one's ability to accurately perceive and respond efficiently to one's environment. It results in conditions such as hypersensitivity to sensation, or sensory defensiveness which creates acute stress and anxiety and a slew of other mental health issues, and sensorimotor dysfunction that creates clumsiness, coordination and balance problems that will create fear and anxiety, while light sensitivity and balance problems creates panic attack (see resources for books and websites). Dr. Harold Levinson, clinical associate professor of psychiatry at New York University Medical Center has found in his practice that *90% of phobia and panic patients actually suffer from inner-ear balance system dysfunction.* Treating the dysfunction eliminates the phobias and panic attacks.

And this book focuses on biological causes of anxiety disorders. It doesn't include the many biological conditions that mimic depression, eating disorders, bipolar disorder, depersonalization, fugue states, schizophrenia or psychosis.

Personal Journey

I know first hand the frustration of having physical problems misdiagnosed as stress and anxiety and left untreated. For twelve years, I walked around day and night in a state of extreme tension -- head squeezed, face and jaw taut, chest compressed, breathing constricted, arms and legs tingling, eyes severely strained, gut in spasms, head in a fog, short-term memory gone, gait unsteady, body weak. Sensations unnerved me. I recoiled if you touched my body, and especially my head, my forehead or anywhere near my ears; my blood curdled if I walked barefoot. I jumped when the phone rang, cringed at the sound of someone chewing, and became instantly unglued from rock music. I swooned at the smell of chlorine and fled a room with musty clothes or pillows. I winced at bright lights, and especially overhead fluorescent lights, or the bright sun. Wearing sun glasses didn't help as any glasses, including my prescription eyeglasses, created eyestrain.

Simple tasks like preparing a meal or shopping at the supermarket overwhelmed me. I couldn't stand upright for longer than 20 minutes or so without collapsing. I got light-headed, weak and unsteady when I changed position, as when rising or sitting down, or when walking a short distance.

Everyone would say, "You look so tired." But I didn't feel tired, which is actually a nice feeling. I felt depleted, overwhelmed, wired, hyped. Inside everything fluttered, tightened, contorted, and spasmed; my stomach felt as if it had been punched, my head as if wrapped in a vice. I felt so overwhelmed and weak that the thought of putting a stamp on an envelope would put me over the edge. *Everything was a struggle.* But I pushed on.

What Was Wrong?

I described my symptoms to doctor after doctor. I was looked at with pity, derision, and amusement and told to learn to control the stress in my life. They prescribed tranquilizers, anti-depressants, and beta-blockers. I didn't take them. Long health conscious, I preferred to heal my anxiety naturally – exercise, the herb kava for relaxing and melatonin for sleep, aromatherapy, progressive relaxation, meditation and so on. Everything helped a little and briefly. I continued to fall apart.

Falling Apart

By my late 40's I was in continual overload, perpetually stressed and anxious, overcome with head pressure, my head in a continual fog and too fatigued to function. I could no longer teach college or write more than in brief spurts and I could barely support myself. Long an exerciser, physical activity became arduous and lost its pleasure. Riding my bike exacerbated my unsteadiness, head pressure, head fog and fatigue, and the longer I rode, the sicker and tenser I felt. Yoga had long been a passion but now getting my weak body into yoga postures was a horrific struggle and I lay sprawled in child pose for much of the class. Friends and family considered my physical problems largely psychosomatic – "You just need a vacation" -- and grew tired of my complaints. I spent more and more time alone. What little energy I had went into survival. My world narrowed to whatever work I could muster to make ends meet, therapy when I could scrape the funds together, and *anything* that might quiet my nervous system. Little did.

First Piece of Puzzle

In 1996, after hearing an occupational therapist talk about *sensory defensiveness* -- the tendency to over-react to ordinary sensation as if it were noxious -- I discovered that my severe over-reactivity to ordinary sensation, which I considered to be anxiety, was an actual condition that *itself* creates enormous stress and anxiety: my inability to cope with the sensory world was not the *result* of my anxiety but one of the *causes*. This filled in one part of the jumpiness puzzle and with a proper "sensory diet" prescribed by an occupational therapist I was able to greatly reduce my irritation to sensation. That perhaps 15 percent of the normal functioning adult population suffer this very common mimicker of panic and anxiety, but don't know it has a name and a treatment, inspired me to write *Too Loud, Too Bright, Too Fast, Too Tight, What to do if you are sensory defensive in an overstimulating world,* published in 2002.

Yet though my defensiveness became more manageable, the other symptoms remained and performing the simplest tasks was an on-going struggle. What was wrong with me?

Second Piece of Puzzle

One day during craniosacral therapy, I felt throbbing and unusual sensations radiating out from scar tissue on my right brow. The scar was a result of an accident I had fifteen years earlier when I had fallen down a flight of stairs and landed on the right side of my head. I didn't relate my neurological problems to the accident because I had not passed out, and an MRI showed no neurological damage. So I forgot about it. Now I wondered if mounds of scar tissue on the right brow could relate to on-going eyestrain, extreme glare and light sensitivity, inability to wear sunglasses (anything with tint), or reading glasses which caused intense, immediate eyestrain.

I told of my accident to Walter Ciao, a developmental optometrist I had been seeing for three years and who had been unsuccessful in getting my eyes to focus with special prism glasses, eye exercises, and light therapy. He concurred that the head trauma likely explained my bizarre symptoms and suggested that I contact Lewis Arrandt, a Miami chiropractor trained in neurocranial restructuring NCR (see chapter eight). I made the appointment for the next day.

Arrandt examined my head and spine. "You've had no life," he said. *Someone understood.* The fall had crunched my skull and spine, creating scoliosis (curved spine) and weakness on my right side: I did not make sense of what I heard in my right ear or saw in my right eye; my right lung was partially collapsed; and the muscles on the right side of my body atrophied and became weak making it hard to coordinate movement of both sides of my body. My jaw was thrown to the right causing TMJD (temporomandibular joint dysfunction characterized by aching and/or clicking in the jaw joints). Chewing food created tension in my jaw and head that further exacerbated head pressure and created tension in my neck and upper chest that constricted breathing. At one point the TMJD became so severe that it created acute myofascial pain syndrome in my upper chest, face and neck and for 6 months I felt as if someone had their hands around my neck, choking me.

Tight muscles in my skull and face from the imbalance, along with mounds of scar tissue above my right eye where I had stitches inhibited the muscles that controlled my vision and my right eye moved up, down, or side to side with difficulty. This explained why wearing glasses not only did not correct my visual processing problems but further exacerbated eyestrain as the prisms in the lenses forced my eyes to work together. With each passing year, the right eye became "lazier" from lack of use and seeing the world created ongoing eyestrain, lightheadedness and loss of balance.

I began NCR immediately. My skull slowly started to realign and my symptoms to abate. My quality of life improved and I was far more functional. But I still felt weak and depleted. What pieces were still missing from the puzzle?

Third Piece of Puzzle

I was born constitutionally sensitive and handled stress poorly. I had always felt anxious and stressed and this wore down my immune system. In my mid-twenties, I got mononucleosis and for one year after I was too ill to work or study. After that, I had chronic mono, or Epstein-Barr syndrome. In my thirties, I taught elementary school in Chicago which constantly exposed me to colds, viruses, and the flu. I was sick from October through April. GI problems further compounded my ill health. In my early twenties and later in my 30's, I took long-term antibiotics that upset the natural flora in my gut and created *Candida* overgrowth or yeast. This led to leaky gut, extensive food intolerances, hypoglycemia -- all common anxiety mimickers. Eating left me weak, dizzy, spacey, irritable, stressed, ill, and fatigued. I went on a cleansing program to help heal my gut, and ate raw, whole food to strengthen my system. I was now able to function out in the world more but overall the weakness, jumpiness, spaciness and fatigue continued. Something was still missing.

Fourth Piece of Puzzle

Though the accident had left me with constant head fog, I had always been spacey, something my family had always joked about. What could have affected my thinking early on? The answer: Head fog likely started with my first silver filling as a child. Silver amalgams are loaded with mercury and some people don't naturally excrete heavy metal from their bodies (see chapter 12). I am apparently one. My body was overloaded with mercury and with lead as well as, over a period of eight years, I had made over one 150 pieces of leaded stained glass.

Puzzle Complete

The puzzle was now complete. In addition to symptoms from head trauma and sensory defensiveness, I had a chronic virus, a slew of GI problems, chemical toxicity, anemia and adrenal exhaustion from the on-going stress that left me tired but wired.

I didn't have one thing wrong with me. I had a multitude of problems that had destabilized and compromised my immune system, nervous system, digestive system, and hormonal balance and that made it hard to determine what made me constantly jittery. Was my head spinning because my skull was misaligned or because of the yeast overgrowth, TMJD, or chronic fatigue? Was I jittery because of sensory defensiveness or sugar imbalance? Was my stomach in spasms because I was anxious or because I had just eaten something to which I was sensitive? Was I dizzy and light-headed from severe eyestrain or from head compression? It took years to realize that the answer was at any point in time a combination of the above, although any one of the problems may have initially set off the symptoms.

Solutions

Now that I knew the problems, I knew the solutions: raw, living foods for maximum nutrition; detoxification; a "sensory diet;" interventions to alleviate eyestrain; therapy for the head trauma; and most anything that would help reduce stress and balance my nervous system. I became a raw food vegan, took whole food supplements, fasted and detoxified, and slept nine to ten hours a night. I did light therapy to help my vision, and used an eye massager to alleviate eyestrain, although this still presents a challenge. I got NCR, biocranial, and osteopathic therapy on an on-going basis for my skull and spine, did body rolling to relax my extremely tight muscles, and magnetic resonance therapy to break down scar tissue to enhance the effectiveness of these therapies. I engaged in sensorimotor activities to reduce my sensory defensiveness, and did yoga, qi gong, meditation tapes, aromatherapy to reduce stress and later an amazing computer program called the Voyager, which bounces scalar waves off your computer and puts you quickly into a highly restorative, deep meditative state (for information, call 1-888-229-9698),

My overall functioning has improved dramatically, along with my relationships, creativity, self-esteem, productivity, and attitude toward life but… only if I maintain my strict protocol. If I regress I pay the price. Fortunately, these episodes are generally short-lived and I quickly return to my "lifestyle."

People tell me I go to an extreme. No. I do what *my* nervous system requires for balance. For me, that's more than for the average person. You will need to find out what *you* need to organize and balance your nervous system and follow that path to the best of your ability, regardless of the generally well meaning opinion of others.

Splitting Mind & Body

Why are physical causes of anxiety so easily overlooked? The answer lies in the centuries old influence of dualism – splitting mind and body.

Under the influence of Christianity, the mind was a real entity that existed independently of the flesh and guided the spirit, a mindset shared today by many New Age proponents. Medieval scholars placed the mind a few inches above the forehead; Leonardo da Vinci placed it inside the skull; Descartes placed it in the pineal gland.

Such thinking profoundly influenced psychiatry. If mind and body are separate entities, then disease is either physical or mental.

In antiquity, people believed mental problems were physical in origin. In ancient Greece the Hippocratic school believed that madness was caused by abnormalities in the humors of the brain and composition of the blood. Such sentiment was echoed throughout history. Then in the nineteenth century two camps emerged in psychiatry: one investigated the "brain," or the biological components of mental disease; the other investigated the "mind."

Body>Mind

Emil Kraepelin (1856-1926), the father of German psychiatry, believed that abnormal behavior, like dementia and manic-depressive psychosis, was caused by organic disturbances. Kraepelin laid the groundwork for the scientific and systematic study of mental disorders. His perspective was strengthened when, borrowing from the new science of bacteriology and the discovery of tiny-disease causing agents know as microbes, psychiatrists discovered some mental illness to come from bacterial illness. A large number of presumably schizophrenic patients proved to be in an advanced state of syphilis, a mimicker of symptoms of schizophrenia. And thousands of "insane" institutionalized in madhouses were suffering from pellagra, a disease caused by niacin deficiency and easily corrected by a balanced diet.

Mind>Body

Unfortunately, the use of treatments like shock therapy and lobotomies smudged medical psychiatry's reputation. Sigmund Freud's cathartic talk therapy of psychoanalysis, on the other hand, seemed to do little harm, and in some cases appeared to cure patients of illnesses like hysteria and neurosis.

Trained as a neurologist, Freud initially believed "anxiety neurosis," or panic attack, entirely biological and not amenable to psychotherapy. But as he developed his theories, this presumably somatic disorder became subsumed under the general category of "neurosis." With his focus on the seething cauldron of desires in the unconscious mind, Freud began to view all behavior as motivated by intrapsychic conflict between the id (the unconscious), the ego (the conscious self) and the super-ego (the conscience) and to result from unresolved childhood issues.

Freud's theory of the unconscious laid the foundation for modern techniques of psychotherapy, and psychiatry's focus shifted from a biological origin of mental illness to a psychological one. With the emphasis now squarely on the "mind" as the origin of mental disorders, even illnesses like schizophrenia and autism were blamed on the cold, uncaring mother.

Body/Mind

Two things happened that created a shift back to a medical model of mental illness: drugs and brain imaging technology. The discovery of miracle drugs, like Thorazine, released millions of patients from the shackles of psychosis so they could lead a more normal life. And brain imaging techniques like the MRI or PET scan identified diseases like schizophrenia as diseases of the brain.

But what about less disabling mental illness like neurosis? Was Freud initially correct that all mental illness would prove to be biologically driven? Indeed. The more we know about the brain, the more Freud's original thesis is proving correct.

Born Anxiety Prone

Anxiety is a normal feeling of unease, edginess and worry in response to feeling endangered. We all experience it from time to time as it prompts us to take protective action and flee or fight the threat. If actual imminent danger triggers the threat, we feel *fear*. If a vague psychological threat, like losing love, self, or soul, triggers the threat, we feel *anxious*: we don't fear getting murdered by our date, we fear getting dumped; we don't fear choking on our food, we fear choking on our words.

In the normal person, anxiety becomes more manageable or disappears when the stressor disappears. But some people are chronically uptight. In the anxiety prone, the rhythms that govern behavior, such as heart rate, breathing, day/night cycles (circadian rhythms), brainwaves and digestion get easily imbalanced and you live in a state of higher arousal than the average person.   Such vulnerability may come from something congenital, like maternal infection or drug use during pregnancy, or you may have inherited an anxiety gene. For instance, studies show that both twins are more likely to suffer from anxiety if they are identical.   And anxiety disorders often run in families.   In other words, even when an anxiety disorder appears *psychological* in origin, it is *biologically* based.

Further evidence for this view comes from research into GABA (gamma-amino butyric acid), an internally produced substance that is the brain's anti-anxiety messenger. Benzodiazepines or anti-anxiety drugs work by enhancing the link between GABA and its receptor sites. The anxiety prone may not produce enough GABA, or substances like it, including endorphins, the brain's own opiate, to shut off anxiety. Less able to handle life's slings and arrows, you handle stress poorly. If it builds beyond your coping capacity, you become constantly "on alert," and anxiety, fatigue and mood swings increase.

Stress, Illness, Angst

Constant stress wears down the systems of the body, creating illness. It happens something like this:

1. **Stress** launches the flight/fight response: heart races, palms sweat, belly contorts, immune system suppresses as all energy goes into "running from the lion."
2. **Chronic stress** depletes the immune system.
3. **Body's** rate of repair slows.
4. **Vital vitamins and minerals** get lost creating malnourishment.
5. **Malnourishment** makes you more susceptible to physical illness like chronic fatigue, infections (viral, bacterial), allergies, autoimmune diseases (lupus, thyroiditis and others), or cancer.
6. **Constant physical tension** causes myofascial pain syndrome, TMJD, or fibromyalgia (a condition of muscular aches and pains, especially in the neck and shoulder areas)
7. **Constant adrenaline overactivity** creates headaches, colitis, irritable bowel, high blood pressure, muscle spasms, eczema, or

ulcers. (People with panic disorder have a higher rate of migraine headache, hypertension, coronary heart disease, ulcer, thyroid disease, and asthma).

8. **Illness** further increases psychological stress, creating anxiety and depression.

This syndrome is termed *adrenal exhaustion* and many consider it a disease in and of itself. We'll talk more about it in chapter two.

What Causes What?

If anxiety creates illness and illness creates anxiety, which comes first -- the anxious-prone egg or the sick chicken. The answer is unclear.

The nervous, endocrine, and immune systems are intimately tied. What impacts one will impact all three systems. For instance, a sick women is more likely to suffer PMS and anxiety than a healthy one. Likewise, the anxiety prone are a more likely candidate for PMS or postpartum blues and probably get colds more often than women who go through the monthly cycle without needing Xanax. In other words, anxiety creates greater stress that impacts the immune system and hormonal system and leads to greater illness. Conversely, illness leads to greater stress that in turn increases vulnerability to anxiety and hormonal imbalance.

All in all, you can be anxious:

➤ **Because** you are an anxious person;

➤ **As** a result of something purely biological, like hyperthyroidism, regardless of your inborn temperament;

➤ **In** response to a highly stressful event, like catastrophic illness in which case the illness is a cause of anxiety, not a mimicker;

➤ **Because** you have both an anxiety disorder and a biological mimicker, and each exacerbates the other.

Where you fall will determine your treatment protocol, including:

◆ Nutritional Changes   ◆ Supplements
◆ Herbs   ◆ Detoxification

- Environmental modifications
- Cranial/Sacral Therapy
- Exercise

- Surgery
- Stress reduction
- Medication
- Psychotherapy
- A combination

Figuring this out is what this book is all about!

Become Your Own Detective

Fortunately, as the following differences demonstrate clear ways exist to establish whether your anxiety is primarily psychologically or biologically triggered.

Onset

Psychologically Triggered Anxiety: Anxiety symptoms generally come on gradually and are pervasive.

Biologically Triggered Anxiety: Anxiety symptoms often happen quickly and may disappear as quickly.

Cause

Psychologically Triggered Anxiety: Anxiety symptoms occur in response to stress or to conflict that creates worry.

Biologically Triggered Anxiety: Anxiety symptoms occur in response to a non-emotional event and follow a pattern:

They occur predictably at certain times of the day, like following a meal, or after consuming too much sugar, carbohydrates, or caffeine.

They occur consistently in response to:

➢ Smoking too many cigarettes
➢ Exercising
➢ Feeling uncomfortably hot or cold
➢ Feeling overwhelmed by an overstimulating environment
➢ Being under the influence of drugs or alcohol, or when trying to stop

➢   Being ill
➢   Menstruation, pregnancy or menopause

Trigger

Psychologically Triggered Anxiety: Anxiety symptoms start with a thought and produce worry. Worry in turn produces more stress or conflict and builds until you have an anxiety attack and, in the extreme panic attack.

It happens something like this:

1. **Worry:**   You worry something bad will happen and feel threatened.
2. **Flight/fight:**   Your brain receives a red flag that you are in "danger" and commands the self-protective flight/fight response in defense. Your brain shouts "run!" or if you can't "attack!" or "freeze" until you can disarm your enemy (real or imagined) enough to get away.
3. **Limbic Activation:**   The amygdala, the seat of fear located in the limbic system (the old midbrain) becomes active and you feel fear or profound unease, often accompanied by loss of control.
4. **Hormonal Release:** Hormones like adrenaline release and the sympathetic nervous system (SNS), a branch of the autonomic nervous system that energizes you for action, sends signals to various parts of the body to produce physiological changes:
   - **Heart** starts pumping to rush fuel to every cell
   - **Breathing** comes in quick spurts to get oxygen in quicker
   - **Sweating** starts to cool you down
   - **Blood** rushes away from the abdomen to the legs to allow you to run faster
   - **Digestion** and other bodily functions halt to conserve energy
   - **Liver** releases sugar to provide quick energy
   - **Pupils** dilate to increase visual acuity

   This flight or fight response takes on different proportions depending on the threat.

Alarm 1 *(Mild Anxiety)*:	Alarm 4 *(Moderate Panic Attack)*:
◆ Nervous ◆ Tense ◆ Butterflies in stomach Alarm 2 *(Moderate Anxiety)*: ◆ Uncomfortably tense & aroused ◆ Heart beating fast ◆ Breathing rapid ◆ Palms sweaty ◆ Muscles tight ◆ In control Alarm 3 *(Intense Anxiety)*: ◆ Uncomfortably spacey or light-headed ◆ Unsteady on feet ◆ Heart pounding or beating irregularly ◆ Chest compressed ◆ Worry about losing control	◆ Palpitations ◆ Difficulty breathing ◆ Chest very tight and compressed ◆ Eyes acutely dilated ◆ Disoriented ◆ Detached & feel unreal ◆ Panic ◆ Loss of control Alarm 5 *(Major Panic Attack)*: ◆ Exaggerated terror ◆ Intense dread ◆ Numb & feel unreal ◆ Fear you are going crazy or dying ◆ Must flee ◆ No control

Biologically Triggered Anxiety: Biologically triggered anxiety begins with bodily sensation and thought follows.

1. **Physical Trigger:** Shopping in the supermarket, you unknowingly feel overwhelmed by the overhead fluorescent lights.
2. **Alarm** set off: heart begins to pound, breathing quickens, and chest feels compressed.
3. **Worry** starts. "What is wrong with me?" "Will I make it out of here without losing it?" "Am I crazy?"

4. **Panic:** Worry escalates into panic.
5. **Panic Attack:** You abandon your full shopping cart and dash out the supermarket.

As you don't know what triggered the panic, you fear that *anything* could set off another unexpected terrifying attack and you become preoccupied with the fear of a second attack. Anticipatory anxiety has set in and perhaps depression. You now have a psychiatric disorder *secondarily* to a biologically triggered condition.

Risk Factors

Psychologically Triggered Anxiety: You have several risk factors associated with developing an anxiety disorder.

Anxiety Risk Factors	
♦ Relationship problems	♦ Trauma
♦ Low self-esteem	♦ Loss
♦ Unstable emotions	♦ Disabilities interfering
♦ Non-productivity	with coping
♦ Non-empathic parenting	♦ Cultural mismatch (living
♦ Dysfunctional family	in foreign land, e.g.)
♦ Neglect, physical or	♦ Stress beyond coping
sexual abuse	capacity
♦ Sensitive constitution	♦ Family history of mental
	disorder

Biologically Triggered Anxiety: You may have few or no risk factors associated with an anxiety disorder.

Emotional History

Psychologically Triggered Anxiety: You have a history of coping poorly with stress.

Biologically Triggered Anxiety: You may have no previous history of reacting to stress with psychiatric symptoms: symptoms emerge "out of the blue" and your behavior and feelings are suddenly radically different from usual. Children may exhibit a sudden decline in school performance or behavior.

Psychotropic Drug Effectiveness

Psychologically Triggered Anxiety: Psychotropic drugs have eliminated or significantly reduced anxiety or panic.

Biologically Triggered Anxiety: You feel heightened agitation or tension that does not respond effectively to psychotropic drugs or therapy.

Nature of Symptoms

Psychologically Triggered Anxiety: Worry, dread or doom accompanies physical symptoms.

Biologically Triggered Anxiety: Heightened agitation or tension may exist without worry, dread or doom or even emotional distress.

Presence of Illness

Psychologically Triggered Anxiety: Anxiety symptoms predominate; physical symptoms, like stomach ache are secondary.

Biologically Triggered Anxiety: You may feel ill much of the time; the cause of your symptoms has eluded medical diagnosis.

	Psychologically Triggered Anxiety	Biologically Triggered Anxiety
Onset	Gradual anxiety	Sudden anxiety
Cause	Emotional event	Physical stressor
Trigger	Anxiety triggered by thought & produces worry	Anxiety triggered by bodily sensations and thought follows
Risk Factors	Have several factors associated with anxiety disorder	May not have risk factors associated with anxiety disorder
Emotional History	Have coped poorly with stress	May have previously coped well with stress
Psychotropic Drug Effectiveness	Effective	Mildly or non-effective
Nature of Symptoms	Worry, dread or doom accompanies physical symptoms	Heightened agitation or tension may exist without worry, dread or doom or even emotional distress
Presence of Illness	Anxiety, not illness predominates symptoms	Feel ill much of the time

How to Use This Book

Now that you've reviewed the differences between psychologically and biologically triggered anxiety, you may find it helpful to fill in a detailed log of your symptoms. Do this for at least one full day but preferably for a whole week.

The more you carefully fill in, the more you will begin to see a pattern for your symptoms and begin to tease out their cause(s).

You may discover your anxiety and panic to have primarily one cause, like hyperventilation, or a multitude of causes, from GI problems to structural problems to a sugar imbalance and you will need to approach the diagnosis and treatment of your symptoms holistically.

Daily Log

Emotional State:
__Calm
__Content
__Sad
__Stressed
__Tense
__Frantic
__Frazzled

Anxiety Symptoms:
__Jumpy/restless
__Edgy/tense
__Explosive
__Worried
__Brain fog
__Forgetful
__Panicked
__Disoriented
__Confused
__Fearful
__Feeling dread
__Sense of doom
__Feeling unreal

Physical Symptoms:
__Headache
__Nausea
__Upset stomach
__Constipation
__Diarrhea
__Dizzy
__Unsteady
__Shaky
__Achy
__Heart thumping
__Breathing rapid
__Chest constricted
__Sweating
__Tingling arms/legs

Quality of Sleep:
__Deep rest
__Restless
__Insomnia

Physical State:
Heart Beat:
__Normal
__Rapid
__Irregular
Breathing:
__Normal
__Quick
__Shallow
__Short of
    breath
__Grabbing for
    air
Muscle Tension:
Hands:
__Open
__Clenched
Shoulders:
__Relaxed
__Hunched

Environment:
Sounds:
__Normal
__Noisy
__Quiet
__Nature sounds
__Pleasing Music
Odors:
__None
__Pleasant
__Noxious
Lights:
__Comfortable
__Overbright
__Dim

Activity:
Physical:
__Active
__Sedate
__Changing head
    position

__Abruptly sit/rise
Mental:
__Engaging
__Boring

State of Arousal:
__Alert
__Focused
__Distracted
__Drowsy
__Groggy
__Unrested
__Fatigued

Food Eaten:
Protein:
__Meat
__Fish
__Fowl
__Eggs
__Dairy
__Seeds
__Nuts
__Lentils
__Beans
Fats:
__Oil
__Butter
__Avocado
__Mayonnaise
__Nuts
Carbohydates:
__Fruits
__Vegetables
__Grains
__Pasta
__Potatoes
__Beans/Lentils
__Cakes
__Cookies
__Candy

Copy the log on the previous page and fill it in ideally every two hours throughout the day.

After filling in the daily log of your symptoms, you will likely have identified areas that need further scrutiny. The next three sections will provide an in-depth look at non-psychological triggers of anxiety and panic: physical, neurological, nutritional, environmental, structural and sensory.

Part one consists of five chapters that discuss how digestive problems, nutritional deficits, medical illness, drugs, hormonal imbalance, and immune system overload can produce symptoms that mimic generalized anxiety and panic attack.

Part two consists of six chapters that cover nervous system imbalance and produce neuropsychiatric symptoms that can present as an anxiety disorder. It covers brain injury, hyperventilation, structural misalignment, and problems related to sensory processing disorder, including balance issues, and light sensitivity.

Part three consists of four chapters that cover the grand nervous system destabilizers -- toxins from our food, drugs, and environment, as well as electromagnetic radiation -- and protection from such assault.

To help you discover the potential cause or causes of your symptoms, each disorder includes an explanation, symptoms, causes, diagnosis, and treatment options, both conventional and alternative, along with a list of resources at the end of the chapter. The conclusion guides you on how to pursue a thorough diagnosis of your symptoms, and includes a checklist of symptoms for the many different anxiety triggers.

By the end of the book, you should have a good idea of what drives your anxiety or panic – something in your mind, head, body, food, posture, the environment, or a combination thereof – and the various treatment options available from both traditional and alternative medicine.

Part One

Physical Problems & Anxiety

If you suffer anxiety or panic attack, your first step should be to rule out possible medical causes. The next five chapters will cover common and uncommon medical anxiety mimics including:

- ◆ Digestive
- ◆ Endocrine
- ◆ Infection
- ◆ Cardiac
- ◆ Cancer
- ◆ Drugs
- ◆ Hormonal
- ◆ Autoimmune
- ◆ Musculoskeletal

If you suspect that illness may be causing or contributing to your anxiety or panic attack, inform your physician and be certain that you get the necessary medical diagnostics tests for any suspected medical condition. By taking charge of your own health, you will be less likely to fall into the common "it's all in your head, take this red pill for anxiety and this blue one for depression" syndrome with your physician. Remember, *you* not the doctor are in charge of your body.

By the end of this section you will have a good idea as to what, if any medical illness drives your anxiety and panic.

1

★

Food & Its Discontents

Let food be your medicine.
-Hippocrates

Shortly after 27 year-old Charles Darwin returned to England in 1836 after his five-year voyage on the *Beagle*, the father of evolutionary theory began complaining of "constant attacks" – heart palpitations, trembling, shortness of breath, vomiting, extreme fatigue, depression, and "swimming in the head." He declined a secretaryship at the Geological Society of London because "anything that flurries me completely knocks me up afterward." Two years later the adventurous explorer retreated to his country home in Kent and became a recluse, rarely leaving his home and then traveling in a carriage with darkened windows. Darwin never learned the true nature of his malady. For forty years, he complained to over twenty doctors who diagnosed his problems as anything from "dyspepsia with aggravated character" to "suppressed gout."

Today, many books and papers have explained Darwin's mystery illness as psychiatric – as psychosomatic, hypochondria, bereavement syndrome, an expression of repressed anger toward his father, or genetic, noting a familial vulnerability to the symptoms Darwin described. But the general consensus has been that Darwin probably suffered *panic disorder with agoraphobia*, which would explain his secluded lifestyle and difficulty in speaking before groups and meeting with colleagues.

Other researchers have looked for an organic cause, including arsenic poisoning, Chagas' disease from an insect bite in South America, or multiple allergies. Drs. Campbell and Mathews of the Darwin Centre for Biology and Medicine, Milton, Pembrokeshire, UK believe otherwise. To them, all evidence suggests a food link: *lactose intolerance* which appeared to run in his family.

Lactose intolerance results when the body doesn't produce enough lactase, an enzyme needed to break down lactose, the main source of carbohydrates in milk, into simple sugars. Two to three hours after he ate, the time it takes for lactose to reach the large intestine, Darwin experienced vomiting and gut problems. Darwin only got better when, by chance, he stopped taking milk and cream.

If these researchers are correct, Darwin's heart palpitations, trembles, shortness of breath, vomiting, extreme fatigue, and "swimming in the head" were signs not of anxiety and panic but food sensitivities. His agoraphobia was not a fear of leaving the safety of his home but of being too ill to do so. Likewise, the solution to his woes was not probing his psyche but not ingesting milk products.

Food is a drug. What we eat directly impacts the physiology and biochemistry of our brain. Yet many don't make the food/mood connection.

To get our system going, we drink a cup of coffee, unaware that too much caffeine can make us jittery and even cause panic attack in some. To mellow out, we eat pasta, ignorant that processed flour acts as a fast acting sugar that can upset sugar imbalance and trigger anxiety and even panic attack in some, or that refined foods rob us of the nutrition the nervous system requires to function well, clouding our mind and destabilizing our emotions. And like Darwin, we may be unaware that we suffer from food related problems like food sensitivities, blood-sugar imbalance and other gut-related problems that restrict the body's ability to properly assimilate food and feed our brain the nutrients needed to be alert, calm, and balanced.

Conversely, how we *feel* profoundly affects what we choose to eat, and how well we digest and assimilate our food. Our emotions are intimately tied to our gut, our "second brain." Containing over 30 hormones, many of which also act as neurotransmitters -- the chemical messengers of mind and emotions -- the gut directly "talks" with the central nervous system. Serotonin, the neurotransmitter that governs mood, is concentrated in the gut – 90% of it lies in your digestive tract. This makes the gut highly sensitive to turbulence: anxiety and digestive disorders, like irritable bowel and spastic colon, go hand in hand. If you raise serotonin level through proper food and supplements, these stress related conditions abate. Further, when anxious, our body goes into flight/fight and digestion and other body functions slow to conserve energy and we don't digest our food well. The poorly digested food ferments and plays tricks on the brain, and we get sleepy and lethargic, or jumpy and anxious.

Let's look at the myriad of ways in which what we swallow can eat us up physically, mentally, and emotionally.

Food Sensitivities

Other than sex, little in life imparts more pleasure than eating. But if you have food sensitivities, you often feel better *not* eating.

When we think of an adverse reaction to a food, we imagine someone eating peanuts and shortly after breaking out in hives, vomiting, or having problem breathing. This person has a food *allergy,* a rare life threatening defensive response that triggers the immunoglobulin-E (IgE) system.

Far more common are *food sensitivities* or *food intolerance*, which are delayed immune reactions to common foods like milk, wheat and corn. They can occur from minutes after eating a food to a few hours or even a few days after exposure, as it takes up to four days for some foods, like meat, to leave the system.

Typically, people will react to an offending food if they've eaten an excessive amount, if they eat several offending foods together, or if they're ill and their resistance is low. But some highly sensitive people will eat an olive and go over the edge.

Triggers

Food sensitivities appears to result when foods, and particularly their protein component, are not completely digested and some of the food putrefies and allergens, undigested food or bacteria slip into the bloodstream – a condition referred to as *leaky gut syndrome* or excessive permeability of the digestive tract. Your immune system reacts to these components as foreign bodies and goes on the defense to destroy the invader, Once in the bloodstream, this foreign matter can cause havoc almost anywhere in the body. You might break out in a rash, or get diarrhea, joint pain or migraines, and, as the immune system is intimately tied to the nervous system, anxiety and depression. To understand how *leaky gut* happens, we need to first look at the normal digestive process.

Digestive Process

1. **We** chew food.
2. **Enzymes** in our saliva begin to break it down and digest it.
3. **Food** travels to the stomach and hydrochloric acid breaks it down further by activating stomach enzymes. This process can take up to thirty minutes.
4. **Partially** digested food goes to the small intestine, where digestive enzymes from the pancreas and bile produced by the liver break down the food's fats, proteins, and carbohydrates into particles that get absorbed across the intestinal lining.
5. **Some** particles travel to the liver, the body's main detoxifying organ to be metabolized; others are carried away by the lymph, an important part of the immune system.
6. **Remaining** unusable food material passes into the large intestine, or colon, where water is removed and the waste gets evacuated from the body.

The more smoothly and quickly food passes through our system, the better the body absorbs and assimilates it and the quicker the waste gets eliminated, avoiding toxic build up. Unfortunately, pizza, steak, bacon, cheeseburgers, hot dogs, French fries, doughnuts, ice cream, chocolate, and many other processed and high "alarm" foods that typify the Standard American Diet (SAD!) are high in saturated fats, sugars, and animal protein that make them hard to digest. Consequently, the process slows, toxins build up, and *leaky gut syndrome* results.

Digestion now takes on a different trajectory.

1. **You** are sensitive to milk, wheat, corn, and eggs and have a few minor symptoms.
2. **Food** stays too long in the stomach because of food sensitivity or imbalanced flora.
3. **The** malabsorbed food putrefies and ferments (you experience bloating, cramps, and gas).

4. **Undigested** food travels to the small intestine, and mucus builds up to protect the lining of the intestinal wall and counteract the bacteria created by fermented food.

5. **Toxic** bacteria from the fermented food overpower the good bacteria in the intestinal tract, slowing down the digestive process.

6. **Undigested,** putrefied food moves slowly through the colon, forming toxic chemicals that irritate the 25 feet of the lining of the digestive tract.

7. **Irritation** worsens and toxic chemicals "leak" through the intestinal membrane into the circulatory and lymph system.

8. **Toxic** chemicals hit the bowel and the entire body soon becomes toxic as the liver, lymph, kidneys, skin, and other organs involved in detoxification become overwhelmed.

Once this happens, your whole system becomes compromised/

1. **Metabolism** slows, energy depletes, immunity reduces, and brain chemistry destabilizes, making thinking fuzzy and emotions labile.

2. **Nutritional** deficiencies, sugar consumption, exposure to environmental molds and chemicals (see chapter 14), or illness further batter the immune system (see chapter two).

3. **You** develop adverse reactions to additional foods, even healthy foods like almonds, green beans, olives, papaya, garlic, and so on.

4. **Health** further deteriorates and you develop other GI problems, respiratory problems, aches and pains, and even chronic fatigue and fibromyalgia.

5. **You** feel bad all over, irritable, anxious, lethargic, and can't think clearly.

6. **Doctors** give you medications to combat illness that further destabilize the gut and increase irritability, nervousness or anxiety.

FOOD SENSITIVITY SYMPTOMS

PSYCHOLOGICAL

Feelings
- Anxiety
- Irritability
- Tension
- Mood swings
- Depression

Thoughts
- Poor concentration
- Brain fog
- Poor memory
- Confusion
- Disorientation

Behavior
- Volatile
- Hyperactivity
- Drug, alcohol addiction

PHYSICAL

Nose
- Itchy, runny, stuffed nose
- Altered smell
- Sinusitis
- Hay fever
- Sneezing attacks

Eyes
- Irritated eyes
- Dark circles under eyes
- Blurred vision
- Spots before eyes

G.I./Urinary
- Indigestion
- Constipation, diarrhea
- Nausea, vomiting
- Belching
- Gas
- Bloating
- Stomach pains, cramps
- Heartburn
- React to MSG, additives food coloring, nitrates, sulfates, aspartame
- Feel better not eating

Joints & Muscles
- Muscle aches & pains
- Stiffness
- Arthritis
- Weakness
- Numbness
- Swollen hands & feet

Weight
- Binge eating/drinking
- Food cravings
- Anorexia
- Fluid retention--puffy face; swollen ankles; wt fluctuation

Skin
- Hives & rash
- Acne
- Itching & burning
- Body odor

Mouth & Throat
- Chronic coughing
- Frequently clearing throat
- Frequent sore throat
- Hoarseness
- Metallic taste
- Canker sores
- Dry or itching mouth
- Bad breath

Ears
- Itching
- Ear aches, infections
- Drainage
- Ringing, hearing loss

- Fullness
- Loss of balance
  Lungs
- Shortness of breath
- Chest congestion

- Difficulty breathing
- Excess mucous
  Heart
- Irregular h.b.
- Rapid or pounding heart

NEUROLOGICAL

Head
- Headaches
- Dizziness
  Arousal
- Unexplained grogginess or fatigue, particularly after eating
- Groggy after night's sleep
- Restlessness

- Apathy, lethargy
- Hyperactivity
- Insomnia
- Hypersomnia
  Sensory
- Sensitivity to chemicals, pollution, cigarette smoke, perfume

OTHER

- Allergies
- Frequent colds & infection
- Anemia
- High cholesterol

- PMS
- Genital itch or discharge
- Food cravings, e.g., bread or cheese

Familiarity Breeds Cravings

The most likely allergens that cause food sensitivities are common foods like wheat, corn, and dairy as frequent exposure overwhelms the immune system. Generally, we don't make a connection between cause and effect as we eat these foods often. The day after eating nachos, for instance, we feel dizzy, irritable, confused, tired, depressed, anxious and even panicked. As we eat corn and milk products daily we don't connect these feelings to the corn, cheese or other ingredients in the long-digested nachos. Instead, we assume our symptoms are from stress and self-medicate by eating nachos again for lunch! This happens all the time because our body begins to *crave* commonly eaten food. What would we crave foods that should be good for us? The answer? They're not!

Most of the food we eat on the Standard American Diet is cooked and processed, containing unnatural substances. Our body reacts to this dead food as foreign, activating the immune system.

Cooked Food Stimulates Immune Response

In 1930, Swiss researchers at the Institute of Chemical Chemistry discovered that heating food beyond a certain temperature, or processing food increased the number of white cells in the blood, a reaction found only when a dangerous pathogen invades the body or by trauma. The worst offenders were:

♦ *Refined, processed foods such as white flour and white rice*

♦ *Pasteurized foods, where milk is flash-heated to high temperatures to kill bacteria*

♦ *Homogenized foods, where the fat in milk is subjected to artificial suspension, or preserved by adding chemicals to delay spoilage, or to enhance texture or taste*

In addition, some of this food contains endorphins, our brain's natural morphine and, like a drug, we desire more and more. Gluten, found in wheat, oats, rye, corn, lentils, buckwheat, and peanuts contains endorphin mimics called exorphins, as does casein, a cow's milk protein. Since most processed foods, and especially junk food, contain either gluten or casein and often both – pizza, cheeseburger, nachos, and cheesecake for instance – the body craves these foods. Eating flesh foods in particular is addictive as they make you sluggish and you become addicted to stimulating substances to rev you up. When you abstain from eating these "foods" you experience withdrawal symptoms and crave the food even more. Such cravings affect your moods, thinking, and behavior and, in some, lead to extreme behavior like eating disorders and learning disabilities.

Eating Disorders

According to Dr. Doris Rapp, a pediatric allergist and environmental specialist, food cravings in some people underlie eating disorders, like *bulimia* and *anorexia nervosa.*

Alcoholism

Food addictions may be implicated in *alcoholism*. For instance, if you are sensitive to corn, you may drink a lot of beer. You think you're addicted to the beer but actually you're addicted to the corn.

Learning Disabilities

For years, many have made a connection between learning disabilities, attention disorders, and food sensitivities. According to Benjamin Feingold, M.S., perhaps forty to fifty percent of hyperactive children are sensitive to artificial food colors, flavors, and preservatives, and to naturally occurring salicylates and phenolic compounds.

Hotly debated for years, his theories have not been borne out in the medical community though virtually every study done demonstrated that some hyperactive children consistently show behavior problems in response to specific food additives. One possible reason for inconclusive research findings is that, even when these substances are removed on the "Feingold diet," children may continue to be hyperactive because unidentified food sensitivities have *not* been removed from the diet!

Bed Wetting & Food Sensitivities

Around 60% of bed wetters wet the bed because they are eating or drinking foods to which they are sensitive. The same statistics apply to ear infections from milk intolerance, while Lancet, the British medical journal reported that 93% of migraines were triggered by food sensitivities.

Autism

Recently, scientists are discovering a link between autism, food sensitivities and a weak immune system. Karyn Seroussi, author of *Unraveling the Mystery of Autism and Pervasive Developmental Disorder: A Mother's Story of Research and Recovery,* removed milk and wheat from the diet of her autistic child and he no longer behaved autistically.

Causes

Many things can cause food sensitivities, including:
- ➤ **Genetics**
- ➤ **Lifestyle**
- ➤ **Drug-like** effects of chemicals naturally occurring in foods or added to them
- ➤ **Poor** nutrition
- ➤ **Long-term** antibiotic use
- ➤ **Chemical** exposure
- ➤ **Poor** metabolic function such as:
  - ○ Increased or decreased thyroid activity
  - ○ Adrenal insufficiency
  - ○ Hypoglycemia (low blood sugar)
  - ○ Estrogen overload relative to progesterone
- ➤ **Inability** to digest a component of a food -- lactose intolerance, for instance, is caused by an enzyme deficiency

---

Food Sensitivity & Food Chemicals
Well known nutritionist and author Gary Null relates how his body always reacted to eating apples. One day he ate an organic apple. To his surprise, he digested it without problem.

Diagnosis

Most people have only a few food sensitivities. But if you've had unidentified food sensitivities for years, you may be intolerant to many different foods -- sometimes as high as twenty or thirty. These can include even healthy foods, like celery or garlic. You will need a diagnostic test to determine your specific intolerances.

Knowing little about food sensitivities, conventional allergists will give you a scratch or prick-puncture test to detect food allergies and sensitivities, a procedure that is only around 20% accurate. Alternative practitioners recommend tests like the ELISA blood test, designed specifically to assess food allergies and to pinpoint delayed allergic reactions, or the Immuno 1 BloodprintTM.

You can also use your body as a laboratory and systematically monitor your own reaction to foods. One way is to take your resting pulse and then again twenty minutes after eating a particular food. Elevation above 10 beats of your normal rate is a likely sign of an allergic reaction. Start self-testing with the foods you eat the most, as these are the foods to which you are most likely sensitive. A simple home urine test is also available.

Smoking Sugar

Did you know that tobacco contains sugar? It is used to cure the tobacco. If you are a smoker, you may become sensitive to the sugar in the cigarettes. Both sugar intolerance and the nicotine addiction act as a powerful stimulant to keep you smoking.

Treatment Options

The key to managing food sensitivities is to establish a healthy digestive track. To do this you will need to:

- ➤ **Remove** offending foods from your diet
- ➤ **Rotate** foods
- ➤ **Supplement** nutritional deficiencies
- ➤ **Detoxify** (see chapter 13)

Removing Allergens

The first step in recovery is to remove offending, addictive foods from your diet. As you do so, you will experience brief withdrawal symptoms. **DON'T GIVE IN TO YOUR CRAVING AND SNEAK A BITE OR TWO!** Remember, the food is poison for you and after you eliminate the offending foods, you will feel better.

If you are unsure what foods you react to, start by removing the most common allergens listed below.

Wheat: The casein and gluten found in wheat, rye, barley and oats make it hard to digest and eliminate as it coats the bowel and creates malabsorption -- mix water and wheat flour and you get glue! As such, it makes you sleepy (and bloated) and can also cause thyroiditis, a common and debilitating low thyroid condition. **Replace wheat with: pure rye; brown rice; quinoa; millet; teff; buckwheat.**

Gluten Intolerance: While wheat especially is hard for everyone to digest, as many as one out of three people suffer gluten intolerance, an inherited condition that leads to mucus and inflammation. The condition is found most frequently in those with Irish, English, Scottish, Scandinavian, and other Northern European and Eastern European heritages. Gluten intolerance prevents the absorption of nutrients that the brain needs to function and sufferers are low in serotonin, the mood altering brain chemical and, since 1979 gluten has been implicated in mental illness. Not surprisingly, when some people remove wheat, rye, barley and oats from their diet, anxiety and panic attacks disappear.

Celiac Disease (CD): An autoimmune disease, *Celiac disease* is gluten intolerance in the extreme and a serious disease. Gluten destroys the villi, miniscule "fingers" in the lining of the small intestine that takes in nourishment and you suffer malnutrition and vitamin deficiencies. Switching to a gluten free diet generally removes the symptoms. Celiac disease may be twice as common as thought and hugely undiagnosed. A Finnish study of 3,654 kids, ages 7 to 16, found it in 1 out of 99 children. Yet just 1 in 2,500 cases are diagnosed, and pinpointing the disease may take up to 12 years.

Celiac Disease Symptoms	
PHYSICAL	**MENTAL**
♦ Chronic diarrhea ♦ Stomach pain ♦ Blood in stool ♦ Steatarhea (undigested & unabsorbed fat in stool ♦ Bloating ♦ Non-epileptic seizures ♦ Dermatitis herpetiformis-(skin rash)	♦ Delayed learning ♦ Developmental delays ♦ Poor short & long term memory ♦ Anxiety ♦ Depression ♦ Poor concentration ♦ Withdrawn behavior

Dairy: In spite of those TV ads, you do *not* want a white mustache from milk. Dairy lines the intestine with mucus, making it hard to digest, assimilate and eliminate your food and results in clogged arteries, congestion and fat. An estimated 60% of Americans can't stomach dairy and are lactose intolerant, including Asians (no dairy served in Chinese, Tai, or Japanese restaurants except ice cream for Westerners), African Americans, and Eastern European Jews. **Replace dairy with rice, almond or goat milk, rice or coconut milk ice cream (delicious!), goat yogurt & cheese.**

Calcium & Dairy Myth

Contrary to popular belief, you do not need dairy products, and especially milk, for sufficient calcium intake. The cow does not drink milk for its calcium. We are the only mammals that drink milk past infancy and it's not even human milk. Little wonder many people are lactose intolerant. Osteoporosis, believed caused by insufficient calcium, is uncommon in countries, like Japan and China, that consume large amounts of soy (non GMO) and little if any cow's milk.

You can get as much as and even more calcium from non-dairy products. A cup of quinoa has the calcium content of a quart of milk. A cup of collard greens, cooked soybeans, or three ounces of sardines

with the bones contains as much calcium as a cup of skim milk.
Other good sources of calcium are kale and sesame butter (tahini).

Sugar, Corn & Soy: Many people find sugar, corn & soy hard to digest. Unfortunately, sugar and corn are hard to avoid. Most foods have sugar, while corn unwittingly finds its way into many prepared food as cornmeal, cornstarch, and corn syrup. As soybeans and soy flour have become more widely used, more people have become intolerant to soy as well. Soy creates mucus and suppresses thyroid function, lowering metabolic rate. Further, it interferes with the production of stress-coping hormones in the adrenals limiting your ability to handle stress. Pass up the soy!

Food Additives: Unknowingly, many people react with anxiety and even panic after eating foods with food additives, such as:

➢ **Monosodium glutamate (MSG)**
➢ **Aspartame** (a low-calorie sweetener used in foods &beverages and as table sweetener; sold under name NutraSweet & Equal)
➢ **Food coloring**

Aspartame Jitters

Containing aspartic acid, one of the most excitatory of nutrients, aspartame can be neurotoxic for some people and block serotonin in the brain. Research has found that eating foods with the sweetener can result in insomnia, anxiety, hostility, depression, ADD, headaches, panic disorder, depersonalization, brain fog, memory loss, dizziness and fatigue and worsen symptoms of PMS. Some suggest that mitral valve prolapse, a minor heart murmur and common anxiety mimicker, increases the likelihood of reacting adversely to aspartame. Food containing additives should be replaced with natural, whole foods. READ LABELS!

COMMON FOOD SENSITIVITY TRIGGERS

- ➤ **Mold/Yeast:** on/in nuts (especially peanuts); cheeses; dried fruit; mushrooms; sourdough, beer, and so on
- ➤ **Wheat:** bread; cakes; cookies; cereals; muffins; bagels; pasta; pizza
- ➤ **Gluten:** wheat; oats; rye; barley; spelt; kamu; soy sauce
- ➤ **Dairy:** milk; cheese; ice cream; yogurt; anything else made with dairy
- ➤ **Corn & Corn Grain:** corn; corn chips; corn oil; cornstarch; corn syrup
- ➤ **Food Additives & Preservatives:** MSG (monosodium glutamate) added to many processed foods and, most notably, much Chinese food
- ➤ **Eggs**
- ➤ **Chocolate**

Food Allergens & Environmental Allergens

When you eliminate food allergens, you may better tolerate environmental allergens like pollens, dust, animal dander, and so on as all these allergies are tied together. This may partly explain why you may react to a food one time and not another. For instance, you may have wheat sensitivity only during the grass pollen season when your immune system is overworked. If you don't eat wheat in the spring, you may not have hay fever in the blooming summer.

Reintroducing Food

Unlike food allergies, food sensitivities are generally temporary and typically disappear when you eliminate the reactive food for 60 to 90 days. After this time your body has cleaned out some toxins and you can reintroduce the food. But you must do so slowly. If you react to wheat and decide to have a sandwich made with white bread for lunch and a few cookies for desert, you will overload your system and the symptoms may reoccur dramatically.

Rotating Your Diet

Imagine being sensitive to dairy and not knowing it. If you've had milk with your cereal for breakfast, cottage cheese for lunch and a cheeseburger for dinner and ice cream for desert, you've eaten dairy all day long! To avoid frequent exposure to an allergen, rotate your foods.

It takes four days for the food you eat to leave your body. On the rotation diet, you eat a particular food once every fifth day and don't overload your system. For instance, you may have apples and pears on day 1, cherries and plums on day 2, blueberries and cranberries on day 3, and oranges and lemons on day 4 as they are all in different food families.

If you are allergic to one food, you are likely allergic to other foods in the same food family. If you react to soy, you may also react to peanuts – two common foods that cause allergic reactions. Likewise, if you react to cauliflower, you probably also react to other cruciferous vegetables like broccoli and Brussels sprouts. On a true rotation diet, you eat foods from the same category on the same day and then not again until the fifth day.

Supplementing

As food sensitivities keep the immune system running overtime, they use up the body's nutrients and deplete necessary vitamins, minerals, and amino acids. To replenish these, follow a whole food healthy diet (see chapter 12) and supplement missing nutrients. As you restore body balance, food cravings and allergy symptoms often relieve. Some people, like holistic psychiatrist Dr. Hyla Cass have found that correcting nutritional deficiency and restoring balance often breaks the addictive eating cycle of those with eating disorders and often the food cravings completely disappear.

Include the following in your diet, especially if you have food addictions:

➤ **Magnesium:**   Eat foods high in magnesium as shortage is implicated in addictions and food sensitivities (see page 44 for a list).

> **Digestive Enzymes:** Take digestive enzymes with meals to help the intestinal tract break down food more completely and to minimize small undigested fragments leaking into the blood.
> **Probiotics:** Take daily good intestinal bacteria, naturally occurring in certain yogurts, and fermented foods or take probiotic supplements that contain acidophilis, bifidus and other friendly bacteria (suggested, Dr. Ohiro). HSO, homeostatic soil based organisms are the most powerful (suggested, Primal Defense, BioticGuard; E3Live probiotics).
> **L-glutamine:** Take this amino acid daily as it helps heal leaky gut and reduce cravings, and particular alcohol cravings; dosage – 500 to 1000 mg daily.

Looking to the East

Acupuncture and acupressure have been found to help eliminate food allergies.

Candida Overgrowth

If you have a slew of food sensitivities, you likely also have *Candida* overgrowth, or yeast, a common but easily missed food-mood related problem that makes you feel hyped and muddled. It affects as many as 40 million Americans of all ages and is especially prevalent in women – it's the cause of vaginitis -- and in children with ADD and hyperactivity.

Triggers

A systemic fungal infection appears to trigger yeast overgrowth. Fungi escape into the gastrointestinal tract and travel into the bloodstream and to many parts of the body, weakening the immune system and creating a variety of symptoms. Anxiety is one of the most common psychiatric symptoms, along with head fog.

SYMPTOMS OF CANDIDIASIS

Feelings	Physical
◆ Anxiety	◆ Cravings for sugar or breads
◆ Irritability	◆ Chronic bloating & cramps
◆ Feeling hyped	◆ Diarrhea & constipation
◆ Mood swings	◆ Flatulence
◆ PMS	◆ Undigested food in stool
◆ Depression	◆ Aching joints & muscles
	◆ Ear infections
Thinking	◆ Chronic congestion
◆ Poor concentration	◆ Coughing
◆ Head fog	◆ Frequent infections
◆ Memory losses	◆ Vaginal itching or discharge
◆ Lightheaded	◆ Rashes
Sensory	◆ Food allergies/sensitivities
◆ Increased sensitivity to tobacco smoke, perfumes, fabrics, & chemical odors	◆ Allergies to antibiotics, such as penicillin, sulfa drugs, & tetracycline
◆ Light sensitivity	◆ Headaches
	◆ Dizziness
	◆ Fatigue

Causes

Bacteria and yeast, including *Candida Albicans*, are present on the skin and in the mouth, nose, and digestive tract. Normally, the micro-organisms living in the lower digestive tract assist in digesting food and in synthesizing essential vitamins. But repeated use of antibiotics, oral contraceptives, steroids, many prescription medications, poor diet, stress and anything that depresses immune function, like autoimmune disease such as Crohn's, allow *Candida Albicans* to overgrow. Often, illness will bring on further antibiotic use, exacerbating the yeast problem and intensifying symptoms.

Diagnosis

Candida overgrowth can be detected from blood tests or a stool analysis given by your medical practitioner.

Treatment Options

Candida thrives in a sugary environment and causes you to crave the sweets and carbohydrates that feed it. As *Candida* is a hard condition to eliminate, you will need to follow a strict nutritional protocol to discontinue its growth. So before you sprinkle sugar on your cereal remember that you will be feeding the yeast breakfast as well!

The following steps are suggested:

Restrict Diet

➢ **Eliminate** sugars, wheat, oat, barley and rye, dairy products, yeast and any product that may contain mold, like mushrooms, peanuts, vinegar, aged cheeses, and cantaloupe.
➢ **Limit** or eliminate carbohydrates such as bread, pasta, muffins.
➢ **Limit** fruit to granny smith apples, lemons and limes or eat no fruit.
➢ **Avoid** alcohol which contains sugar; the yeast in alcohol also worsens allergic symptoms.

Kill the Yeast

Conventional
➢ **Antifungal** medication

Natural
➢ **Grapefruit** seed extract
➢ **Caprylic** acid
➢ **Olive** leaf extract and wild oregano, which work synergistically
➢ **Cranberry** extract which also acts as a powerful antioxidant
➢ **Yucca** juice extract
➢ **Garlic**, a potent natural detoxifier that also protects the body from the toxins causing the infection
➢ **Enzymes** cellulose and protease which literally digest *Candida* cell walls
➢ **ScFOS**, a product from Japan

➤ **Probiotics**:   acidophilus   and   other   friendly   bacteria;
    homeostatic soil organisms (HSOs); yogurt
➤ **Alkalizing** food and supplements – see page 48

What to Expect

Initially, you might feel awful as you restrict your diet. Don't be alarmed. As the yeast die off, headaches, fatigue, gastrointestinal problems and sugar cravings are common. This will pass. Most people begin to experience relief from their symptoms within two weeks of initiating treatment. Length of treatment varies by how closely you restrict diet. Typically, you will need to follow dietary restrictions for three to six months.

If you find your Candidiasis chronic and can't seem to get rid of it, you may have an underlying infection that needs to be diagnosed. Candidiasis is also hard to get rid of if you are overly acidic.

Acidity of the Gut

Do you know your daily pH? You should. Based on degree of acidity or alkalinity of the body's blood or other fluids, the cells, organs, and fluids of the body have a pH value and this value determines how well they operate. When the body's pH is too high or too low, the cells become stressed and cannot utilize the nutrients they need or eliminate wastes efficiently. This happens primarily when eating acidic foods that include meat, poultry, dairy and cheese products, eggs, sugar and refined foods, excess fatty and rich foods, and coffee, tea and alcohol, as these foods increase the transit time of food through the digestive tract and vitamins and minerals might not adequately be assimilated. The worst offender is meat which stays in the body for at least three days, producing much acid waste.

When the body's pH balance is disrupted, the body restores balance by pulling essential minerals such as potassium, magnesium, calcium, and sodium from the nervous system and you feel head fog. The resulting under-absorption of minerals and vitamins, especially B and C further stresses the body. Over time, an animal-product based diet creates a metabolic breakdown in the body and you feel increasingly more sluggish, tired and congested with excess mucous or sinus problems that further stress the body and aggravate tension and anxiety. *All* pharmaceutical drugs too have an acid reaction in the body and create similar problems.

Taking supplements won't correct over-acidity, as you might not adequately absorb them. Rather, you need to correct your diet. In the 1950's, Dr. Watson discovered that the brain appears to function optimally at an acid/alkaline balance (pH) of 7.46 of the body's terrain, or slightly *alkaline*. If the blood pH is off, he found people were anxious, depressed, paranoid and even schizophrenic. When he used proper diet to normalize pH in over 300 people, their psychiatric symptoms went away. For information on how to balance pH, see chapter 12, p.268.

Nutritional Deficiency

Overly acidic food, food sensitivities, yeast overgrowth, leaky gut, and illness -- all drain the body of necessary vitamins, minerals, enzymes, amino acids, and essential fatty acids. Such deficiency starves the brain of needed nutrients and creates psychiatric symptoms. Stress is also a major cause of nutritional deficiency. When stressed, our adrenal glands work overtime and vitamins, like C and B, and minerals, like calcium and magnesium get depleted, creating anxiety symptoms.

Vitamins and Minerals

If you suffer anxiety or panic, you need to refurbish your nervous system with the necessary vitamins and minerals. How do you know what vitamins and minerals your system lacks? Holistic practitioners can provide you with specific blood tests to determine your nutritional needs.

Making Serotonin
Vitamin C along with sufficient quantities of vitamin E and the minerals magnesium, zinc, copper, manganese and iron is needed to make serotonin, which governs mood. In some people, supplementing these nutrients has greatly reduced or alleviated symptoms of panic and anxiety.

Vitamins

The most crucial vitamins for optimizing brain function are the Bs first and foremost and then Vitamin C. B vitamins are necessary to deliver oxygen to the brain and protect it from harmful free radicals (toxic chemicals that cause disease and early aging), and to turn glucose into energy in the brain cells to aide in manufacturing neurotransmitters. Especially necessary are B_1, B_2, B_3, B_6, and B_{12} as deficiencies can lead to anxiety, irritability, restlessness, fatigue, emotional instability and depression. Alcoholics for instance commonly show B_1, B_3, and B_{12} deficiencies.

B_1 **(thiamin)** is essential for extracting energy from glucose, the brain's fuel.

B_2 **(riboflavin)** is necessary for releasing energy from carbohydrates, and to make many nerve chemicals and hormones that regulate thinking and memory.

B_3 **(niacin)** is necessary for oxygen transport of the blood. Taking niacin greatly reduces anxiety and depression by helping to regulate GABA, a brain chemical that works by limiting the nerve cell activity in the areas in the brain associated with anxiety. **PF5** is the active, coenzyme form of *B_3* and can be taken along with "Pharma Gaba," a new potent form of GABA.

Pellagra

At the beginning of the twentieth century, pellagra, a disease caused by niacin deficiency in the diet, reached epidemic proportions. Initially, patients became anxious and agitated but as the disease advanced they exhibited dementia, psychosis, mania, and catatonia and were committed to mental institutions. In 1937, the vitamin was added to commercial food products and pellagra essentially disappeared. Today it is seen primarily in alcoholics, drug abusers, the elderly, victims of liver disease, and those with Parkinson's disease as some drugs used to treat the disease can lower niacin levels in the body.

B_5 **(pantothenic acid)** is vital to synthesize hormones and support the adrenal glands.

B₆ (pyroxidine) influences the immune and nervous systems and is needed to convert the amino acid tryptophan to the neurotransmitter serotonin. It is also replete with antioxidants needed for all neurotransmitter activity. So essential is **B₆** for the brain and nervous system that if your diet is short even 1 mg. your nervous system could go haywire. Even minor depletion produces abnormal functioning of several enzymes responsible for metabolizing a variety of nerve chemicals, including serotonin, dopamine, and GABA, which regulate behavior. As toxins from these neurotransmitters don't get broken down, they build up and irritate the nerves. Fruits are naturally high in **B₆** .

Serotonin and Drug Side Effects

Mood swings and depression that occur as side effects of medications such as hormone replacement therapy, oral contraceptives, and anti-tuberculosis drugs might be caused by drug-induced suppression of vitamin B₆ metabolism that in turn under-produces serotonin. For more information, see chapter three.

A condition called *pyroluria* occurs when, due to an inborn error in metabolism, people cannot convert B₆ and the mineral zinc into usable compounds. This inability affects serotonin and other neurotransmitters in the brain making you prone to chronic tension and a low stress threshold. Physically, you are prone to knees that crack, a tendency to sunburn and stretch marks. More than 40% of alcoholics may suffer pyroluria.

B₁₂ (cobalamin) is necessary to form the myelin sheath surrounding nerve cells to speed transmission of chemical messages from one nerve cell to the next. Deficiency from poor diet or the body's inability to absorb the vitamin results in faulty formation of myelin. It comes mostly from animal products. If you are a strict Vegan and do not eat flesh products, take a B₁₂ supplement (see www.mercola com).

B₁₂ & OCD

*A study in Acta Psychiatrica Scandinavica in July, 1988 found
B₁₂ deficiency implicated with some obsessive compulsive patients.*

C is required by the adrenal glands to make hormones that regulate
stress, blood sugar, and other necessary hormonal functioning, as
well as to feed the brain to help nerve transmission by producing
neurotransmitters like serotonin and norepinephrine.   Vitamin C
deficiency is relatively rare in the US because of the wide
availability of citrus fruits and leafy green vegetables.   It takes
approximately 200 mg of Vitamin C (the amount obtained from six
ounces of orange juice or 1 cup of broccoli) to keep the immune
system running smoothly and to meet extra demands of stress.

VITAMINS	VITAMIN DEFICIENCY	FOOD SOURCES
B_1 (thiamine)	◆ Blood sugar imbalance ◆ Fatigue ◆ Weakness ◆ Brain fog ◆ Memory loss ◆ Anxiety ◆ Irritability ◆ Emotional instability ◆ Poor attention & concentration ◆ Aggression ◆ Personality changes	◆ Sunflower seeds ◆ Pine nuts ◆ Sesame seeds ◆ Pecans ◆ Pinto beans ◆ Millet ◆ Lima beans ◆ Filberts ◆ Wild rice ◆ Rye ◆ Brewer's yeast
B_2 (riboflavin)	◆ Depression ◆ Irritability ◆ Confusion ◆ Disorientation	◆ Cayenne pepper ◆ Almonds ◆ Wild rice ◆ Mushrooms ◆ Millet ◆ Kelp ◆ Collard greens ◆ Watercress ◆ Dandelion greens ◆ Kale ◆ Brewer's yeast

B₃ (niacin)	• Muscle weakness • Apathy • Anxiety • Fatigue • Irritability • Depression • Delirium • Memory loss • Dementia	• Cayenne pepper • Wild rice • Sesame seeds • Sunflower seeds • Pumpkin seeds • Mushrooms • Peas • Millet • Kelp • Meat • Chicken • Fish • Peanuts • Wheat germ • Brewer's yeast
B₅ (pantothenic acid)	• Fatigue • Irritability • Restlessness • Nervousness • Insomnia • Depression	• Legumes • Liver • Meat • Chicken • Whole grains
B₆ (pyroxidine)	• Fatigue • Depression • Irritability • Learning problems • Noise sensitivity • Seizures	• Cabbage • Beet • Orange & lemon • Brewer's yeast • Whole grains • Legumes • Nuts • Seeds • Avocado • Dark, leafy green vegetables • Turkey • Tuna
B₁₂ (cobalamin)	• Anemia • Disorientation • Numbness • Tingling in hands & feet • Moodiness • Confusion • Agitation • Dizziness	• Meats • Most fish, especially trout, mackerel, herring • Egg yolks • Yogurt • Dulse (sea veg) • Algae • Wheatgrass

C	Rare	
		♦ Citrus fruit, lemon & orange with peel
		♦ Cantaloupe
		♦ Cayenne pepper
		♦ Red/green pepper
		♦ Kale
		♦ Parsley
		♦ Collard greens
		♦ Broccoli
		♦ Watercress
		♦ Cauliflower
		♦ Persimmons
		♦ Papaya

Minerals

Minerals serve diverse functions, including activating enzymes that are responsible for transmitting nerve impulses and muscle contraction. They cannot be formed in the body but must be obtained from the diet. Deficiencies can lead to anxiety symptoms.

Calcium

Calcium is the most abundant mineral in the body and plays a crucial role in nerve transmission, muscle contraction, heart rhythm and hormone production, in addition to other functions.

Hypocalcemia

Hypocalcemia is marked by too little calcium in the blood and caused by hypoparathyroidism, kidney failure, pancreas inflammation, or Vitamin D deficiency. It occurs mostly in children and mostly girls. Initial symptoms include irregular heartbeat, depression, anxiety, emotional lability, irritability, and fatigue, making it an easy mimicker of an anxiety disorder. It is easily diagnosed through blood tests and readily treated with calcium and Vitamin D supplements.

Magnesium

One of the first minerals depleted in processed foods and also one of the first to deplete under stress, magnesium plays a major role in nerve and muscle function. Deficiencies produce anxiety, irritation and other psychiatric symptoms. In laboratory animals, one study found that a magnesium deficiency increased sensitivity to noise and overcrowding, whereas the animals were better able to cope when their diets were high in magnesium.

Writes Dr. Sherry Rogers in *Food, Mood and Behavior* by Gary Null, "In 27 years of medical practice, the one nutrient I have been very impressed with is magnesium. In treating people with panic disorders, anxiety, insomnia, fatigue and depression, just by merely correcting their magnesium … has made a dramatic difference" (p. 30).

Magnesium deficiency is also associated with several anxiety mimickers, including drug side effects and cardiac arrhythmia.

Chocolate & Magnesium

Depressed people often crave chocolate, which can be a sign of magnesium deprivation as chocolate contains magnesium. Meeting magnesium needs may explain in part why eating chocolate makes you feel better.

The best way to supplement magnesium is with a skin spray or to drink it in a tea called ***Calm*** by Natural Vitality. For better absorption, take magnesium along with taurine, an amino acid.

Potassium

Found primarily within cells, potassium is energizing and necessary for nerve impulse transmission and heart muscle contraction. High in potassium, bananas contain antidepressant serotonin and sleep inducing melatonin, though it won't put you to sleep. Melatonin is activated by darkness.

Phosphorus

A major mineral found mainly in bones and teeth, phosphorus is the most common mineral in the body after calcium.

Copper

Copper is an important trace mineral for the functioning of the central nervous system. Too much copper however also causes problems. According to orthomolecular medicine, which deals with nutritional treatment of mental health problems, excess copper overstimulates the brain and therefore can make you anxious. Excess copper also raises estrogen levels and is implicated as well in female hormone depression. Niacin, vitamin C, and zinc are antagonistic to copper and help neutralize the copper overload.

We are exposed to copper primarily from copper plumbing which can leach into drinking water and from a copper tea kettle (you will see a green stain) and produce similar psychiatric symptoms as Wilson's disease. Some drugs will also exacerbate copper overload, including: neuroleptics; antibiotics; antacids; cortisone; Tagamet; Zantac; diuretics.

SOURCES OF COPPER EXPOSURE	
◆ Copper Plumbing ◆ Birth control pills ◆ Copper sulphate treated jacuzzi's or swimming pools	◆ Drinking water ◆ Prenatal vitamins ◆ Copper IUD's

Wilson's Disease

Severe copper deficiencies occur in Wilson's disease, a rare genetic disease that disables the body's ability to metabolize copper and it builds up, mainly in the liver and the brain. Victims are generally between ages six and twenty. Signs of the disease include distinctive golden-brown or gray-green rings around the corneas in around half the cases. Hepatitis is common because of the toxic effects of excessive amounts of copper in the liver.

WILSON'S DISEASE SYMPTOMS	
Psychiatric Symptoms	**Other Symptoms**
◆ Anxiety ◆ Depression ◆ Mania ◆ School phobia ◆ Hysteria ◆ Hyperactivity	◆ Tremors, jerkiness, subtle twisting of extremities ◆ Blank emotional expression ◆ Emotional lability-inappropriate crying, laughing ◆ Psychosis ◆ Paranoia

Initially, around 20% of cases display psychiatric symptoms. As copper increasingly accumulates, nerve cells are damaged and other symptoms may occur. Psychiatric symptoms often occur before physical symptoms and patients commonly get initially referred to a psychiatrist. This mistake can be fatal: if detected early Wilson's disease can be medically treated and reversed; if left untreated the young person will die prematurely. Chelating treatments eliminate the excessive copper.

Zinc

A trace mineral required for an array of metabolic processes, zinc is necessary for enzyme function, digestion and blood sugar regulation. Constant stress will deplete it and may be the cause of eating disorders like anorexia, bulimia, and obesity. Diminished zinc also leads to altered taste and smell sensitivity and may be implicated in sensory defensiveness.

Zinc Deficiency & Eating Disorders

A study at the University of Kentucky funded by the National Institutes of Health found that most patients with eating disorders were zinc deficient. In some bulimic patients, liquid zinc supplements alone eliminated cravings and binge-purge behavior, while another study published in 1987 in the Journal of Adolescent Health Care found supplemental zinc to alleviate anxiety and depression in anorexic girls.

Whole Food Supplements

Get needed vitamins and minerals from food sources and whole food supplements, as they have been processed at low temperatures to keep them alive, thereby preserving oxygen and enzymes to slowly to build your immune system into vital health. Included in this group are green power powders, which use fresh water single-cell algae as the principal ingredient. Even better, take live blue-green algae like E3Live or BSP (Biosuperfood), or phyloplankton (FrequenSea). In contrast, multivitamins which are synthetic and processed do not assimilate well into your system. In fact, man-made and especially most isolated vitamin and mineral products may actually attack your immune system as everything in the body depends on synergy.

MINERALS	DEFICIENCY SYMPTOMS	FOOD SOURCES
Calcium	♦ Insomnia ♦ Agitation ♦ Palpitations ♦ Muscle spasms & weakness ♦ Irritability ♦ Nervousness ♦ Arm & leg Numbness ♦ Hyperactivity ♦ Depression ♦ Memory Impairment ♦ Delusions	♦ Sesame seeds ♦ Sea vegetables ♦ Collard greens ♦ Kale ♦ Turnip greens ♦ Quinoa ♦ Almonds ♦ Filberts ♦ Parsley ♦ Citrus peel
Magnesium	♦ Anxiety ♦ Muscle tremors ♦ Confusion ♦ Irritability ♦ Short attention span ♦ Sleep problems ♦ Pain	♦ Dulse ♦ Kelp ♦ Almonds ♦ Walnuts ♦ Filberts ♦ Sesame seeds ♦ Lima beans ♦ White beans ♦ Red beans ♦ Millet

Potassium	• Insomnia • Nervousness • Fatigue • Cardiac arrhythmia • Depression	• Bananas • Cantaloupe • Grapefruit • Watermelon • Avocado • Winter squash • Kelp • Mustard greens • Oranges • Potato peelings • Peas • Beans • Fish • Beef liver • Milk
Phosphorus	• Anxiety • Irregular breathing • Fatigue • Tremulousness • Weakness	• Fish • Meat/Poultry • Milk • Eggs • Nuts • Beans • Peas
Copper	• Erratic heartbeat • Sleep interference	• Nuts • Seeds • Legumes • Leafy greens • Whole grains • Fruit • Beans • Liver
Zinc	• Eating disorders • Altered taste & smell sensitivity	• Seafood • Meat • Poultry • Brewer's yeast • Whole grains • Bran

Essential Fatty Acids

Essential fatty acids -- the good fats -- are brain food. Omega-3s alone make up around a quarter of our brains. Deficiency causes brain cells to malfunction and can result in anxiety symptoms. For instance, panic attack has been linked to a deficiency of alpha-linolenic acid, the essential omega-3 fatty acid found in high concentrations in flaxseed oil. In one study, three out of four patients with a history of agoraphobia for ten or more years improved within two to three months after taking flaxseed oil daily. All patients showed signs of a deficiency of this essential fatty acid: dry skin, dandruff, brittle fingernails that grow slowly and nerve disorders.

Omega-3's also regulate mood: the more omega-3s in the diet, the less likely someone will be depressed. As fish is a major source of omega-3s, a country's consumption reflects prevalence of depression. In Japan, where fish is a staple in the diet, the rate of depression is low. In Germany, where fish is not a mainstay in their diet, the rate of depression is high. Fish oil effectively helps treat manic depression or bipolar disorder, and even schizophrenia.

Your body can't make essential fatty acids you must get them from your food.

Food Sources Omega-3:		Food Sources Omega-6:
◆ Hemp	Deep sea fish such as:	◆ Hemp
◆ Flax		◆ Sesame
◆ Chia	◆ Salmon	◆ Pumpkin
◆ Pumpkin seeds	◆ Mackerel	◆ Sunflower seeds
◆ Unsaturated oils	◆ Herring	
◆ Walnuts	◆ Sardines	
◆ Green leafy spinach	◆ Krill	
	◆ Fresh tuna	

As a rule of thumb, always eat a food first before its oil as the food is alive and unprocessed: sunflower seeds rather than sunflower oil; olives rather than olive oil; and so on. And oil is fat!

"High 5"

If you are a vegetarian, a great way to get your essential fatty acids is by throwing the "high 5" seeds onto your salads, in your cereal, or deserts. Using an herb or coffee grinder, grind together:

- **Flaxseed:** healthy alpha-linolenic acid
- **Hemp seeds:** high in the digestion aiding nutrient edestin protein
- **Pumpkin seeds:** high in magnesium, zinc, iron, enzymes & alpha-linolenic acid
- **Sunflower seeds:** high in calcium, vitamin E, potassium & folate
- **Sesame seed** (unhulled): iron, calcium, protein, potassium, & zinc.

Store the mixture in a sealable, airtight jar in the refrigerator.

Amino Acids

Amino acids come from the protein we eat and produce neurotransmitters -- the brain's chemical messengers. Eight essential amino acids create many other amino acids needed by the brain to function. Of note is tryptophan, the building block of the neurotransmitter serotonin. Tryptophan can be gotten from foods (see box) or supplemented (recommended www.nutrabio.com). A form of tryptophan, 5-Hydroxy-Tryptophan (5-HTP), is sold over the counter in health food stores.

SOURCES OF TRYPTOPHAN		
◆ Carrot	◆ Spinach	◆ Chicken
◆ Beet	◆ Turnip	◆ Tuna
◆ Celery	◆ Pineapple	◆ Eggs
◆ Dandelion greens	◆ Bananas	◆ Yogurt
◆ Fennel	◆ Turkey	◆ Milk

Do not take tryptophan if you are on anti-depressants. For more information on amino acids, see pages 114-115.

Enzymes

Enzymes are essential living proteins that enable the body to digest and assimilate food and clear out toxins. Special enzymes digest proteins, carbohydrates, fats, and plant fibers. If they don't do their job, mental and physical health are compromised.

Physical Enzyme Deficiency Signs	
♦ Bloating	♦ Heartburn
♦ Belching	♦ Endocrine gland
♦ Gas	♦ Imbalances
♦ White coated tongue	♦ Diabetes
♦ Bowel disorders	♦ Obesity
♦ Abdominal cramping	♦ High cholesterol
♦ Food allergies or	♦ Arthritis
sensitivities	♦ High stress

Anxiety & Digestive Enzymes

Protease

Protease digests protein and creates acidity. If you don't produce enough to digest protein, your blood can become excessively alkaline which can cause anxiety and insomnia. Inadequate protein digestion also leads to hypoglycemia, or low blood sugar.

Lipase

Lipase digests fat, fat-soluble vitamins, and balances fatty acids. When the enzyme is deficient, vertigo, common with panic attack, can result. Lipase deficiency is also a possible cause of Ménièré's disease, a disturbance of the inner-ear balance system in which the fluid-filled chambers swell and cause periodic vertigo (see chapter 10).

Sucrase

Sucrase is necessary for getting glucose into the brain. Deficiency produces: anxiety; panic; depression; mania; severe mood swings; hypoglycemia; gluten intolerance.

Maltase

Maltase digests maltose, a sugar from starch digestion. Intolerance creates environmental hypersensitivities.

Getting Enzymes

All of us lose our ability to produce concentrated digestive enzymes as we grow older and therefore do not digest our food as well and this can lead to malnutrition. *It's not what you eat but what you assimilate!* Stress, fatigue, aging, low body temperature, and malnourishment all create deficiencies and produce different symptoms, including psychiatric.

The only way to replenish this enzyme potential and conserve our bodies' limited enzyme-producing capacities is to eat natural sources of enzymes -- raw fruits and vegetables. Broccoli, for instance, contains cellulase to break down the cellulose cell walls of the fiber. That people who eat a large percentage of their diet as raw foods are more youthful, energetic, and healthy relates in large part to their greater enzyme reserve. For more information, see chapter 12.

Enzyme Rich Foods

➤ **Sprouts** seeds with a ¼ inch sprout. They literally grow as you bite into them.
➤ **Chlorophyll** rich greens. If you have a "green" vegetable drink in the morning, you feel charged … full of life and energy.
➤ **Fermented** foods such as raw sauerkraut, kim chi, and raw seed and nut cheeses.
➤ **Soy**, miso and tempeh (if your system can tolerate soy).

Enzyme Supplements

In addition to eating enzyme rich food, take digestive enzymes to aid digestion, and systemic enzymes to build up enzymes and destroy free radicals, slowing the aging process. Take digestive enzymes thirty minutes before a meal to empty the stomach and activate digestion, and especially when eating any cooked meal, which lacks naturally occurring enzymes. Take systemic enzymes one hour before or two hours after a meal so the enzymes will absorb quickly into the body to boost the immune system.

Methylation

Methylation is an internal process of adding or removing a methyl group (one carbon connected to three hydrogen atoms) to a compound or other element. In simple terms, receiving a methyl group starts a reaction like turning on a gene or activating an enzyme, while losing it stops the reaction and the gene is turned off or the enzyme is deactivated.

William Walsh, chief scientist at the Pfeiffer Treatment Center in Warrenville, IL, believes that around 45% of the population is under-methylators and 15% are over-methylators, while 60% or so are neither.

Psychiatric and physical conditions associated with under or over-methylation include:

Undermethylation:

- Anorexia
- Bulimia
- Shopping and gambling
- Depression
- Schizo-affective disorder
- Delusions
- Oppositional-defiant disorder
- OCD
- Seasonal allergies
- Perfectionism
- Strong will
- Slenderness
- High libido

Overmethylation:

- Anxiety/panic disorders
- Anxious depression
- Hyperactivity
- Learning disabilities
- Low motivation
- "Space cadet" syndrome
- Paranoid schizophrenia
- Hallucinations
- Absence of seasonal allergies
- Food/chemical sensitivities
- Dry eyes
- Low perspiration
- Artistic/music interests/abilities
- Intolerance to Prozac & other SSRI's

Histamine levels, determined by a blood test from your physician, will indicate whether you are an over or under-methylator. Elevated histamine indicates undermethylation, and taking supplements like taurine, GABA (both precursors to methyl activity in the brain), and SAMe help normalize the level. Low histamine indicates over-methylation and taking such supplements would be detrimental.

Methylation turns on serotonin, and melatonin production. If you are an under-methylator, increasing methylation may balance out these neurotransmitters, lessening depression and improving sleep without drugs. Getting methyl groups also turns on detox reactions to rid the body of chemicals and increasing methylation will help you better detoxify. If an over-methylator, you need folic acid, B_{12} and B_3 to decrease methylation and turn off reactions that need to be off and you may become less hyper or aggressive. You may also have elevated copper levels that need chelating. For more information, check out the *Pfeiffer Treatment Center website* listed at the end of the chapter.

Sugar Seesaw

Sugar – we all crave it. And for good reason. Sugar is glucose, our brain's only fuel source. As 20 percent of the glucose we ingest feeds the brain energy needed to sustain life, desiring sugar is hard-wired into our brain and starts with the sweet taste of mother's milk.

And so, as energy starts to deplete, often by the middle of the afternoon, you reach for a pick up. If you opt for an apple, your sugar level will stabilize gradually as sugar in its natural form of fructose is slow-releasing and balanced by the fiber content. If you reach for a glazed doughnut, you will experience a quick high -- refined sugar, stripped of fiber and nutrients, is rapidly absorbed and broken down into glucose and quickly reaches the brain – and then crash.

Here's what happens.

1. **Adrenal glands** release adrenaline and cortisol to stabilize sugar level, prompting the liver to pump sugar into your blood stream.
2. **Ten** to fifteen minutes later your blood sugar rises to above-normal levels; you feel more aroused and energetic or, if sugar sensitive, hyperaroused and nervous.
3. **Twenty-five** to forty minutes later your blood sugar falls dramatically to below-normal levels; you become cranky and exhausted as your brain is again starved of its fuel.
4. **You** reach for another doughnut to get energized.

Ultimately, nervous tension, anxiety, and irritability become inevitable as sugar depletes the body's B-complex vitamins and minerals, creating stress. Stress in turn rapidly burns up glucose and quickly exhausts it, starving your brain. Further, a diet high in refined sugar increases blood lactate levels and may induce panic in susceptible persons.

Alcoholism & Sugar Cravings

Alcoholics have either high or low blood sugar levels and this causes sugar cravings. Alcohol is full of processed sugar. When blood sugar drops, alcohol boosts sugar and satisfies their need. When on the wagon, they turn to doughnuts and chocolate bars to satisfy their sugar needs. The sugar and grain ferment in their digestive tract and, within 30 to 60 minutes, turn into alcohol satisfying their cravings. If you reduce the sugar cravings by eating whole food and natural sugars, need for alcohol should reduce as well.

Hypoglycemia Mimics Panic Attack

When the brain is starved for fuel, some people become tremulous, confused, spacey and anxious. They have *hypoglycemia*, or periodic drops in blood sugar below normal which produces symptoms similar to a panic attack.

HYPOGLYCEMIA & PANIC ATTACK SYMPTOMS	
◆ Palpitations	◆ Agitation
◆ Anxiety	◆ Blurred vision
◆ Light-headedness	◆ Panic feelings
◆ Trembling	◆ Chest pain
◆ Unsteadiness or weakness	

Nicole, a warm, friendly shiatsu massage therapist is a typical example. For over ten years, she rarely left her house. Before that, she had a thriving practice and was studying to be an acupuncturist. Now going to her mailbox was a challenge.

Nicole suffers from agoraphobia, or fear of the marketplace. It started with a panic attack while shopping in Bloomingdale's in New York one afternoon. While browsing the clothing section, she suddenly felt horrific dread. Shaking, dripping with sweat, and her heart pounding, she dropped a dress she was holding in her hand and ran out the door. She hailed a taxi, a luxury she could ill-afford but *she had to get home*! Two weeks later, she had another attack while in the supermarket. After that, the attacks came on frequently, unpredictably, and anywhere – even at home, and often in the middle of the night. Even her home no longer appeared safe.

She became severely depressed and, though happily married, started to fight bitterly with her husband and to avoid him. "I can't get him to understand the nightmare I'm going through." She started to think of ways to kill herself. Her husband insisted that she see a psychiatrist who put her on the anti-depressant Zoloft. This stopped the suicidal thoughts but Nicole felt dead inside and lost all sexual interest. Her marriage deteriorated further and she felt her life rapidly going downhill.

One day, she read an article on how hypoglycemia or low blood sugar can cause panic attack. She knew she was hypoglycemic, a condition that runs in her family, but she didn't make the connection between her panic attacks and low blood sugar. Now it hit her. That day at Bloomingdales she had neglected to eat breakfast or lunch as she had felt somewhat nauseous all day and that set off hypoglycemia which likely set off her panic attack. After that, the panic attacks seem to occur on days when, busy massaging clients and interning as an acupuncturist she would forget to eat or snack on cookies, which destabilized her sugar level. She started to eat frequently to prevent her blood sugar from dropping, and slowly cut out sugar. Her panic attacks stopped. She discontinued her medication and slowly gained enough confidence to resume her practice and acupuncture internship.

COMMON SYMPTOMS OF HYPOGLYCEMIA

- ➤ **Anxiety**, nervousness, light-headedness, weakness, irritability
- ➤ **Rapid** heart beat:
    - o 2-3 hours following a meal
    - o Middle of night from release of cortisol & other stimulating hormones
    - o Early in morning - blood sugar lowest from fasting all night
- ➤ **Symptoms** disappear soon after eating
- ➤ **Feeling** high after eating sugar & 20-30 minutes later feeling depressed, irritable, or spacey

---

If hypoglycemia evokes a panic attack and you don't make the connection between food and terror, as Nicole did not, you begin to become fearful of having another panic attack under the same circumstances. Anticipatory starts to set in and you become *phobic*. For instance, if you panicked during work because you skipped lunch, you fear returning to work. In the extreme, you become *agoraphobic*, like Nicole. You now have an anxiety disorder secondary to a biological condition. Or hypoglycemia may co-exist with an anxiety disorder and, in the very least sugar instability aggravates both anxiety and panic attacks caused for another reason. If you become hypoglycemic during sleep, when your body metabolizes sugar and demands more, you wake up in a fright – a condition called *nocturnal panic*.

Cause

The cause of hypoglycemia is unknown. Some believe it is not a condition but a symptom of other conditions that can be triggered by stress, infection, exhaustion, or yeast overgrowth and food allergies.

Here's the scenario:

1. **You** have yeast overgrowth and crave sweets, as the yeast live on sugar.
2. **You** gorge on chocolate ice cream.
3. **You** are sensitive to chocolate – remember, the foods you most crave are the ones you are likley allergic to – and your sugar gets unbalanced and you crash.
4. **Cravings** reset and you spoon down a pint of rocky road ice cream.

Chemical poisoning can also create sugar intolerance. Mercury poisoning especially kills the zinc in the body and inactivates the enzymes necessary for digestion (see chapter 14). As you don't burn sugar, you become sugar-intolerant.

Diagnosis

If you suspect hypoglycemia, your doctor can give you a 6-hour glucose tolerance test. After fasting for 12 hours, you drink a highly concentrated sugar solution and your blood sugar is measured every half hour for six hours. Beware though! This test will not pick up milder cases of hypoglycemia. If you test negative but have the above symptoms, you need to follow dietary restrictions. You should also get checked for food sensitivities as 80% of people with hypoglycemia have them.

Treatment Options

Fortunately, sugar-imbalance, or hypoglycemia can be overcome by restricting simple sugar intake. This is hard. Whereas our Stone Aged ancestors had to travel far to find an apple in season or the rare honey comb, jelly beans are on every corner today.   Take heart. As you get off the sugar seesaw, sugary food will lose its appeal.

To balance sugar level, avoid the following foods:

Simple Sugars:	High GI FOOD*	Simple Starches:
♦ Candy ♦ Cookies ♦ Cakes ♦ Colas ♦ Ice cream ♦ Honey ♦ Corn syrup ♦ Molasses ♦ High fructose	♦ White bread ♦ Puffed rice ♦ Puffed wheat ♦ Instant rice ♦ Instant potatoes ♦ Corn chips ♦ Raisins	♦ Pasta ♦ Refined cereals ♦ Potato chips ♦ White bread **Sugar at top of top list of ingredients:** ♦ Salad dressings ♦ Soft drinks ♦ Baked beans

*GI - Glycemic Index

GI measures how quickly food is turned into glucose causing a quick rise in blood sugar and raising insulin. Some healthy foods, such as carrots, corn, flax seeds, bananas, apricots, papaya, and watermelon have a high GI and some suggest eating these foods in moderation. Others claim that unless you mix them with other high GI foods, you can't eat enough at one sitting to destabilize your sugar level.

➢ **Eat** complex carbohydrates, like whole grains, fruits and vegetables, as the sugar in these foods is digested slowly and released gradually into the blood circulation.

➢ **Get sufficient chromium, iron, B vitamins and C:**

  ♦ **Chromium** carries sugar to your cells and helps to stabilize sugar level. Deficiency leads to glucose intolerance, anxiety and fatigue. Eat chromium rich foods such as:

    o Whole grains
    o Apples
    o Bananas
    o Spinach
    o Brewer's yeast
    o Wheat germ
    o Potatoes
    o Eggs

- o Beef   o Liver
- o Chicken

If necessary supplement with daily chromium.

- ◆ **Iron** deficiency can lead to anemia, a possible cause of hypoglycemia. Eat iron rich foods such as:
  - o Pumpkin, sesame, sunflower seeds
  - o White beans
  - o Lima beans
  - o Cayenne
  - o pepper
  - o Chickpeas
  - o Millet
  - o Parsley
  - o Organ meats
  - o Egg yolk
  - o Blackstrap
  - o molasses
  - o Lecithin
- ◆ **Vitamin B-complex and vitamin C** increase your resiliency to stress, while vitamin-B helps regulate the metabolic process that converts carbohydrates to sugar.

➢ **Don't Gorge:** To regulate your sugar level, eat five or six small, frequent meals divided evenly throughout the day. Eat breakfast and snack between meals. What kind of snack? Some feel eating protein and complex carbohydrates, like peanut butter spread on a whole wheat cracker, controls sugar level. Others recommend that every meal should consist of 30% protein, 30% fat and 40% carbohydrates, snacks included. Whole food nutritionists recommend *not* combining protein, starches, and fruits, as food digests at different rates and in different acid/alkaline environments. As a rule of thumb, they recommend eating vegetables with protein, or with starches or with avocado, and fruits with other fruits, although melons should be eaten alone. For a snack, you could have fruit, *or* nuts with dates, *or* corn chips and beans. As food is quickly digested, assimilated, and eliminated, sugar regulation is not a problem.

➢ **Get Moving:** Exercise, like aerobics or weight bearing exercise, weight lifting or yoga help control sugar level by building muscle mass as the more muscle you have, the better your body is able to regulate glucose levels.

Not Quite Hypoglycemia

What if your symptoms are similar to those of hypoglycemia but don't entirely fit the profile? The pancreas is subject to stimulation through the vagus nerve, which goes through the hypothalamus, the seat of emotions. Stress alone can force the pancreas to secrete insulin and determine how much glucose is converted to energy.

Caffeine Jitters

Ever wonder how some people can drink coffee all day and sleep at night? It's their liver – it easily detoxifies the caffeine. But if your system is easily overaroused, it's a bet that your liver does not quickly detoxify and a cup of coffee makes you jumpy.

Found in coffee, tea, colas, cocoa and chocolate, and some over-the-counter drugs, caffeine stimulates by increasing adrenaline in the brain and you feel alert and awake. But the effect doesn't last.

Here's what happens:
1. **You** drink a cup of coffee.
2. **Almost** immediately you feel more alert and focused.
3. **An** hour or so later, you begin to feel lethargic, drowsy, cranky, and foggy.
4. **You** grab another cup of coffee or a chocolate candy bar to perk up again.
5. **You** become addicted and up your intake.

The worst offender is coffee as it contains two other stimulants: theophylline and theobromine, which are also found in decaffeinated coffee. A mere four cups per day can make you nervous and jittery. In a study published in the *American Journal of Psychiatry*, 1,500 psychology students were divided into four categories based on coffee intake: abstainers; low consumers (1 cup or equivalent a day); moderate (1-5 cups a day); and high (5 cups or more a day). The moderate and high consumers demonstrated higher levels of anxiety and depression than the abstainers. Further, the high consumers had higher incidence of stress-related medical problems with lower academic performance. Caffeine injections also produce panic in healthy volunteers participating in anxiety studies.

COMMON SYMPTOMS OF CAFFEINE USE	
PSYCHOLOGICAL	PHYSICAL
♦ Nervousness	♦ Headache
♦ Restlessness	♦ GI irritation
♦ Anxiety	♦ Rapid heart beat
♦ Irritability	♦ Rapid breathing
♦ Excitement	♦ Ringing in the ears
♦ Trembling	♦ Frequent urination
♦ Insomnia	

If you are already suffering anxiety and panic episodes, even a little caffeine will make you feel uncomfortable and jittery and aggravate the frequency and severity of episodes.

Causes of Caffeine Jitters

➤ **Caffeine** stimulates the release of stress hormones from the adrenal glands, like cortisol, triggering fight or flight -- fast pulse, quick breathing, and muscle tension, physiological responses typical of anxiety states.

➤ **Caffeine** interferes with adenosine, a brain chemical that normally has a calming affect, and raises levels of lactate, a biochemical implicated in producing panic attacks. Even in normal people, eight cups of coffee quickly ingested can produce symptoms that mimic a panic attack.

➤ **An** allergic reaction to caffeine appears as anaphylaxis and the body enters the fight or flight mode, which may be mistaken as hyperactivity, anxiety, or panic disorder.

➤ **A diuretic**, caffeine speeds elimination of many minerals and vitamins, such as potassium, zinc, magnesium, calcium, vitamin C, and the B vitamins, and especially the anti-stress vitamin B_1. Deficiency increases anxiety, mood swings, and fatigue.

➤ **Caffeine** causes a rise in blood-sugar levels in the first hour, followed by a drop in glucose to subnormal levels.

Breaking the Habit

Avoid Caffeine Products Like:
♦ Coffee   ♦ Teas

- ◆ Soft drinks
- ◆ Chocolate
- ◆ Caffeinated waters
- ◆ Chocolate

- ◆ Ice cream & yogurt with coffee, mocha, or cappuccino
- ◆ OTC drugs, like NoDoz, Excedrin, Anacin, Dexatrim

Replace Caffeine

➢ **Drink** decaffeinated coffee but choose one that uses a non-chemical-based method of decaffeination, such as the "Swiss water process."

➢ **Substitute** with an herbal coffee substitute like Teecchino.

➢ **Include** arousing ginger, cayenne, and peppermint in your diet.

➢ **Give** your system an early morning boost naturally:
- Drink something with intense flavor, like pure cranberry juice, or suck on a lemon.
- Eat something that makes you chomp and bite, like an apple, as heavy work to the jaw is energizing and alerting.
- Take a cold shower.
- Do quick, intense physical activity, like jumping jacks or push-ups.
- Listen to upbeat music.

➢ **Use** herbal energizers, or "adaptogens": ginseng, ashwaganda, licorice root, reishi mushroom, rhodiola rosea.

➢ **Include** stimulating amino acids in your diet or supplement:
- Phenylalanine (natural caffeine), found in meats, wheat germ, dairy products, granola, chocolate and oatmeal
- Tyrosine, made from phenylalanine, rapidly alerts you. Too much however can make you jittery.
- Green tea (decaffeinated)
- Coenzyme Q_{10}

➢ **Detoxify** your liver (see chapter 13), as the more sensitive you are to the caffeine jitters, the less well your liver is metabolizing the drug and clearing it from the body.

➢ **Reduce** caffeine gradually to avoid caffeine withdrawal as it takes around four days to break the coffee habit. Expect headaches and drowsiness during withdrawal.

Quick Review

➢ **Food is a drug**. What we eat directly impacts our physiology and biochemistry of our brain.

➢ **Food** related problems, like food sensitivities and Candida overgrowth eat up the gut, affecting the nervous system and creating symptoms that easily mimic an anxiety or panic attack.

➢ **Processed**, pasteurized, salted, sugared, colored, artificial, overly cooked, acidic and toxic food leaves us overfed but malnourished. Nutritional deficiency affects brain chemistry and makes thinking fuzzy and emotions labile.

➢ **Nutritional** deficiencies create anxiety or panic symptoms. These include especially the B Vitamins and C, and the minerals calcium and magnesium, as well as deficiency in essential fatty acids, particularly Omega 3s, amino acids, and enzymes.

➢ **Sugar** instability is a major mimicker of anxiety. Hypoglycemia, or low blood sugar triggers panic attack in an untold number of people diagnosed with panic disorder.

➢ **Caffeine** is a stimulant that, often unknowingly, creates the jitters and even panic in those whose systems easily react to stimulants.

Resources

Suggested Books

General
- *Food-Mood-Body Connection* by Gary Null (Seven Stories Press, 2000).
- *Nutritional Influences on Illness* (Third Line Press, 1993).
- *Food and Mood* by Elizabeth Somer (Owl, Henry Holt, 1995).
- *Nutrition and Mental Illness: An Orthomolecular Approach to Balancing Body Chemistry by Carl C. Pfeiffer* (Healing Arts Press, 1988).
- *What Your Doctor May Not Tell You About(TM) Anxiety, Phobias, and Panic Attacks : The All-Natural Program That Can Help You Conquer Your Fears* by Douglas Hunt (Warner, 2005).

Food sensitivities
- *Coping with Food sensitivities*, by Dick Thom (Sterling, 2002).

- *Unraveling the Mystery of Autism and Pervasive Developmental Disorder: A Mother's Story of Research and Recovery* by Karyn Seroussi (Simon and Schuster, 2000).
- *Food Sweeteners – Aspartame and Its Adverse Reactions, Strange Symptoms, Illness Behavior & Controversy*, by Miladie L. Dillard (Abbe, 1994).
- *The Complete Guide to Food Allergy and Intolerance* by Jonathan Brostoff & Linda Gamlin (Inner Traditions International Limited, 2000).
- *Brain Allergies: The Psychonutrient and Magnetic Connections* by Willam H. Philpott (McGraw Hill, 2000).

Candida Overgrowth and Parasites
- *Guess What Came to Dinner* by Ann Louise Gittelman (Avery, 2001).
- *The Yeast Connection Handbook* by W. G. Crook (Professional Books, 1999).

Sugar Intolerance
- *Sugar Blues* by William Dufty (Warner Books, 1974).

Vitamins, Minerals, Amino Acids
- *The Miracle of Magnesium* by Carolyn Dean (Ballantine, 2003).
- *The Mood Cure: The 4-Step Program to Take Charge of Your Emotions—Today* by Julia Ross (Penquin, 2003).

Nutritional Intervention for Psychiatric Disorders

Pfeiffer Treatment Center
4575 Weaver Parkway
Warrenville, IL 60555-4039
(630) 505-0300 - (630) 836-0667 fax
http://www.hriptc.org

2

★

Disease and Dis-Ease

James suffered debilitating panic attacks. His first one hit like lightning. Found lying on a neighbor's patio screaming, "I'm dying! I'm having a heart attack!" James was rushed in an ambulance to the nearest hospital. The emergency room physician found nothing physically wrong with him and referred him to a psychoanalyst.

After four years in analysis, James felt understood. But the panic attacks continued. He saw a psychiatrist who diagnosed him as depressed and put him on antidepressants. The panic attacks continued. Finally, James was referred for electroconvulsive therapy (ECT). Fortunately, before being hospitalized, he met with Dr. Marc Gold, a biopsychiatrist and author of *The Good News about Panic, Anxiety and Phobias.* Dr. Gold suggested a complete medical, neurological and endocrinological testing. James glucose-tolerance test revealed he had non-insulin dependent diabetes. His panic attacks were apparently triggered by wild fluctuations in his blood sugar levels. He was treated medically and the panic attacks ceased.

Many medical illnesses mimic anxiety or panic. And as happened to James, frequently they go undetected. Often the major symptoms are purely psychiatric and the illness goes undiagnosed: symptoms of hypoglycemia, for instance, are a dead ringer for panic attack. Or psychiatric symptoms emerge before physical symptoms, and the condition doesn't get diagnosed in its early stages when it's most treatable. For instance, the initial symptoms of lupus, a chronic auto-immune disease, may be anxiety and obsessive-compulsive behavior.

In a typical scenario, people will feel ill and run to their doctors with a litany of common physical complaints like headache, weakness, insomnia, dizziness, a racing heart, or just feeling unwell. Doctors perform routines tests that fail to uncover a problem. For instance, mild hypoglycemia may not show up on a 6-hour glucose tolerance test. Rather than exploring further, doctors assume the symptoms are stress induced and prescribe Xanax and Zoloft. The patient gets sicker and tries another doctor with similar results. This can go on for years and with serious consequences. Delayed diagnosis can result in serious impairment or death, as in brain tumor, pancreatic cancer, heart attack or Lyme disease.

In this chapter we explore how **cardiovascular disease, infections, endocrine and metabolic disorders,** and even **cancer** can all mimic an anxiety disorder.

Endocrine Disorders

Among the biggest mimickers of anxiety and panic are endocrine disorders and especially those of the thyroid gland.

The endocrine system produces hormones that work with the nervous system to maintain internal balance and harmony. \

Endocrine System	
◆ Thyroid	◆ Hypothalamus
◆ Parathyroid	◆ Pituitary
◆ Adrenals	◆ Ovaries & testes
◆ Thymus	

Endocrine Disorders as Psychological Mimickers

A 1978 study conducted by researchers Hall and Popkin and reported in Archives of General Psychiatry showed that endocrine disorders, especially thyroid, account for over 20% of psychological masquerades. When hormones are out of balance, endocrine disorders, such as **hyperthyroidism, hypothyroidism, hypoglycemia** *(see chapter one),* **diabetes mellitus** *and* **Cushing's syndrome** *result and frequently mimic an anxiety disorder. When the adrenals are overworked,* **adrenal exhaustion** *results, depleting your immune system and creating a state of constant stress and anxiety.*

Thyroid Disorders

Located at the front and base of your neck, the thyroid gland plays a role in metabolizing the nervous system. When it over- or under secretes thyroid hormone, psychiatric symptoms emerge:

> **Too little** thyroid hormone, or hypothyroidism, mimics depression
> **Too much** thyroid hormone, or hyperthyroidism, mimics anxiety and panic disorder

Hyperthyroidism

In **hyperthyroidism**, an overactive thyroid gland pumps high levels of thyroid into the body and raises metabolic rate. The brain immediately detects this imbalance and anxiety, jitteriness, irritability, emotionality, distractibility and hyperactivity result along with a plethora of physical symptoms. The heart can race as high as 200 beats a minute and, assuming you are having a heart attack, you rush to the emergency room. A cardiologist will conduct tests, find nothing, and send you home recommending that you see a psychiatrist. In one study of hyperthyroid patients, twenty-three of twenty-nine had symptoms of anxiety that could have met the DSM-IV criteria for panic disorder. When given thyroid medication (propanolol), 91% of the patients experienced relief from anxiety.

Symptoms of Hyperthyroidism	
◆ Rapid heartbeat	◆ Thinning fine & silky hair
◆ Excessive sweating	◆ High energy" fatigue
◆ Fatigue	◆ Flushed, warm skin (in
◆ Heat intolerance	contrast to cold, clammy
◆ Weight loss	hands of anxious person)

More common in women than in men, hyperthyroidism tends to develop during puberty and in middle life and is often precipitated by severe stress. The onset can be slow or abrupt.

Detecting hyperthyroidism is complex and can't be identified in the office by the usual blood chemistry. Consequently, physicians easily miss the medical markers until symptoms become extreme. Some people become symptomatic during the night and awaken with their mind racing, heart pounding, and anxious and nervous. Often, they will get diagnosed as having a sleep disorder and prescribed sleeping pills, or as having panic attack, and prescribed anti-depressants. As the latter helps reduce stress, which sets off thyroid problems by causing the body to pump out antibodies to the thyroid gland, the pills may help reduce the incidents of nocturnal panic. Such relief will confirm that the problem is psychiatric not physical and cause further delay in diagnosis.

Thyroid problems are serious and should be treated promptly or they will worsen. Often they exist as part of an infection syndrome that combines any combination of parasites, *Candida* overgrowth, and viral syndromes like the common Epstein-Barr virus. The existence of these possible co-existing illnesses should be investigated as well.

Hashimoto's Thyroiditis

Hashimoto's thyroiditis produces hypothyroidism, along with some signs of hyperthyroidism and you may be both depressed and anxious. Swinging from low to high thyroid, you experience profound fatigue, poor memory and concentration, depression, and nervousness ranging from mild anxiety to full-blown panic attacks.

Diabetes Mellitus

Diabetes can create anxiety and depression and an anxiety disorder co-exists with the medical illness. In this case, both the diabetes and the anxiety disorder need to be treated.

Hyperglycemia (high levels of blood glucose) frequently occurs in diabetics who consume too much food to be metabolized by their insulin, and produces severe anxiety. One study found generalized anxiety disorder six times higher in diabetics than in the general population. Once blood glucose levels are stable, the anxiety abates.

Cushing's Syndrome

Also known as hyperadrenalism, **Cushing's syndrome** results from excess circulation of the steroid cortisol and is caused either by hyperactivity of the adrenal cortex or by cortisol-secreting tumors elsewhere in the body. In some cases, steroid abuse by athletes or others or prolonged stress brings on the syndrome. More women than men have the condition.

About half with Cushing syndrome experience anxiety and depression, the latter more common. Though distinctive physical markers accompany the syndrome, they generally don't appear until later, making the disease an easy anxiety mimicker.

Cushing Syndrome Physical Markers	
♦ Moon-faced appearance ♦ Weight gain mostly around trunk	♦ Purple stripes on abdomen ♦ Easy bruising

Depending on the cause, treatment includes surgery, radiation, or drugs that block the effects of the excess cortisol.

Pheochromocytoma

A rare tumor of the adrenal gland, **pheochromocytoma** produces excessive levels of catecholamines, like adrenaline, which helps you respond to stress, or dopamine or noradrenaline, the feel good neurotransmitters, and these excessive levels throw off the body's hormonal balance. This can trigger a range of intense symptoms that mimic a panic attack making pheochromocytoma an easy mimicker of panic disorder.

Symptoms of Pheochromocytoma	
♦ Severe anxiety ♦ Pounding headaches ♦ Nausea ♦ Diarrhea ♦ Sweating	♦ Difficulty breathing ♦ Heart palpitations ♦ Pallor ♦ Vertigo

Distinguishing pheochromocytoma from panic attack:

➤ **Generally** occurs in those under twenty-five who complain of panic or severe anxiety.

➤ **High** blood pressure which may occur only during panic attack.

➤ **Sneezing,** laughing, sexual intercourse, and urinating triggers it though emotional stress alone can also trigger it.

➤ **History** of endocrine tumors.

The disease is diagnosed by identifying increased levels of catecholamines in the blood or urine. Surgical removal of the non-malignant tumor cures this condition in 90 percent of cases.

Carcinoid Syndrome

Marked by upper-body flushing, diarrhea, abdominal cramps, and color changes in the skin from pallid white to blue, *carcinoid syndrome* refers to symptoms brought on by secretions of carcinoid tumors that affect the endocrine cells in the small intestine, stomach, or appendix. Forty percent of patients suffer psychiatric symptoms, with heightened anxiety as the most common. Certain foods or alcohol, physical exertion, excitement, or epinephrine infusion can trigger the syndrome. A serious condition, it requires immediate medical attention as these tumors often spread to other organs.

Panhypopituitarism

Panhypopituitarism results when the anterior pituitary gland produces decreased hormones in response to tumors, injury, radiation, or infectious diseases. Three fourths of patients experience depression, anorexia nervosa, or anxiety. Treatment consists of hormone therapy and, in some cases removal of the pituitary gland.

Panhypopituitarism Physical Markers	
◆ Lowered sex drive	◆ Hypothyroidism
◆ Infertility	◆ Hypotension
◆ Hypoglycemia	◆ Susceptibility to infection

Adrenal Exhaustion

The stress response, commonly known as flight/fight was designed to enable us to survive an immediate threat: the charging lion, impending tidal wave, or writhing snake. Such life threatening danger required an immediate response and energy-producing chemicals coursed through the bloodstream to prepare for fleeing or fighting danger. If that wasn't possible, the animal played dead long enough to escape the predator's attention and to run for its life.

In modern life, life threatening danger is uncommon for most. Rather, we fight traffic, the bill collector, the screaming siren, stale indoor air, a nagging child, and a demanding boss. As these threats don't put us in immediate danger, often we can neither flee nor fight these stressors and stress chemicals build up and stew inside. Over time, stress and over-reactivity become chronic and a constant stream of stress hormones wears down the body. Eventually the immune system is depleted and the body succumbs and breaks down.

The adrenal glands drive the endocrine system's stress response, primarily through the release of two stress hormones that drive flight/fight, adrenaline and cortisol. Under prolonged stress, the adrenal glands become overtaxed and go into a state of temporary underfunctioning. Over time, constant stress uses up the defensive's energy reserves and they eventually reach the last stage of exhaustion.

- **The body** becomes overworked and depleted of its normal energy reserves.
- **Fatigue** becomes chronic, and the person tends to have a difficult time handling any stressful situation without overreacting or becoming unglued: while awake you feel agitated, anxious, easily confused and exhausted; while asleep you remain revved up and you feel restless, startle easily from noise, arouse from temperature changes, and awaken fatigued.
- **Panic** or mood swings, irritation to light, noise and touch, depression, lack of attention to personal care, and addiction to coffee, cigarettes, and stimulants and alcohol and drug abuse are likely.

Symptoms of Adrenal Exhaustion

Sensory
- Sensitivity to exhaust fumes, smoke, fog, petrochemicals
- Aversion to strong odors
- Low noise tolerance noise
- Sensitivity to bright light

Psychological
- Rapid mood swings
- Nervousness
- Depression

Emotional
- Emotionally stressed
- Easily frustrated
- Cry easily

Mental
- Lack of alertness
- Inability to concentrate
- Head fog

Neurological
- Dizziness upon standing
- Startle easily
- Lightheadedness
- Headaches
- Fainting
- Insomnia
- Poor sleep
- Awake unrested
- Clumsy

Physical
- Post exercise fatigue & stress
- Dark circles under eyes
- Poor immune functioning - frequent colds; chronic infections
- Breathing difficulties
- Edema
- Heart palpitations
- Indigestion
- Chronic heartburn
- Infrequent urination
- Lack of thirst
- Salt cravings
- Fatigue
- Need caffeine to get going
- Low blood sugar symptoms
- Low blood pressure
- Food allergies/sensitivities
- Weak & shaky
- Hands/feet sweat easily
- Teeth clenching/grinding
- Chronic back pain
- Low cholesterol
- Trouble breathing – asthma
- Small jawbone or chin

Treatment

Once you reach the last stage of adrenal exhaustion, you need a holistic approach to build your nervous system. Covered in part III, this includes nutritional support, detoxifying body and environment, and alleviating EMF's. Balancing emotions is a must, as is learning to think more positively, engaging in exercise and, importantly, stress reduction activities like meditation or progressive muscle relaxation. In addition, some holistic doctors recommend adrenal tonics, such as the Chinese kidney "yin" formulas. For more information, see kitchendoctor.com and *The Mood Cure* by Julia Ross (see Resources).

Cardiac Disease

The scene is repeated nightly in emergency rooms. People come in with hearts racing, gasping for breath and terrified they're having a heart attack and about to die. Their EKG is normal. The diagnosis is panic attack. The patient is sent home on tranquilizers and referred to a psychiatrist.

While many *are* only suffering panic attack, others may actually *have* undiagnosed cardiac problems. Cardiac-related problems, which includes the heart and all the veins and arteries that transport blood throughout the body, commonly mimic an anxiety disorder. Further, one of three cardiac patients suffers panic disorder.

Mitral Valve Prolapse

The foremost cardiac anxiety mimicker is mitral valve prolapse (MVP), a common and generally benign inherited heart condition. The heart is a pump with four chambers. Blood moves through the mitral valve, the valve separating the upper and lower chambers on the left side of your heart, as it passes from the upper to the lower chamber. With mitral valve prolapse, a slight defect prevents the valve from closing completely; some of the blood can flow back from the lower to upper chamber, creating a slight heart murmur.

Though not serious in most cases, the resulting rush of blood from an MVP episode can feel like a fluttering or a racing heart, sometimes accompanied by difficulty breathing and even chest pain. Not surprisingly, many become anxious and may even have a panic attack. So strong is the relationship between MVP and anxiety disorders that studies have found that 30 percent of patients diagnosed with generalized anxiety disorder or panic disorder and 44 percent of patients with bipolar disorder has MVP. The incidence is far higher in women and especially young women, the group most likely to experience panic attacks. As MVP sufferers seem more volatile and emotionally unstable than others, some researchers believe that people with MVP are wired differently. Normal stresses and surprises set off an exaggerated response, flooding their systems with stress hormones that leave them "wired and tired."

The sign of MVP is a heart murmur, or click, and can generally be picked up using a stethoscope. But this procedure can overly diagnose a murmur or miss it altogether. Only an echocardiogram (a procedure using sound to image the internal structures of the heart) can give a definitive diagnosis of MVP. After receiving an echocardiogram in my thirties, I was diagnosed with MVP but not symptomatic. In my 40's, I began having cardiac arrhythmia which caused intense anxiety. I saw a cardiologist who, using a stethoscope, did not detect a heart murmur and, without ordering an echocardiogram, told me I did not have the condition. I went to a different cardiologist who gave me an echocardiogram. It revealed moderate mitral valve prolapse and, though innocent, needs to be watched.

If MVP is benign, generally cardiologists recommend monitoring the condition. If MVP presents symptoms, you may, according to a large study, be low in magnesium. The study found that taking 600 mg of magnesium one to three times daily improved symptoms. If you decide to self-treat with magnesium supplements, don't take more than 600 mg of magnesium per day. A suggested product is *Calm* by Natural Vitality. Consult a holistic doctor for a specific protocol for mitral valve prolapse.

Essential Hypertension

Millions of Americans suffer hypertension or high blood pressure. Though the exact cause is unknown, a number of conditions, such as adrenal, thyroid, and kidney disorders, may result in secondary hypertension. Hypertension may be symptomless, or present with symptoms easily mistaken for an anxiety disorders, such as headaches, ringing in the ears, lightheadedness, and fatigue.

Cerebral Arteriosclerosis

Arteriosclerosis is marked by the thickening, hardening, and loss of elasticity of the artery walls.

Internal Hemorrhage

A serious condition that requires prompt medical intervention, an internal hemorrhage is a large loss of blood within the body from arteries, veins, or capillaries.

Subacute Bacterial Endocarditis

A serious bacterial infection, endocarditis is the inflammation of the lining of the heart or heart valves that, left undetected, can result in potentially fatal heart valve damage. Until it becomes acute, a patient may appear to be suffering only from anxiety-like symptoms such as weakness, loss of appetite, joint pain and night sweats.

Cardiac Arrhythmias

The heart must maintain a continuous flow of oxygen-laden blood by uninterrupted pumping. Arrhythmia or alternations in the rhythm of the heart can create symptoms like rapid heartbeat, palpitations, chest pain, breathlessness, and irritability that, until the condition is diagnosed can appear as anxiety. Magnesium and potassium deficiencies can cause cardiac arrhythmia and should be supplemented. The herb Hawthorne can treat minor arrhythmias.

Paroxysmal Atrial Tachycardia

A heart condition characterized by sudden, explosive episodes of rapid heartbeat, paroxysmal atrial tachycardia can create profound unease, anxiety, unsteadiness and explosive behavior. Swollen ankles are a marker.

Myocardial Infarction (MI)

A heart attack or MI may be caused by a blood clot that interrupts the flow of blood, resulting in damaged heart tissue. Sometimes people experience a sudden and sharp pain that starts in the chest and may radiate to the neck, left arm, or upper abdomen and generally seek immediate medical attention. But sometimes the symptoms are deceptively milder, including indigestion, mild discomfort, and irregular heartbeat, and may be mistaken for an anxiety attack: heart attacks and panic attack have at least ten symptoms in common.

	Symptoms	Cause(s)
Mitral Valve Prolapse	◆ Fluttering or racing heart ◆ Difficulty breathing ◆ Anxiety ◆ Panic	Defective heart valve
Essential Hypertension	◆ Headaches ◆ Ringing in the ears ◆ Lightheadedness ◆ Fatigue	Unknown
Cerebral Arteriosclerosis	◆ Headache ◆ Dizziness ◆ Memory defects masked as anxiety attack	◆ Hypertension ◆ Kidney disease ◆ Diabetes ◆ Excessively high fats in blood
Internal Hemorrhage	◆ Rapid pulse ◆ Low blood pressure ◆ Dizziness ◆ Thirst ◆ Cold hands or feet	◆ Fainting ◆ Fear, restlessness ◆ Loss of blood
Subacute Bacterial Endocarditis	◆ Weakness ◆ Loss of appetite ◆ Joint pain ◆ Night sweats	◆ Bacterial infection
Cardiac Arrhythmia	◆ Palpitations ◆ Rapid heartbeat ◆ Tachycardia (very rapid heartbeat) ◆ Breathlessness ◆ Chest pain ◆ Behavioral changes, e.g., sudden irritability & flying off handle	◆ Coronary artery disease ◆ Electrolyte imbalances, e.g., sodium or potassium ◆ Changes in heart muscle ◆ Injury from a heart attack ◆ Healing after heart surgery ◆ Magnesium & potassium deficiency

Paroxysmal Atrial Tachycardia	◆ Tachycardia ◆ Profound unease ◆ Anxiety ◆ Unsteadiness ◆ Explosive behavior ◆ Swollen ankles	◆ Cardiac disorder ◆ Metabolic disorder ◆ Effects of certain drugs ◆ Emotional stress ◆ Physical stress ◆ Hyperthyroidism
Myocardial Infarction (MI)	◆ Chest pain ◆ Indigestion ◆ Mild discomfort ◆ Irregular heartbeat	Blood clot

Infectious Disease

Infectious diseases, viral and bacterial, sudden or chronic (e.g., dental infections) have a profound effect on normal brain function and cause symptoms easily mistaken for anxiety.

Infectious Disease Symptoms	
◆ Apathy ◆ Exhaustion ◆ Confusion ◆ Appetite & memory loss	◆ "Nervous stomach" ◆ Social withdrawal ◆ Lethargy ◆ Loss of sex drive

In some cases, infections can lead to serious mental illness. In "The Role of Infections in Mental Illness," Frank Strick notes that infectious disease can be a common cause for inducing psychiatric symptoms. Mental patients, for instance, have much higher rates of parasitic infection than the general population.

Common viral infections include:

➢ **Mononucleosis** (the "kissing" disease), a type of herpes virus that attacks the body's disease-fighting white blood cells as well as Herpes Simplex Type 2

➢ **Hepatitis**, a common viral liver infection

➢ **Encephalitis**, an inflammation of the brain

> **Brucellosis,** a chronic disease of farm animals that can be transmitted to humans

---

Herpes & Schizophrenia

Research done at the John Hopkins Children's Center found that mothers with Herpes Simplex Type 2 infection at the time of pregnancy had children almost six times more likely to later develop schizophrenia.

Let's look closely at two particularly insidious and well recognized infectious diseases that are great mimickers of anxiety: **lyme disease** and **strep throat.**

Lyme Disease

Eight-year-old Sammy was a seemingly well adjusted child and an average student. One day out of the blue he became agitated, forgetful, and defiant. He started to suffer persistent headache, lack of coordination, and joint pain. The quality of his schoolwork began to plummet and the school staff suggested that his parents take him for a neuropsychological evaluation.

The evaluation revealed that Sammy had ADD and the neuropsychologist suggested putting Sammy on Ritalin. Luckily his parents first took him for a full neurological assessment. The results revealed Lyme disease. After a course of antiobiotics, Sammy's symptoms of "ADD" disappeared and his grades improved.

Lyme disease begins with a tick bite that spreads the bacterium Borelia burgdorferi from birds, mice, and chipmunks into people. The infected person breaks out with a bull's-eye rash and mild flu-like symptoms that respond quickly to oral antibiotics. In some cases, the disease will stabilize for months, even years. But in other cases, Lyme disease goes unrecognized or patients don't respond to treatment. The disease quickly attacks the central nervous system and becomes a chronic, debilitating neurological condition. Anywhere from 15 to 40% will exhibit neuropsychiatric symptoms and be misdiagnosed as having a psychiatric disorder. In the US, Europe, and Japan, some individuals who develop schizophrenia later in life closely mirror the seasonal distribution of Ixodes ticks at the time of conception.

Neuropsychiatric Symptoms of Lyme Disease	
♦ Moodiness	♦ Fatigue
♦ Confusion	♦ Unsteadiness
♦ Compulsive behavior	♦ Personality changes
♦ Irritability	♦ Psychosis
♦ Anxiety	♦ Oppositional behavior in
♦ Panic attacks	children

If your anxiety or panic emerged suddenly and you suspect that you could have been exposed to ticks that carry the Borrelia burgorferi organism, seek immediate medical care.

Strep Throat

Following a bout with strep throat, some children suddenly wake up counting and recounting their stuffed animals and avoiding sidewalk cracks or other senseless rituals, appearing obsessive-compulsive. Apparently, streptococcal antibodies find their way into the brain and attack a region called the basal ganglia, causing characteristic clumsiness and arm-flapping along with obsessions and compulsions. About 25% to 30% of children with obsessive-compulsive disorder may actually have this autoimmune disorder, called **PANDAS** (pediatric autoimmune neuropsychiatric disorder associated with Group A streptococcal infection). And though the virus itself is not mistaken for an anxiety disorder, the subsequent **obsessive-compulsive behavior** is assumed psychiatric.

What distinguishes OCD from PANDAS?

OCD

➢ **Uncontrollable** replay of thoughts or actions.

➢ **Obsessions** produce anxiety.

➢ **To** reduce anxiety, people engage in actions or rituals that involve washing and cleaning, checking (that the stove is off), symmetry, counting, repeating, redoing, and hoarding.

➢ **Such** behavior develops over many years and is often preceded by a major stressor, such as illness or job loss.

➢ **OCD** patients respond well to SSRIs and behavior therapy and symptoms change gradually.

PANDAS

➢ **Symptoms** appear quickly and increase and decrease sharply.

➢ **Obsessive-compulsive** behavior isn't the only symptom.

➢ **Child** may have tics, trembling, twitches, grimacing, clumsiness, loss of math skills, sensitivity to touch and clothing tags, poor attention span, distractibility, irritability, impulsivity, separation anxiety, and bedtime fears.

Cancer

When my vivacious, cheerful and highly social grandma Pearl was sixty-seven, she complained of never feeling well and retreated to the couch. She had constant crying jags and felt anxious *about everything*: any problem in her family *or* in the world at large -- distant earthquakes; car bombings; famine. One day she called me crying because she learned that the opera singer Beverly Sills had breast cancer. Illiterate and lacking culture, my grandmother never heard an opera. But my grandmother had breast cancer fifteen years earlier and Beverly Sills was Jewish: she was a part of the family. Other than the usual age related aches and pains, doctors could find nothing wrong with my grandmother and so we all ignored her complaints. Six months later she was dead from pancreatic cancer.

A lethal cancer, pancreatic carcinoma attacks the pancreas, an organ necessary for healthy digestion. The first signs are psychiatric: depression, weeping fits, anxiety and insomnia. It is not until the cancer has dangerously progressed that physical symptoms like pain, weight loss, and jaundice appear to indicate serious illness. By this time, it's often too late, as it was for my grandmother, and the person may die within the year.

Brain tumors, which I discuss in chapter six, and tumors that attack the endocrine system also produce behaviors that, until diagnosed, may appear as an anxiety disorder.

Quick Review

➤ **Many** medical illnesses mimic an anxiety or panic attack, including:
- o Cardiovascular disease
- o Infections
- o Endocrine and metabolic disorders
- o Cancer

➤ **Often** major symptoms are purely psychiatric, as in hypoglycemia whose symptoms resemble panic attack. Or psychiatric symptoms emerge before physical symptoms.

➤ **Some** illness is serious and if not diagnosed early will result in serious impairment or death, as in brain tumor, pancreatic cancer, Lyme disease, or insulin dependent diabetes.

➤ **Endocrine** disorders are among the biggest mimickers of anxiety and panic and include: hyperthyroidism
- o Diabetes mellitus
- o Cushing's syndrome
- o Pheochromocytoma
- o Carcinoid syndrome
- o Panhypopituitarism

➤ **Cardiovascular** disease is a common mimicker of anxiety and especially mitral valve prolapse. Other cardiovascular disease that can be initially mistaken for an anxiety attack includes:
- o Essential hypertension
- o Cerebral arteriosclerosis
- o Internal hemorrhage
- o Subacute bacterial endocarditis
- o Cardiac arrhythmias
- o Paroxysmal atrial tachycardia
- o Myocardial infarction (heart attack)

➤ **Infectious** diseases, viral and bacterial, often manifest with anxiety symptoms. These include:
- o Mononucleosis (the "kissing" disease)
- o Hepatitis
- o Encephalitis
- o Brucellosis
- o Lyme disease & strep throat can in some cases produce symptoms identical to obsessive-compulsive disorder and be misdiagnosed as such.

> ➤ **Brain** tumors, pancreatic carcinoma, and tumors that attack the endocrine system can mimic anxiety.

Resources

Suggested Books

- *The Good News about Panic, Anxiety and Phobias* by Marc Gold (Villard, 1989).
- *Understanding Mental Disorders* by Ghazi Asaad (Brunner/Mazel, 1995).
- *Distinguishing Psychological from Organic Disorders, Screening for Psychological Masquerade* (2nd edition) by Robert L. Taylor (Springer, 2000).
- *Psychiatric Disorders with a Biochemical Basis* by David Donaldson, (Pantheon, 1998).
- *Preventing misdiagnosis of women: a guide to physical disorders that have psychiatric symptoms* by Elizabeth A. Klonoff (Sage, 1996).
- *It's not All in Your Head* by Susan Swedo (HarperSanFrancisco, 1997).
- *Natural Therapies for Mitral Valve Prolapse* by Ronald L. Hoffman (McGraw Hill, 1999).
- *The Mood Cure: The 4-Step Program to Take Charge of Your Emotions—Today* by Julia Ross (Penguin, 2003).
- *A Dose of Sanity* by Sydney Walker (Wiley, 1997).

3

★

RX Jitters

There are some remedies worse than the disease.
-Publilius Syrus

Think back on when your anxiety or panic first began. Were you taking any drugs or medication, prescribed or over-the-counter? If so, when did you start taking these pills? These are important questions in your hunt for answers to your anxiety symptoms.

Like many, you may take an aspirin for headache, an antacid for heartburn, antihistamines for allergies, beta-blockers for palpitations, antibiotics for the flu, and caffeine to wake up and alcohol to calm down. And you may be, or have been on tranquilizers to relax and anti-depressants to cope with the blues. Before you swallow another pill, beware. All these are drugs and *any drug can produce psychiatric symptoms including anxiety, panic or depression.*

Whether illicit, prescribed, or over-the counter, all drugs can cause side effects that upset brain chemistry and alter mood, perceiving, thinking, behavior, and sleep. This likelihood increases especially when drugs are combined. Particularly among the elderly, who are often on several medications, a drug cocktail may be an invitation for all sorts of psychiatric mayhem, including anxiety.

Certain drugs also create dependency, both psychological and physical. Withdrawing from them, even slowly, can create unbearable anxiety; some people contemplate or attempt suicide.

According to biopsychiatrist Dr. Mark Gold, author of *The Good News about Panic, Anxiety & Phobias* these problems are of great concern.

Since both therapeutic medications and illegal drugs are so widespread, since the symptoms they produce are so convincingly mental, and since so many psychiatrists fail to investigate thoroughly for drugs before diagnosing, I believe that drugs are the most dangerous and common of all (anxiety) mimickers (p. 176).

Those most at risk for drug intolerance are people with a compromised nervous system. They may have always had a delicate system or become sensitive from conditions that interfere with the liver's ability to rid the body of drugs such as:

➢ Illness	➢ Chemical sensitivity
➢ Drugs	➢ Sensory defensiveness
➢ Food related problems	➢ Brain trauma

Some if not all of these people probably don't excrete drugs well. Autopsy studies of some antidepressant-induced suicides show patients to have had low levels of the liver enzymes that metabolize antidepressants. Thus, despite being on recommended doses, they had abnormally high levels of antidepressants in their blood

If you easily experience drugs side effects, you too may be poor at metabolizing drugs. So before you pop another pill to ease your angst, remember the nasty potential aftermath.

Drug Side Effects

Though all drugs have the potential to create anxiety, the drugs most likely to cause psychiatric symptoms are those that stimulate the nervous system directly, such as: amphetamines, certain antihistamines and decongestants, over-the-counter and prescription diet pills, anti-depressants, and recreational drugs including nicotine and caffeine. All these potentially create *nervousness, impulsivity, hyperactivity, anxiety and panic.*

Prescription Drugs

When your doctor prescribes medication, you tend to take it on faith and often fail to ask about potential side effects. They can be numerous and even dangerous – as drug commercials enumerate! -- and in some cases greatly outweigh the drug's benefits.

The following include some but not all of the prescription medication that can mimic anxiety and panic.

Psychiatric Medications

Psychiatry has made enormous strides in helping the anxious, the depressed, the manic, and even psychotic with psychotropic drugs. At the same time, the side effects of these drugs can in some cases cause their own brand of psychic torture.

Antidepressants

Half of all people who suffer anxiety also suffer depression. In fact, at times there's little clinical distinction between the two. You can be in the doldrums and listless or you can be in the doldrums and jumpy. If you are one of the latter, you have likely taken anti-depressants at some point. The "Prozac nation," we not only routinely control our moods through medication but those of our children as well: in an average week, some 20 million Americans, including over one million teens and children, take an antidepressant, such as Paxil, Prozac, Zoloft, Effexor or Wellbutrin.

Antidepressants fall into three categories.

1. *Tricyclics.* The oldest antidepressant, tricyclics such as Elavil, Tofranil, or Norpramin can cause anxiety, restlessness, confusion, disturbed concentration, drowsiness, disorientation, insomnia and nightmares.
2. *Monoamine Oxidase Inhibitors.* Less commonly prescribed as they interact adversely with many foods, MOI's such as Nardil or Marplan can cause anxiety symptoms, nervousness, insomnia, and euphoria. If unmonitored, these side effects can mushroom into symptoms indistinguishable from panic, mania, or schizophrenia.
3. **SSRIs** (selective serotonin re-uptake inhibitors). Though effective for many people, SSRIs, including Prozac, Zoloft, Paxil, Celexa, Luvox, Lexapro, and other drugs, all have side

effects, from mild to severe, and that includes anxiety, agitation, fatigue, drowsiness, dizziness, apathy, and insomnia.

Other newer antidepressants don't fit into these categories, including *Wellbutrin, Effexor, Cymbalta, Remeron, Symbiax, and Serzone,* but can also cause side effects.

Today, the SSRIs are the most commonly prescribed anti-depressants since Prozac revolutionized psychiatry. For many desperately depressed people, they have been a godsend: they're not only highly effective in helping people cope with major depression but generally have minor medical side effects.

But they're also overprescribed, limit the highs as well as the lows, creating a zombie-like effect, and can *create* anxiety. As Peter Breggin explains in *Talking Back to Prozac* the drug acts as a stimulant to the nervous system, similar to taking amphetamines. Agitation, anxiety, or panic occurs in particular when starting antidepressants or increasing the dose. Feeling anxious on top of depressed heightens anxiety unbearably and has prompted suicidal behavior and even suicide in some Prozac users. Such extreme side effects have provoked a host of lawsuits against Eli Lilly & Co. the drug's manufacturer. In a span of two years, the Food and Drug Administration (FDA) received almost twice as many reports of adverse reactions to Prozac than it did to Elavil, a tricyclic antidepressant, in 20 years.

Anti-Anxiety Drugs

Buspirone (Buspar) is a popular anti-anxiety drug that has the advantage of not being habit forming, as are the benzodiazepine tranquilizers, like Valium, Librium, and Xanax, which are addictive. And while you need to wean gradually off benzodiazepines or suffer serious withdrawal symptoms, Buspar can be stopped abruptly. But unlike the benzodiazepines, which increase GABA activity, thereby dulling awareness and other brain activity, Buspar is actually stimulating than sedating. At the onset of therapy, it can cause nervousness, excitement, drowsiness, fatigue, light-headedness, headache and confusion, and worsen panic attacks. For this reason, some people immediately stop taking the drug before its effect kicks in.

Non-Psychiatric Drugs

Who do you know who is not on some medication? Probably few people. And while doctors may inform people of some common physical side effects of many drugs, like upset stomach or headache, they rarely tell you that many non-psychotropic medications create anxiety and panic in some people. Herewith is a list of some, but by no means all of the more commonly prescribed drugs that have psychiatric side effects.

1. *Lidocaine.* Used to treat cardiac arrhythmias (irregular heartbeats), as well as for general and local anesthesia, it can cause "doom anxiety."
2. *Prednisone.* A corticosteroid anti-inflammatory drug, it can cause panic attacks, depression, mild mania, sleeplessness, disorientation, confusion, and even psychosis.
3. *Indomethacin.* A nonsteroidal anti-inflammatory drug, it can produce anxiety, along with hostility, disorientation, depression, hallucinations and even psychosis.
4. *Vinblastine.* An anticancer drug, one study showed it to produce anxiety and depression within two to three days of treatment in eighty percent of patients.
5. *Nalorphine.* A preanesthetic to the main anesthetic given, it can mimic panic disorder, creating immediate sensations of panic, suffocation, and fear of impending doom.
6. *Thyroxine.* A thyroid hormone, it can produce anxiety and insomnia in high doses.
7. *Ethosuximide.* Used to treat petit mal epilepsy, it can produce anxiety, depression, delusions, hallucinations and psychosis.
8. *Salbutamo.* Given to asthmatics, it can produce anxiety.
9. *Birth control pills.* Oral contraceptives involve powerful hormones and can cause anxiety, panic attacks, depression and even psychosis. They also deplete magnesium, an essential mineral for balancing the nervous system.
10. *Keppra.* An anticonvulsant, it can cause agitation, aggression, anger, anxiety, apathy, depersonalization, depression etc.
11. *Phentermine..* A diet pill, it can cause restlessness or tremor, nervousness or anxiety, headache or dizziness.
12. *Pseudoephedrine.* Used to relieve nasal or sinus congestion, it can cause nervousness, anxiety and insomnia.

13. **Ditropan.** Used to treat the symptoms of overactive bladder, it can cause agitation, fast heartbeat, confusion, and mood changes.

14. **Miralax.** Prescribed for constipation, it can apparently cross the blood-brain barrier and some parents of children with autism and sensory processing disorder report their children's behavior to regress. For instance, some autistic children whose speech and language has improved through therapy will go back to babbling or not speaking.

15. **Interferon.** An antiviral agent used in the treatment of AIDS and chronic viral hepatitis, it can cause irritability, depression, extreme emotional lability, paranoia, and confusion. In one study, it produced such side effects in one out of five patients.

Drug GI Side Effects & Psychiatric Symptoms

Many drugs upset the gastrointestinal system and create food related anxiety mimickers, like yeast overgrowth and leaky gut syndrome. These conditions rob the nervous system of needed nourishment to maintain emotional equanimity and, along with the drug's effect on the brain, further increase anxiety, nervousness, and irritation (see chapter one).

Non-Prescription "Drugs"

Like many people, you may not realize that over-the-counter medication are drugs and may omit telling your doctor that you use them. Nor may your doctor have warned you of their potential side effects. In fact, some have powerful mind altering effects.

Some of the over-the-counter medications that produce symptoms that mimic anxiety and panic include:

➢ **Laxatives** may contain mercurous chloride and, when overused, lead to mercury poisoning which can mimic heightened anxiety and phobic behavior (see chapter 14).

➢ **Diet pills** are a stimulant even when over-the-counter.

➢ **Decongestants & antihistamines**, contained in many cough and cold medicines, stimulate the heart and make people jumpy.

> ➤ *Caffeine*, the main ingredient in No-Doz, and found in the cold remedy Dristan and many pain relief and menstrual relief formulas such as Midol, Excedrin, and Anacin, can produce instant panic in the panic-prone and panic-like symptoms in normal people (see chapter one).

Recreational Drugs

In my early 20's, I smoked marijuana at a party. I lost all connection to my body. People seemed far away and unreal, as if I were looking through a window. Time seemed to stand still as the terror lingered for agonizing hours. I was experiencing *depersonalization,* a psychiatric symptom of panic attack.

From the cannabis plant to the peyote cactus and the poppy flower, humans throughout history have sought out mind altering drugs, for healing and for recreation. Such drugs, including cocaine, heroin, amphetamines, hallucinogens, and alcohol, create instant euphoria and many anxiety sufferers turn to them for self-calming. Be warned: They are a major anxiety mimicker. These drugs greatly alter neurotransmitters such as serotonin, norepinephrine, dopamine, and endorphins, and throw off the body's chemical balance. Such imbalance triggers a wide variety of psychiatric disorders, from anxiety and panic to depersonalization, paranoid states, and hallucinations.

Nor does the euphoria last. The brain has its own negative feedback mechanisms to prevent us from overstimulation. When we boost our feel-good neurotransmitters, the receptor sites in the brain gradually shut down and we need more of the stimulant to feel good: we need two joints of pot or two snorts of cocaine or two shots of vodka to get a similar effect. Eventually we may become addicted and unknowingly worsen our anxiety.

Yet not everyone does. Why do some people become addicted to recreational drugs and not others? Scientists have now discovered faulty genes that predispose us to addictions by programming deficiencies in particular brain sites. Writes Julia Ross in her book *The Mood Cure,*

> Depending on whether you've inherited deficiencies in serotonin, norepinephrine, endorphin, and/or GABA, you'll

be attracted to drugs that affect that particular deficiency zone (or zones) (p. 254).

Ross was able to successfully wean people from their addictions through the use of amino acids. See pages 114 for information on using amino acids in place of psychotropic drugs.

Alcohol

Freeing our inhibitions and producing a sense of well being, alcohol is a natural and expected part of many social settings and has been for at least 6,000 years of recorded history. Refuse a drink and you are a party pooper. But if you suffer anxiety or panic attack, think twice before you sip away at Merlot. Alcohol readily crosses the blood-brain barrier and releases dopamine to stimulate you, quickly followed by endorphins to make you feel high, and GABA to help you relax. But as the effect wears off, you begin to get edgy, your thinking gets fuzzy, and you might feel sleepy. If you have a compromised nervous system, these aftereffects multiply and you get anxious or even panic.

Further, alcohol is metabolized as a simple carbohydrate, or sugar, and rapidly absorbed by the body. This can deplete vitamins and minerals and trigger panic symptoms. If you use it to calm yourself, as many do since it initially acts as a depressant, you may unknowingly cycle your panic attacks. As it wears off, your anxiety will return more intensely and create an immediate need for more alcohol. One study found that anywhere from 18 to 32 percent of patients hospitalized for alcoholism may be suffering from panic disorder alone or with agoraphobia, or from social phobia, when you fear embarrassing yourself when socializing. Further, when people drink, they tend to not eat, which causes nutritional problems and further intensifies symptoms of anxiety and panic.

If you are a woman with moderate to severe anxiety, mood swings, and depression due to PMS, menopause, or emotional causes, you should avoid alcohol entirely or limit its use to occasional small amounts. Like other sugars, alcohol increases hypoglycemia symptoms which can mimic a panic attack or at the very least increase anxiety and mood swings, and especially if you suffer PMS related hypoglycemia.

Marijuana

Commonly known as cannabis, hash, or pot, marijuana has been used as an intoxicant for thousands of years in Asia and the Middle East. In the US, it is the most widely used illegal drug.

Almost with the first inhale, you begin to feel mild euphoria, sense of slowed time, and increased sensitivity to sound. But you may also feel anxious, as marijuana lowers blood sugar, as well impaired judgment, paranoia, and, as happened to me, depersonalization. Many agoraphobics report their first "out of body" experience while smoking marijuana.

Cocaine

Whether sniffed, injected, or smoked (as freebase or crack), cocaine is a stimulant and can produce anxiety-mimicking side effects: increased heart rate, irregular heart beat, high blood pressure, restlessness, and irritability.

Panic attack is common with cocaine use. EEG tracings of the brain following cocaine injection show activity in the same area of the brain responsible for flight or fight -- the exact reaction during a panic attack. One survey conducted by the national helpline 800-CO-CAINE found that 50 percent of the callers reported cocaine-induced panic attacks. After repeated use, *kindling* may cause cocaine users to panic even when not under the drug's influence. After repeatedly stimulating a part of the brain, the brain's activity threshold lowers and you react to a stimulation level previously tolerated.

Amphetamines

Widely used for staying awake, dieting, and revving up the system, amphetamines -- "speed" or "uppers" – are stimulants that help you focus, feel energized, and productive. But in some they also produce side effects that can easily mimic an anxiety attack.

Amphetamine Side Effects	
◆ Hyperactivity	◆ Elevated blood pressure
◆ Rapid speech	◆ Over-stimulation
◆ Fast heartbeat	

If you have a history of panic attacks, avoid the following drugs that contain amphetamines:

- ➢ Benzedrine (bennies)
- ➢ Dexedrine
- ➢ Methedrine

- ➢ Ritalin, used to treat ADHD in children

Drug Withdrawal

Following his divorce from a woman that he had deeply loved, Raffi became clinically depressed. He couldn't sleep, couldn't eat, and couldn't stop crying. He felt like dying. His physician prescribed Zoloft and Raffi willingly took it. Within three weeks, his depression lifted but he felt like a zombie. He lost his creative edge in his profession of developing product names, something at which he excelled. Even worse, he felt like a "eunuch" as his girlfriend no longer turned him on. Accusing him of pining for his former wife and not loving her anymore, she broke off with him.

Raffi felt lost. Hoping to regain libido, he stopped taking the Zoloft. Within days, he felt jumpy, ill-tempered, anxious, restless and despondent. He called his girlfriend and quickly got into a fight, screaming at her that she was a shallow person for not understanding that his sexual difficulties were drug induced. She told him he was crazy and hung up on him. He paced the floor, pulling at his hair, whimpering, and contemplating suicide. The next morning, he resumed the drug, terrified of living without it. His anxiety soon abated.

When doctors start you on a pill, often they don't monitor your progress and many people decide to stop taking their drugs without first consulting their physician. This can produce withdrawal symptoms that can be worse than the symptoms that led to initially taking the drug. Some of the worst offenders are anti-depressants, tranquilizers, sleeping pills, narcotics, nicotine and caffeine – precisely the pills many anxiety sufferers take for relief! Withdrawal from these drugs can initially produce jitteriness and anxiety that intensifies to panic, and especially if you stop "cold turkey." To be safe, you should discontinue these drugs gradually and under doctor supervision.

Anti-Depressants

Some 78 percent of people on antidepressants experience horrific withdrawal side effects upon terminating the drug or in the beginning while decreasing the dosage to establish therapeutic effect. Side effects that start to occur three days to weeks after lowering the dosage or terminating the drug can be mistaken for anxiety or for depressive relapse which takes typically one to two months or more to slowly develop. Consequently, people continue usage. After taking Paxil for two years and then abruptly stopping, one man had his first nocturnal panic attack and felt as if his body had gone into shock. He immediately resumed Paxil. Unknowingly, he had become dependent on the drug. This happens not necessarily because someone needs continued usage but to suppress withdrawal reactions that mimic the original psychiatric condition, explains Dr. Joseph Glenmullen, in his book, *The Antidepressant Solution, A Step-by-Step Guide to Safely Overcoming Antidepressant Withdrawal, Dependence, and "Addiction."* Further, elaborates Glenmullen, some patients experience withdrawal symptoms not from terminating the drug but because they've forgotten to take the drug for a day or two. They feel worse and the doctor ups their dosage, which may increase side effects.

Psychiatric Anti-Depressant Side Effects	
◆ Anxiety	◆ Vivid dreams
◆ Agitation	◆ Impulsivity
◆ Panic attacks	◆ Akathisia
◆ Insomnia	◆ Hypomania
◆ Irritability	◆ Mania
◆ Hostility	◆ Excessive anger
◆ Suicidal feelings	◆ Dizziness

Suicide Potential

Of great concern are suicides that have resulted from the severity of the withdrawal symptoms. In response, the FDA has urged

pharmaceutical companies to include warning labels of such
potential risks on all thirty-two anti-depressants currently on the
market. And though we tend to think of depression as the leading
cause of suicide, studies show that anxiety, by making you
frightened, impulsive, panicky and unable to think clearly, equally
puts you at risk for suicide, and especially as anxiety and depression
often co-exist. Even worse, SSRI's produces akathisia in some, a
severe form of drug-induced agitation long linked to suicide and
violence.

Creating extreme anxiety, tension, irritability, hostility, paranoia,
rage reactions, and violence that make you want to jump out of your
skin, akathisia, a profoundly serious drug effect, is basically
unrelenting, maddening sensory defensiveness (hypersensitivity),
similar to what some autistic people experience (see chapter nine).
The abnormal bodily sensations and anxiety interfere with being able
to think clearly and you feel confused and unreal. Some become
suicidal and violent, even though such behavior feels alien and out of
character. They will start to depersonalize and, feeling out of their
body, observe what is happening but feel unable to stop though a part
of them feels horrified. Some commit suicide as their only means of
ending the horrific bodily upheaval. Women, who typically attempt
suicide by overdosing rather than more violent means, will mutilate
themselves with knives, hang themselves, shoot themselves, or jump
off buildings.

Karen: A Case Study

In *The Antidepressant Solution,* Glenmullen describes Karen, a
compelling case study of how anti-depressant withdrawal can lead to
suicidal behavior and how easily psychiatrists fail to recognize anti-
depressant side effects.

A paralegal in her late twenties living in San Francisco, Karen
was in a warm, supportive relationship with her boyfriend for three
years and looking forward to applying to law school. She was in
great shape and jogged five miles every other day. Life was good.

One day she felt a sharp pain in her abdomen. She knew it was
an ovarian cyst bursting, as it had happened three times before in the
last six months. To stop the pain, her gynecologist suggested she go
on birth control pills. Ovarian cysts burst because they grow too

large and by regulating female hormones birth control pills suppress their formation. Karen started the pill.

Within two weeks, Karen started having crying jags and couldn't get out of bed. Knowing depression is a well known side effect of birth control pills her gynecologist immediately stopped the pill and referred her to a psychiatrist. The psychiatrist recognized that the birth control pills caused her depression. But rather than waiting first to see if the depression would pass, he suggested that she go on Paxil, an anti-depressant. Karen reluctantly agreed. Apparently he did not warn her that Paxil is commonly associated with side effects.

From Paxil to Panic

Soon after starting the drug, Karen became jumpy, unable to sleep, startled easily, and couldn't concentrate. Noise drove her batty. She felt dizzy, nauseous, started vomiting, and had a rash that covered her neck, back, and legs and that lasted the whole time she was on the drug.

Within weeks she had the first panic attack of her life. Thereafter, she had panic attacks regularly, and fainting spells as well, sometimes following the panic attack. Not recognizing the panic attack as a side effect of Paxil – ironically Paxil is popularly used to *treat* panic attack -- her psychiatrist thought she had panic disorder and started her on an anti-anxiety drug, and increased her Paxil dose. Her symptoms worsened. He felt she needed a higher dose and continued to increase her dosage about every two weeks. Karen continued to get worse. She barely slept, became paranoid, had violent dreams and was afraid to leave the house.

Paxil to Celexa

After three months on Paxil, her psychiatrist decided it wasn't working, and switched her to Celexa, another anti-depressant. Karen continued to get worse. Assuming, she had not yet reached therapeutic dose, he continued to increase dosage and with each up in dosage her insomnia, panic attacks, rash, nausea, vomiting, fainting spells, nightmares, and paranoia worsened.

Celexa to Suicidal

On New Year's Eve, Karen became suicidal. Convinced that he hadn't yet found the right dosage of medication, her psychiatrist assured her that the Celexa would kick in "and you'll feel back to normal again." She began having hallucinations. Her psychiatrist prescribed an anti-psychotic to reduce the hallucinations. She was now on eight to ten pills a day – antidepressants, anti-anxiety pills, and antipsychotics.

In the early spring, Karen cut and scratched herself with a kitchen knife. In May, she began self-medicating with alcohol and by June cocaine. She felt better. Over the summer, she stopped the alcohol and cocaine and her symptoms came back full force.]

Celexa to Lexapro to Excruciating Headaches

By now she had been on anti-depressants for a year and her psychiatrist suggested switching from Celexa to Lexapro, as it had fewer side effects. She made the change in October and within weeks began having debilitating headaches. One night the headaches were so severe she became suicidal and went to the emergency room. The ER doctors gave her a CAT scan, found nothing and sent her home. The next day the headache was so excruciating that she checked herself into a psychiatric ward, afraid she would harm herself.

From Depressed to Bipolar & Back to Celexa

Greatly concerned about her welfare, her family flew her home to Boston. Karen's mother arranged for her to meet with a psychiatrist on the staff of Massachusetts General Hospital. He felt she had been misdiagnosed. She wasn't depressed she was bipolar, a psychiatric illness manifested by depression, mania and at times hallucinations and psychosis. He felt Karen was bipolar II, meaning she experienced depression and hypomania, a milder form of mania. He took her off Lexapro and switched her back to Celexa. The maddening headaches went away and Karen felt somewhat better.

Fortunately Karen also met with a psychotherapist that she had seen briefly in college. She saved her life.

Drug Toxicity!

Having known Karen before, the psychotherapist knew Karen had not had the pre-existing conditions consistent with the symptoms she now exhibited. The psychotherapist suspected that Karen's problems were *drug toxicity*. Having read *Prozac Backlash* by Joseph Glenmullen, she felt Karen had been put on an antidepressant too quickly after the birth control pills. The doctor should have waited to see if her depression would lift.

Withdrawal Nightmare

Karen knew she had to get off the Celexa. That proved difficult. The psychotherapist and Karen's mother spoke to a dozen or so psychiatrists, none of whom were willing to wean her off the drug as they were convinced of the bipolar hypothesis. Finally, one did agree to taper her off the Celexa. But he did so too steeply giving her extreme side effects and she experienced horrendous withdrawal symptoms. She had severe dizziness; nausea and vomiting so severe it had to be treated with compazine, an antivomiting drug; aches and pains; muscle spasms; buzzing in her ears; twitching all over; electric shock-like sensations radiating down her back to the rest of her body and she would shake for several minutes; and "brain freezes" – painful shock-like sensation behind her eyes, accompanied by disorientation and brief amnesia without loss of consciousness. A number of the symptoms indicated she was having a seizure. This was confirmed by an abnormal EEG (a brain wave that looks for evidence of seizures) and she was put on an anticonvulsant.

Even worse were the psychiatric withdrawal symptoms. She had severe anxiety, agitation and irritability that was even worse than when she started to taper off the Celexa. She cried "all the time." She felt so confused that one day she stepped off the curb in front of an oncoming car. She had violent thoughts, suicidal urges, and finally auditory hallucinations – voices were telling her to kill herself and her parents. She shared the hallucinations with her parents and for her own safety she was admitted to a Harvard hospital where she was watched around the clock.

While in the hospital, she was finally withdrawn completely off the Celexa but despite high doses of antipsychotic medication, she heard voices the entire twelve days she was in the hospital, although they continued to get lower in volume and intensity and finally stopped nine days after stopping the Celexa. Within a month, almost all of her symptoms disappeared, though she continued to have insomnia and muscle cramping for many months. As her symptoms improved, she slowly weaned off all her medications, including sleeping pills, anti-anxiety meds, antipsychotics and the anticonvulsant. After three months of living with her family, she returned to San Francisco to reclaim her life. A year after she was completely off Celexa, Karen described her traumatic experience to the department of psychiatry at Harvard hospital where she was treated.

Ignoring a "Red" Flag

Looking back on her experience, Karen wondered why her on-going rash wasn't a red flag that something was triggering an allergic reaction to the antidepressants. The psychiatrists, it seems, were too focused on her psychiatric symptoms to consider the possibility of a medical problem and too quick to dish out an anti-depressant. Her case illustrates the potential danger from the side effects of anti-depressant drugs that get quickly dismissed as mental rather than biological in origin.

Benzodiazepines

If anyone wanted to know how anxious we are in the U.S., they need only look at the 25 million prescriptions written annually for benzodiazepines like Valium, Librium or Xanax. The most widely prescribed medications in the U.S., these minor tranquilizers are also addictive. Excessive or prolonged use creates "wear out" and you need higher and higher doses to calm, creating psychological dependency.

Knowing they are addicted, some users suddenly stop taking the drugs cold. This is dangerous. Abrupt withdrawal has serious side effects.

Benzodiazepine Abrupt Withdrawal Side Effects	
♦ Tremulousness ♦ Insomnia ♦ Extreme anxiety ♦ Panic attack	♦ Confusion ♦ Perceptual disturbances ♦ Paranoia

If you are taking a tranquilizer and want to quit, do it slowly and under medical supervision. Expect to initially feel agitated and for withdrawal to take a long time.

Amphetamines

A widely abused drug, amphetamines, or speed produces drug dependence and withdrawal symptoms, such as jitteriness and hyperactivity that easily mimic an anxiety disorder.

Narcotics

In this day and age, almost all of us have witnessed on TV or at the movies the horrific withdrawal symptoms from narcotics like heroin, morphine or Demerol. The addict instantly becomes nervous, agitated, restless and anxious, to say nothing of the horrendous physical symptoms like tremors, vomiting, and profuse sweating. If you are taking a narcotic and wish to discontinue use, it's urgent that you do so under medical supervision.

Nicotine

Many people smoke and most have tried to stop at least once. Eight of ten smokers who do try to stop experience withdrawal symptoms that mimic anxiety disorders. These panic-like symptoms keep people smoking, and even prevent them from inhaling cigarettes with less nicotine as reducing nicotine also creates panic. Like with any other drug, you should stop smoking gradually to let your body adjust slowly to the lack of the stimulant.

Interestingly, women but not men who suffer panic attack are more likely to smoke. One study that compared 217 patients with panic disorder to 217 age-matched controls found more female patients with panic disorder to smoke at the time of their first panic attack than did control subjects (54% versus 35%). Current smoking prevalence was also higher in those patients with panic attack versus controls (40% versus 25%).

Caffeine

If you are a heavy caffeine consumer and suddenly decide to replace that cup of coffee with herbal tea, you may become anxious and even experience a full-blown panic attack. If cutting back causes nervousness, tension, or anxiety, decrease your caffeine intake slowly.

Natures Pharmacy

Do you need to take drugs? Unless you have a life threatening disease, many holistic practitioners feel the answer is, in most cases, no. Many alternative natural therapies exist to balance your biochemistry naturally – for instance by boosting low serotonin which can cause anxiety, panic and sleeplessness. Unlike Xanax and Zoloft, alternative substances within nature's pharmacy work with not against your body's design to modify brain chemistry without side effects.

While natural cures to illness are beyond the cope of this book, below are options to anti-anxiety drugs. Though you may wish to experiment at the suggested dose to see what works or you, it is always best to take these supplements under the guidance of a holistic physician or naturopath. Books listed in the resource section can guide you as well.

Herbs

Generally safe, effective, and non-addictive, herbs have been used to relax body and mind for centuries. And while the FDA does not routinely study them in the US, the E Commission in Germany studies them for their safety and effect. For instance, German researcher H. P. Volz and colleagues demonstrated that kava provided significant relief of anxiety versus a placebo, and with minimal side effects.

The following herbs have been deemed safe as nature's tranquilizers:

➢ **Kava** enhances GABA activity, thereby relaxing both muscles and emotions and calming without sedating, as prescription tranquilizers often do. Don't use it along with benzodiazepine tranquilizers.

➢ **Valerian root** is a natural relaxant that, taken together with kava, enhances the action of gamma amino butyric acid (GABA), a neurotransmitter that is considered a natural anti-anxiety drug and low in many high-strung people. It works well as a sleep aid. It is also useful for gut related problems as it seems to block the transmission of stressful nerve impulses to the bowel.

➢ **Passionflower** has a mild relaxing effect and induces a deep, restful sleep.

➢ **Gotu kola** mildly relaxes and revitalizes the nervous system, as well as decreasing fatigue and depression while increasing memory and intelligence.

➢ **Ginkgo biloba** improves brain function by increasing cerebral blood flow and oxygenation, helping ease depression, anxiety, headaches, memory loss, tinnitus (ringing in the ears), vertigo, headache, and poor concentration. A blood thinner, don't take before surgery.

➢ **Sceletium** is an herb from South Africa that has been used since prehistoric times to lessen anxiety, stress, and tension and raise spirits and connectedness. It has no serious side effects but should not be taken with antidepressants or with large doses of tryptophan or 5-HTP.

➢ **Holy Basil** is an herb used for over 3000 years in Ayurvedic tradition to reduce anxiety. It is also helpful in regulating blood sugar and insulin metabolism.

➢ **Sensoril** is a proprietary extract of Ashwaganda and a well known Ayurvedic herbal treatment for stress and anxiety. Providing many benefits, it helps increase energy, reduce fatigue, improve sleep, decrease irritability, enhance concentration/focus, reduce stress and increase overall feeling of wellbeing.

There is a downside. Unlike drugs that attack symptoms quickly, herbs work more subtly and slowly and you may not initially feel the POW of a tranquilizer. Don't be fooled into trying a larger dose.

Though generally safe if you adhere to the suggested dose on the bottle, herbs can powerfully affect the body. If the suggested dose isn't doing the trick, consult a licensed herbalist or nutritionist. If you are pregnant or nursing always consult with a physician before taking any herb. If scheduled for surgery, always tell your physician what herbs you are taking as some are blood thinners and must be stopped before surgery.

A few herbs have been shown to cause anxiety.

Yohimbine, an herb derived from the bark of a tree, is a male aphrodisiac with sometimes dangerous side effects. Even standard amounts may occasionally trigger anxiety, panic attack, and mania.

Ephedra is a stimulant used for quick energy and appetite suppression. The "herbal Ecstasy," it's misused for recreation, and in high doses creates rapid heart rate, dizziness, headache, anxiety and insomnia.

Amino Acids

➢ **GABA** (gamma amino butyric acid): An amino acid and neurotransmitter, GABA regulates the neurotransmitters noradrenaline, dopamine and serotonin. The brain's natural Valium, it dampens the nervous system and helps calm by naturally slowing breathing and heart rate, and relaxing muscles. Librium and Valium work by pushing GABA into the brain and blocking the re-uptake. Take it before a known stressful event to help *prevent* anxiety.

➢ **Taurine:** An amino acid, taurine inhibits the release of adrenaline and provides similar calming as GABA. Some get pleasantly high from only a few capsules.

Sleep Aide
Actress Margot Kidder, who manages bipolar disorder via natural means, uses 1000 mg. each of tryptophan, taurine, and GABA before bedtime to help with sleep.

➢ **Tryptophan:** An amino acid that is a source for both 5-HTP and serotonin, tryptophan can be taken in supplement form and has been shown to raise serotonin levels by 200%.

➢ **5-HTTP:** A form of tryptophan, 5-HTTP helps regulate serotonin level, and induce relaxation, elevate mood, and promote healthy sleep, dreaming, and creativity. Take it with vitamin B6. Do not take it if you are on anti-depressants. In one study, 5-HTP eliminated anxiety symptoms in 58% of patients as opposed to 48% on Luvox, a potent popular European anti-depressant.

TMJD & Serotonin

TMJD, a debilitating condition that involves pain in the muscles of the jaw used for chewing and or the temporomandibular joint, interferes with breathing, leading to tension and anxiety. Food and supplements that raise serotonin level alleviate symptoms.

Other

> **Phosphatidylserine:** a fatty acid that helps the hypothalamus to regulate the amount of cortisol produced by the adrenals. **PS** can be bought as an over-the-counter supplement.

> **Reishi:** A relaxing medicinal mushroom, reishi reduces anxiety and insomnia.

> **Aconitum Napellus:** A homeopathic remedy for panic attack, aconitum napellus has been reported to stop a panic attack within 30 seconds. Try 30C potency.

> **L-Theanine:** Abundant in green tea, L-theanine increases brain GABA and significantly affects neurotransmitters like dopamine and serotonin, resulting in improved memory and learning ability. It is effective in treating anxiety, nervousness, sleep disturbances, premenstrual syndrome (PMS) and ADD/ADHD.

> **Relora:** A new all-natural anti-anxiety and stress relief ingredient to control stress-related eating and drinking, relora is both non-sedating and a potential anti-depressant. Taken from Chinese medicine, it helps quiet the hypothalamic-pituitary-adrenal axis without causing drowsiness, and reduce anxiety by acting as a "precursor" to DHEA, the hormone that helps counteract the negative effects of the stress hormone cortisol. In one study, 80% of stressed adults studied felt more relaxed with Relora. And preliminary results of a pilot study to normalize cortisol levels in stressed individuals suggest that Relora can decrease the cravings for high fat, high sugar foods, presumably because it normalizes stress hormone levels that cause these cravings.

➢ **Chinese Red Date (**Red Jujube) has been used for thousands of years in traditional Chinese Medicine to treat of anxiety and insomnia. You can find Red Jujube in Chinese markets, and also as an ingredient in many natural anxiolytic preparations.

➢ **Adaptogens** - Two adaptogens shown helpful for anxiety are Rhodiola and Ashwaganda.

➢ **Calmes Forte** – Homeopathic remedy for reducing stress.

Amino Acids & Mood Cure

In her book, **The Mood Cure,** *Julia Ross discusses the powerful role of amino acid supplementation on mood. For bipolar disorder, hyperactivity, depression, stress and anxiety, she suggests a trial dose of amino acids of 500 to 1000 mg. of L-carnitine in the morning and 3 to 5 capsules of phosphatidyl choline, a fatty acid. This will slow the spontaneous rate of neuronal firing in the brain, and, in the bipolar, does so as well as lithium without negative side effects. Proper vitamin and mineral supplementation must accompany the amino acids. A caveat: people respond differently to amino acids so try them ideally under a physician's care.*

Abbreviations: SE-standardized extract; TF-tincture form

Herbs

	Use	Dosage
Kava	Relaxes both muscles and emotions; calms without sedating **Warning:** Don't take with alcohol or tranquilizers, or if you have liver problems.	60-75 mg kavalactones, 2 to 3xs daily; 60-250 mg 30 mins. before sleep; take daily for no more than 3 months *
Valerian Root	Anti-anxiety; sleep aid; digestive aid **Warning:** Don't take with alcohol, tranquilizers, antihistamines, muscle relaxants, narcotics	50-100 mg, 2 to 3xs daily; 150-300 mg 45 mins. Before sleep *
Passionflower	Sleep aid	100-200 mg daily*
Gotu Kola	Relaxes and revitalizes; decreases fatigue & depression; increases memory & intelligence.	As directed on label

Gingko Biloba	Improves brain function by increasing cerebral blood flow & oxygenation; eases depression, anxiety, headaches, headache, memory loss, tinnitus, vertigo, & poor concentration; **Warning:** a blood thinner, don't take it before surgery.	SE 120-240 mg daily in two doses*
Sceletium	Lessens anxiety, stress, and tension; raises spirits and connectedness; heightens sensory perception. **Warning:** don't take with antidepressants, large doses of tryptophan or 5-HTP.	50-100 mg daily for mood; 100-200 mg daily to increase connectedness*
Holy Basil	Reduces anxiety; regulates blood sugar & insulin metabolism	As directed on label
Sensoril	Increases energy, reduces fatigue, improves sleep, decreases irritability, enhances concentration/focus, reduces stress; increases overall wellbeing.	As directed on label

Amino Acids

	Use	Dosage
GABA	Relaxes both muscles & emotions; calms without sedating	100-500 mg, 1-3 xs daily** Suggested: Nutrabio.com
Taurine	Inhibits release of adrenaline and provides a similar calming effect as does GABA.	100-500 mg, 1-3 xs daily** Suggested: Nutrabio.com
5-HTP	Boosts serotonin, helping stabilize mood, control anxiety & diminish stress. **Warning**: Do not take with anti-depressants.	50-100 mg daily; 50 to 200 for sleep one hour before bedtime*
Tryptophan	Boosts serotonin, helping stabilize mood, control anxiety & diminish stress	500-1,500 mg daily**

Abbreviations: SE-standardized extract; TF-tincture form

Other

	Use	Dosage
Calmes Forte	Reduces stress	1-2 capsules or as needed
Reishi	Adaptogen; reduces anxiety & insomnia; calms & energizes	TF (20%), 10 ml 3xs daily; tablets, 1,000 mg, 1 to 3xs daily*
Aconitum Napellus	Stops panic attack	30C potency**
L-Theanine	Improves memory & learning ability; produces alert relaxation; reduces anxiety, nervousness, sleep disturbances, (PMS), ADD/ADHD	As directed on label
Relora	Relaxes; decrease cravings for high fat, high sugar foods	As directed on label
Chinese Red Date	Treats anxiety & insomnia	As directed on label
Rhodiola	Adaptogen; reduces anxiety by stabilizing adrenal hormones; improve concentration	SE 100 mg 2- 3xs daily w/meals*
Ashwaganda	Adaptogen; reduces stress; acetylcholine enhancer; both energizes and calms	300 mg of SE, 2 to 3xs daily*
Calmes Forte	Homeopathic; reduces stress	As directed on label

* Information taken from: *Natural Highs* by Hyla Cass (Avery, 2002).

** Information taken from: *The Mood Cure: The 4-Step Program to Take Charge of Your Emotions—Today* by Julia Ross (Penguin, 2003).

A word of caution. If you are taking any medication, check with your physician to see if they interact with herbal supplements. Many herbs will interact with anti-depressants and other medication.

Quick Review

➢ **Whether** illicit, prescribed, or over-the counter, all drugs can cause side effects that upset the chemical balance essential to normal brain communication and alter mood, perceiving, thinking, behavior, and sleep. Such side effects are common and easily misdiagnosed.

➢ **Drugs** that stimulate the nervous system directly easily produce nervousness, impulsivity, hyperactivity, anxiety and panic. These include:
  ➢ Amphetamines
  ➢ Certain antihistamines and decongestants
  ➢ Over-the-counter and prescription diet pills
  ➢ Anti-depressants
  ➢ Recreational drugs including nicotine and caffeine
  ➢ Psychotropic drugs and especially SSRIs

➢ **Many** non-psychotropic medications create anxiety and panic, such as Lidocaine, Prednisone and oral contraceptives.

➢ **Some** over-the-counter medication can produce symptoms that in some cases mimic anxiety and panic. These include:
  ➢ Laxatives
  ➢ Diet pills
  ➢ Decongestants and antihistamines
  ➢ Drugs containing caffeine like No-Doz, Dristan, Midol, Excedrin, and Anacin

➢ **Drug** withdrawal, and especially from anti-depressants, tranquilizers, sleeping pills, narcotics, nicotine and caffeine, can initially produce jitteriness and anxiety that intensifies to panic. Discontinue these drugs gradually and under doctor supervision.

➢ **Many** alternative natural therapies exist that help your body to regain its natural state of health and vibrancy without side effect and that modify brain chemistry without side effects.

Resources

Suggested Books

General
• *Talking Back to Prozac* by Peter Breggin (Tor Books, 1994).

- *The Antidepressant Solution* by Joseph Glenmullen (Free Press, 2005).
- *Panic Free: Eliminate Anxiety and Panic Attacks Without Drugs and Take Control of Your Life* by Dr. Lynne Freeman (Arden Books, 1999).
- *How to Quit Drugs for Good* by Jerry Dorsman (Prima Communications, 1999).
- *Spontaneous Healing* by Andrew Weil (Knopf, 1995).

Natural Cures

- *Natural Highs* by Hyla Cass (Avery, 2002).
- *Miracle Cures* by Jean Harper (HarperCollins, 1997).
- *The Mood Cure: The 4-Step Program to Take Charge of Your Emotions—Today* by Julia Ross (Penguin, 2003).
- *Balance Your Brain, Balance Your Body* by Jay Lombard and Christian Renna (Wiley, 2004).
- *Prescription for Nutritional Healing, A Practical A-Z Reference to Drug-Free Remedies Using Vitamins, Minerals, Herbs, and Food Supplements* fourth edition, James E. Balch and Phyllis A. Balch (Garden City Park, NY: Avery Publishing, 2004).
- *Natural Energy* by Mark Mayell (Three Rivers Press, 1998).
- *Beyond Prozac, Brain-Toxic Lifestyles, Natural Antidotes & New Generation Antidepressants* by Michael Norden (Regan Books, 1995).
- *Nature's Prozac: Natural Therapies and Techniques to Rid Yourself of Anxiety, Depression, Panic and Stress* by Judith Sachs (Prentice Hall, 1997).
- *Prozac-Free: Homeopathic Medicine for Depression, Anxiety, and Other Mental and Emotional Problems* by Judy Reichenberg-Ullman (Prima, 1999).

Websites

Holisticonline.com
Moodcure.com

4

★

Hormone Havoc

Far too many women are given a psychiatric diagnosis and psychotropic medication, without the realization that the "symptoms" are occurring around the menstrual period and may be triggered by hormonal changes.

Elizabeth Lee Vliet, M.D.,
Screaming to be Heard

Do you feel at the mercy of your hormones -- snapping at those you love, jumping when your dog barks, crying at the drop of a hat at certain times of the month, after childbirth, or when you've reached a certain age or?   Countless women do.

At puberty, in pregnancy, after delivery, around menstruation, and at menopause, changes in female hormone levels of estrogen and progesterone can produce emotional turmoil: agitation, crying jags, despair.   In an article published in the 1996 *Journal of Reproductive Medicine,* the authors proposed that when estrogen levels fall below the minimum required, the brain becomes dysfunctional.   Some women experience panic attack preceding menstruation when estrogen levels are low. As much as 80% of women suffer PMS and baby blues after delivery. Many women suffer pronounced anxiety and depression relating to menopause.   Little wonder that anxiety disorders and depression are two to three times more common in women than in men.

Hormones or the Psyche?

So common is mild to moderate anxiety, depression, sleep disorders, and lethargy during hormonal changes women will often feel their symptoms are normal and expected – something to live with.   Consequently, they hesitate to seek help, and especially as professionals tend to dismiss a woman's complaints as "just hormones." When they do seek help, many women are falsely given a psychiatric diagnosis like generalized anxiety disorder, or panic disorder, and put on tranquilizers and antidepressants.

Of course many women have both PMS and core psychological issues. But until you tease out and treat the underlying biochemistry that might be throwing off hormones, you can't know what causes what. Often psychological problems reduce or even disappear when your hormones regulate.

How do you know causes your anxiety: hormones or the psyche? Two indications are timing and culture.

Timing

When anxiety or panic happens will clue you as to their source.

Generalized Anxiety
➤ **Psychological**: Anxiety is present almost daily.
➤ **Hormonal**: Anxiety is cyclic or episodic and generally subsides as hormones regulate, following pregnancy, menstruation, and menopause.

Panic Disorder
➤ **Psychological**: Panic attacks occur unpredictably.
➤ **Hormone Fluctuation**: Panic attack preceded menstruation and following childbirth. Your panic attacks will have begun after puberty and stopped after menopause.

Culture

Extreme hormonally induced emotional shifts are, to a great extent, a product of our modern, technological, junk food, drug-taking, couch potato society. Neither PMS, postpartum depression nor menopause-as-nightmare seems to exist in non-industrialized societies. Naturopath Karen Jensen, ND, author of *Menopause, A Naturopathic Approach to the Transition Years* (Prentice Hall, 1999) points out that most symptoms commonly attributed to perimenopause or menopause are the same as those resulting from stressed adrenal and thyroid glands, an overtaxed and underfunctioning liver, and poorly functioning digestive system – all strongly related to poor nutrition and overtoxicity.   In non-technological societies, diets are more nutrition dense, providing more vitamins and minerals necessary to feed the brain and balance hormones and emotions.   Nor are women as likely to live in a chemical cesspool.   Further, lacking cars, computers, TVs, and supermarkets, women in indigenous societies move! Exercise helps reduce the onslaught of hormones, and increases pleasurable endorphins, the brain's natural opium, relaxing you.

Let's now look at how PMS and marching into menopause mimic anxiety attack as well as depression.

PMS

"Next mood swing, 2 minutes," says a bumper sticker. Screaming, crying, restlessness, moodiness -- these and other signs of emotional instability that suddenly emerge in many women every month or so, even when normally even-tempered and confident, have caused a legion of family and friends to quietly disappear for a week or so. Even murder has been attributed to PMS!

The butt of endless jokes, premenstrual syndrome or PMS was, until recently, cast aside by the medical profession as a symptom of the female's tendency toward hysteria for which she needs a tranquilizer. Fortunately in the 21st century, PMS has finally been recognized by most orthodox physicians as a legitimate condition.

PMS refers to a cluster of symptoms that women may experience anywhere from three days to a week preceding menstruation and that disappear when blood begins to flow.

Up to 150 different symptoms have been documented for PMS and fall into *four* general patterns:

1. **Anxiety**:   nervous tension, excessive mood swings, irritability, anxiety & panic
2. **Depression**: depression, increased crying, confusion, brain fog, lethargy, and insomnia

3. **Craving:**   increased appetite, craving for sweets, heart palpitations, headache, fatigue, dizziness, queasiness or nausea, sweating

4. **Hyperhydration:**   physical changes like weight gain, swelling of legs and hands, breast tenderness, and abdominal bloating

PMS sufferers run the gamut from experiencing one combination of symptoms to all, and the symptoms may vary from month to month. Though annoying and troublesome, these symptoms should not greatly interfere with functioning. If they do, you may have PMDD or *Premenstrual Dysphoric Disorder, a* psychiatric disorder suffered by a small percentage of women who experience disabling anxiety and depression during most menstrual cycles, except in the week following menstruation. These women may require psychiatric treatment or, if they choose, holistic treatments outlined in this chapter.

Causes

PMS is caused by an imbalance in the ratio between the primary female hormones estrogen and progesterone. The exact imbalance varies:

➤ **Estrogen** appears to outweigh progesterone immediately preceding menstruation, and this produces anxiety, irritability, and mood swings that respond to extra progesterone.

➤ **Estrogen** appears at its lowest point before menstruation and the first few days of bleeding, while progesterone rises, producing depression more than anxiety.

➤ **Levels** of both hormones drop immediately preceding the onset of bleeding and results in both anxiety and depression.

Of these three, excess estrogen is the most common. Whey would this be? Blame it primarily on modern living. Women today are overly exposed to estrogen-like chemicals in the environment, such as pharmaceuticals (drugs), agrochemicals (including pesticides and fertilizers), and petrochemicals (such as plastics) that can act similarly to the body's own estrogen and exacerbate PMS symptoms, and other problems, such as endometriosis and infertility.

Added to this exposure are conditions that tax the liver, which plays a vital role in recycling and breaking down hormones, and the liver can't do its job.

These include:

➢ **Poor** digestion, detoxification, and elimination
➢ **Bodies** overloaded with alcohol, drugs, coffee, fatty meats, dairy
➢ **Lack** of necessary nutrients (e.g., B vitamins), needed to breakdown estrogen
➢ **Thyroiditis**
➢ **Vaginal** candidiasis

Treatment Options

If PMS symptoms take control of your life, many interventions will help balance the body's hormones and loosen its grip:

➢ **Psychotropic** drugs (if you choose to take them)
➢ **Dietary** changes
➢ **Supplements**
➢ **Regular** exercise

Pop a Pill

To cope with PMS psychiatric symptoms, millions of women are prescribed anti-anxiety or antidepressant medication. Older women especially are likely to take these drugs as PMS related emotional symptoms commonly worsen or first appear in the late thirties and early forties. This is because as women age and estrogen levels decline, serotonin, the mood-altering neurotransmitter decreases as well.

Should You Take Meds?

Positive
➢ **For** many, the drugs greatly help as they alter serotonin levels in the brain.

Negative

➤ **Antidepressants** and anti-anxiety drugs come with risks, including *increased* anxiety and depression in some women.

➤ **As** PMS is hormonally induced, hormone regulation may make anti-anxiety or antidepressant medication unnecessary for some women. Ability of antidepressants and anti-anxiety medications to work optimally appears to be affected by circulating hormones, especially estrogen and progesterone. For instance, the presence of estrogen increases the binding of the antidepressant drug imipramine (Tofranil) to serotonin-2 receptors involved in mood.

➤ **Many** natural alternatives to drugs exist to control anxiety (see pages 112-116).

Get off Sugar Seesaw

Blood-sugar instability is a major trigger for the anxiety, irritability and nervous tension related to PMS, as well as menopause-related emotional symptoms. Both sugar and alcohol cause valuable electrolytes, particularly magnesium, to be lost through the urine. One study published in the *Journal of Applied Nutrition* found that women with PMS symptoms had a 50 percent higher sugar intake than normal volunteers. Another study published in the *American Journal of Psychiatry* found that women with PMS related emotional symptoms were more likely than others to crave sweets pre-menstrually.

If you are stuck on the sugar seesaw, eat a diet high in complex carbohydrates (fruit, whole grains, starches). This allows for a gradual release of sugar into the bloodstream, creating a moderate rise in brain serotonin. For more information on blood-sugar regulation see the information on hypoglycemia in chapter one.

Skip Coffee

Avoid stimulants like coffee, chocolate, cigarettes. A week before their period, some women become sensitive to caffeine. When they give up their morning coffee, many women find their PMS symptoms greatly reduced as the liver can better detoxify. In a study reported in the *American Journal of Public Health,* 216 female college students were questioned as to the severity of their PMS symptoms in relation to caffeine intake. Sixteen percent of women who used no caffeine reported suffering severe PMS symptoms, while 60 percent of those women drinking between 4.5 to 15 cups of caffeinated beverages per day reported severe symptoms.

Rebalance Estrogen and Progesterone

Eat foods rich in phyto-estrogens to help block the effects of excess estrogen and re-balance the ratio between estrogen and progesterone.

Foods High in Phyto-estrogens	
◆ Soy	◆ Wheatgerm
◆ Citrus fruits	◆ Peas
◆ Oats	◆ Carrots
◆ Fennel	◆ Apples
◆ Alfalfa	◆ Pears
◆ Licorice	◆ Herbs:
◆ Celery	○ Sage
◆ Flaxseeds	○ Parsley
◆ Beans	◆ Basil
◆ Rice bran	

Also, eat foods rich in:

◆ Folic Acid (green leafy vegetables)
◆ Vitamin B_6 (whole grains and legumes)
◆ Vitamin B_{12} (animal products or supplements)

Amino acid methionine If you have trouble sleeping the week before your period and are under 35 years of age, you may be low in progesterone which interferes with activation of GABA in your brain. You may need more progesterone during this time.

Eat Healthy

Many women with PMS lack proper nutrition. For instance, many opt for a hamburger for lunch rather than eat a healthy salad. If you are one, you are likely deficient in necessary vitamins and minerals and this can cause or worsen PMS symptoms. For instance, if you don't have enough B-complex vitamins and especially B$_6$, your blood sugar and estrogen levels will be off.

Some nutritional guidelines to improve PMS symptoms:

> **Nutrients**: Eat a diet rich in vitamins E, A, B and especially B$_6$, and C, along with folic acid, calcium, magnesium, selenium, and zinc.

> **GLA**: Get needed gamma-linolenic acid (GLA), an essential fatty acid contained in primrose oil, flaxseed oil, or black currant seed oil.

> **Fiber**: Eat a diet high in fiber to help the colon sufficiently excrete estrogen from the body.

> **Meat-Less**: Avoid eating animal fat which throws estrogen levels off.

Calcium & PMS

A study in the American Journal of Obstetrics in 1998 reported that 1,200 mg of calcium carbonate reduced PMS symptoms like negative mood and food cravings by 48%. For information on how to get these essentials vitamins and minerals in your diet and to learn how to eat a healthy diet, see chapter 12.

Supplement

Many supplemental formulas are available specifically for a woman's body. Look for a whole food supplement consisting of green power powders and blue-green algae as your best choice. In addition, take acidophilus or HSOs to fill the gut with good bacteria needed to help break down metabolites of estrogen.

Detoxify

Detoxifying your body will help alleviate PMS symptoms and remove heavy metals from your body. The U.S. Environmental Protection Agency has linked exposure to mercury vapors to menstrual disorders. Lead is of equal concern as it interferes with the binding of estrogen to its receptors thus reducing its affect. The more severe are PMS symptoms the greater the likelihood of lead toxicity. For information on detoxifying heavy metals, see chapters 13 and 14.

Other Options

> **Progesterone:** Natural progesterone cream eases irritability for some women. The cream is applied topically to the skin on the fatty areas of the body for easy absorption and taken from day 14 until day 28 of the menstrual cycle, with one week off.

> **Herbs:** Many herbs help relieve PMS symptoms, including black cohosh, dong quai, fennel seed, sarsaparilla root, lavender tea, peppermint tea, and St. John's wort.

> **Melatonin:** A study at the University of California-San Diego suggests that some women suffering PMS may be deficient in melatonin. Taking melatonin at night, as directed on the label, will help you sleep better and regulate hormone levels. If you are sleeping well without it, discontinue usage. Only take melatonin for a few months and then stop.

> **Aromatherapy:** Essential oils for psychological and physical well being helps many women relax. To relieve PMS, try lavender, chamomile, neroli or clary-sage. Lavender is the nose's valium. Brain wave studies demonstrate lavender to increase alpha waves, the state associated with relaxation.

> **Light:** Light relieves PMS symptoms. Get more sunlight or try two hours of bright light in the mornings or evenings with an Ott-Lite, a full spectrum fluorescent light box. A dim red light works wonders as well on reversing PMS symptoms.

Change of Life

If you've suffered PMS, you are a more likely candidate for the anxiety, insomnia, headaches, irritability, fatigue and depression, hot flashes and night sweats that hit during perimenopause, the period when a woman's body is preparing for menopause. This doesn't happen suddenly as you hit fifty. Hormonal changes, and especially falling estrogen levels, occur subtly over time, as much as ten years before a woman reaches menopause when her periods stop.

Symptoms of Menopause	
PSYCHOLOGICAL	PHYSICAL
◆ Anxiety	◆ Hot flashes
◆ Irritability	◆ Headaches
◆ Insomnia	◆ Dry skin
◆ Mood swings	◆ Bloating
◆ Poor concentration	◆ Heart palpitations
◆ Fatigue	◆ Nights sweats
◆ Insomnia	◆ Urinary incontinence
	◆ Vaginal dryness & itching
	◆ Weight gain

The emotional havoc that often happens in perimenopause relates primarily to falling estrogen.   As estrogen levels drop so do endorphins, the brain's opium and this drop produces effects similar to withdrawal from heroin or morphine: irritability, tearfulness, anxiety, stomach upset, diarrhea, and sweating.

As changes happen gradually, a woman may not associate her distress with falling hormones and she assumes it emotional. If you are a fortiesh woman and suffer anxiety and panic that seems to be getting worse as you age, a blood test to determine your level of follicle-stimulating hormone (FSH) will tell you if you are in perimenopause. FSH levels increase as estrogen falls. If estrogen is low, many options exist for balancing your hormonal system.

Treating Symptoms

Conventional

Take HRT?

Conventional medicine regards menopause as a disease that requires a cure: HRT (hormone replacement therapy) to the rescue. But over the last ten to fifteen years, numerous studies have surfaced debunking HRT as a panacea for menopausal symptoms and a preventative measure for osteoporosis.   Although it can provide symptomatic relief and some protection for women's bones, HRT produces tremendous, even life threatening side effects.   A national study was terminated midway after a clear increase in strokes, heart attacks, and breast cancer in the hormone-treated group. And anxiety, mood swings and irritability will result if a woman is automatically put on hormone replacement because of her age and her body is still producing adequate amounts of hormones.

Alternative

Many options to HRT exist. Women in more traditional societies rely on natural cures to treat menopausal-related symptoms without the side effects of drugs. Chinese Medicine, for instance, has been treating hot flashes and hormonal emotional distress with acupuncture and herbal medicine for almost 3000 years.

Take Natural Hormones

Natural progesterone cream applied to the skin has proved helpful in regulating hormones for many women. Pregnenolone cream is another option.   Made from diosgenin, a plant compound, pregnenolone is a precursor for DHEA.   It is converted into progesterone, cortisone, testosterone, and estrogen in the body. Some creams also include essential oils known to relieve menopausal symptoms such as lavender, chamomile, neroli, or clary-sage.

Eat Better

Good Fat: Modern diets are notoriously low in nutrition, and especially in the good omega-3 fats.   Many of these oils, including evening primrose, black currant, and flax seed oil have been used specifically for menopause-related complains such as vaginal dryness and hot flashes, the latter of which greatly increases irritability and anxiety.

Phyto-Estrogens: Phyto-estrogens provide a weak estrogen that helps *increase* estrogen in menopausal women. For a list of foods that increase healthy estrogen, see page 127.

Many recommend soy in your diet to help ward off hot flashes and other complaints. Chinese women, who rarely suffer menopausal symptoms, consume this bean in large amounts. Soy contains a type of protein that mimics the body's estrogen but unlike hormone replacement therapy appears protective against breast cancer. Be aware though that soy is not only highly mucus forming and a major allergen but that it is also a genetically modified food and is therefore not considered a natural, whole food.

Adding phyto-estrogens to your diet will also help with insomnia, a common complaint of women in perimenopause and menopause. The brain needs estrogen to stimulate serotonin in the brain which in turn is needed to produce melatonin, the hormone needed for sleep. Low estrogen translates into low serotonin and low melatonin.

Coffee: Watch your coffee intake. Many menopausal women complain that caffeine increases the frequency of hot flashes.

Try Herbs

Many herbs have been successfully used for millenniums to reduce menopausal symptoms. These include:

➢ **Black cohosh**, an excellent natural estrogen promoter, has very low side effects.
➢ **Dong Quai,** licorice and chaste berries all contain components that mimic the body's own hormones.
➢ **Gingko** reduces cold hands and feet, a common menopausal complaint.
➢ **Kava** helps menopausal women better cope with anxiety. In two placebo-controlled, double-blind studies of 80 women with menopause related symptoms, the kava group reported reductions in anxiety symptoms, hot flashes, and other menopausal symptoms, along with improved sleep, mood, and sense of well-being.

Move

Exercise is one of the best anxiety busters, boosting endorphins and altering mood, as well as inducing deeper sleep. And it helps with other menopausal related symptoms. Scandinavian researchers discovered that daily exercise can ward off hot flashes, improve bone density, and increase energy in menopausal women. If you are getting anxiety-producing hot flashes, exercise outdoors in the morning as bright light in the a.m. also eliminates them.

Quick Review

➤ **Hormonal** changes in the female hormones estrogen and progesterone at puberty, in pregnancy, after delivery, around menstruation, and at menopause can produce anxiety symptoms, insomnia, depression, and sleep disorders that can be misdiagnosed as psychiatric.

➤ **Anxiety** or panic attack that is cyclic or episodic and generally subsides as hormones regulate, following pregnancy, menstruation, and menopause, is likely hormone-induced and the symptoms might disappear when hormones regulate.

➤ **Most** women experience some degree of PMS related anxiety and depression during most menstrual cycles, except in the week following menstruation. When it becomes disabling, you may have *Premenstrual Dysphoric Disorder* and may want to investigate psychiatric treatment along with the treatments outlined in this chapter.

➤ **The** closer women get to menopause, the more estrogen levels decline and the greater the likelihood of anxiety attacks and intensified PMS symptoms.

➤ **While** modern doctors often prescribe psychotropic drugs for PMS and menopausal anxiety symptoms, they can be controlled naturally through:
  - Healthy diet
  - Supplementation
  - Herbal supplements
  - Exercise
  - Aromatherapy
  - Light therapy

➤ **Traditionally**, women have been prescribed natural hormone replacement therapy for menopausal related symptoms, including emotional. But recently its safety has been questioned. Many natural alternatives exist, including:
  - Progesterone cream
  - Diet high in phyto-estrogens
  - Herbs such as black cohosh
  - Exercise
  - Aromatherapy
  - Light therapy

Resources

Suggested Books

➢ *The Silent Passage: Menopause* by Gail Sheehey (Pocket Books, 1995).
➢ *Screaming to be Heard* by Elizabeth Lee Vliet (Evans, 2001).
➢ *Natural Hormone Balance for Women : Look Younger, Feel Stronger, and Live Life with Exuberance* by Uzzi Reiss, Martin Zucker (Atria, 2002).
➢ *What Your Doctor May Not Tell You About Menopause (TM): The Breakthrough Book on Natural Hormone Balance* by John R. Lee (Warner, 2004).

5

★

Tired & Achy

If you walk with crutches, sympathy and offers for help will abound. But if you suffer chronic, severe and persistent fatigue, flu like symptoms, headaches, fitful sleep, or pain all over your body-- largely invisible symptoms--you will garner little sympathy and your complaints will often meet with disbelief and misinformation. Such is what happens to those who suffer chronic fatigue syndrome (CFS) and fibromyalgia (FM), two chronic and debilitating illnesses that often co-exist and that render you exhausted, unable to sleep, in pain, spacey, anxious, depressed, and sensory defensive.

Often unable to find any organic cause for CFS and FM, many uninformed physicians and psychiatrists believe they are somatic or physical expressions of depression and anxiety and sufferers hear the familiar "your illness is all in your head:" psychiatry not medicine is the answer for the "yuppie flu." Or physicians treat individual symptoms, like prescribing painkillers or muscle relaxers for fibromyalgia pain, or antibiotics for the flu-like symptoms of CFS, not realizing that the symptoms add up to a syndrome. These band aid interventions barely make a dent and anxiety intensifies. Or your symptoms are considered psychosomatic and physicians, family and friends dismiss you as a hypochondriac. Misunderstood, unsupported, devalued, and unlovable, and too ill to work, parent, love, or play well, your life and self narrows drastically. Who wouldn't feel anxious or depressed?

Chronic Fatigue Syndrome

The story of the horse Seabiscuit, made into a major motion picture, is truly heroic. The horse and his jockey, Red Pollard, both suffered injuries that should have stopped them from ever racing but, with persistence, achieve an amazing comeback. Laura Hillenbrand, the author of *Seabiscuit: An American Legend* on which the movie is based has her own heroic story behind its inception. For over seventeen years, Laura Hillenbrand has been debilitated by CFS and wrote the book against all odds.

Hillenbrand's symptoms began in March, 1987 with nausea, fever and muscles aches that appeared to be food poisoning, as she recounted in a New Yorker article in July, 2003. She felt extremely exhausted and too weak to walk. To get to the bathroom, "I had to drag my shoulder along the wall to stay upright," she writes.

Not knowing what was happening the twenty-year old dropped out of college and retreated to her mother's house and quickly to bed. She had lost twenty pounds, her lymph nodes were painfully swollen, her throat was on fire and her limbs unsteady; during the day she had the chills and at night she was soaked in sweat. Her mind was in a fog and she couldn't make sense of words or shapes or think well enough to finish a sentence. She felt dizzy, disoriented, unsteady on her feet, and depersonalization: "I was at a sensory distance from the world, as if I were wrapped in clear plastic."

Having never been ill before, she didn't have an internist and so she went to see her old pediatrician. He prescribed antibiotics for a fever and strep throat and sent her to an internist. He found nothing amiss and prescribed antacids for her GI problems. She didn't get better. She returned to see him. He told her the problem was not in her body but in her mind and to see a psychiatrist. The psychiatrist felt that she was mentally healthy but had an undiagnosed physical condition. "Find another psychiatrist," the internist advised her.

She went to another internist who found that she had the Epstein-Barr virus. He prescribed some nutritional supplements but they had no affect. She got worse. Her hair started to fall out; her periods ceased; bleeding sores pocked her mouth and throat; she had trench throat and her temperature spiked to a hundred and one every twelve hours. Her world narrowed to her bed and her window.

She saw doctor after doctor who tried to convince her that her problems were psychological. Friends started to concur, accusing her of being lazy and selfish. She felt ashamed, angry, depressed, and horrifically lonely. She contemplated suicide.

Finally, one of the doctors suggested she see Dr. John G. Bartlett, the chief of the Division of Infectious Diseases at Johns Hopkins

University School of Medicine. After a lengthy exam and review of her medical records, he had a diagnosis: chronic fatigue syndrome. A recently discovered condition, CFS is characterized by disabling weakness, exhaustion, flu-like symptoms, mental disorganization and many other symptoms that may continue for months, or even years. Not good news but at least she had a diagnosis!

She began to get stronger but had to be careful not to overextend herself. "One mistake could land me in bed for weeks, so the potential cost of even the most trivial activities, from showering to walking to the mailbox, had to be painstakingly considered."

A friend referred her to Dr. Fred Gill, a renowned infectious-disease specialist. In the following years, he was able to help her manage her symptoms and she got back to something of a life. Having been a writer before the illness began, she began to write articles in spurts, as she could muster the energy. And then she discovered the story of Seabiscuit. Impassioned by the extraordinary courage of a boy and a horse, she could transcend her own sick body to write the story.

Feeling stronger, her boyfriend and her drove to New York to see the racetrack at Saratoga. The ten-hour road trip and a ferocious thunderstorm took its toll. By the time they turned into the farmhouse driveway, she was chilled and sweating profusely. She slid into a delirium. Months went by and she couldn't get down the stairs or bathe herself and had to hire help to assist her. She became extremely dizzy and her eyes were jerking to the left. A neurological exam revealed that her vertigo was neurological and virtually untreatable. It didn't stop. Her ears pounded with a constant shrieking sound. When she looked down to write, the room spun so she perched her laptop on a stack of books. When she was too tired to sit at her desk, she set the laptop in her bed. When she was too dizzy to read, she lay down and wrote with her eyes closed. Yet, obsessed with this fascinating story, she lived in her subjects' bodies and forgot about her own and in two dizzy years finished the book!

How Do You Know If You Have CFS?

If you have chronic fatigue syndrome, there's no mistaking it.

You experience:

➢ **Severe & Disabling Fatigue:**   The least exertion makes you extremely tired and you feel as if your eyelids may droop from heaviness.

➢ **Constantly Ill:**   You have a sore throat, a fever, a headache, achy muscles, trembly limbs, cold hands and feet, PMS, and irritable bowel syndrome.

➢ **Sleep Issues:**   You always want to be in bed and sleep too much; or you can't fall asleep as inside everything races and thumps and, once asleep, continually awaken.

➢ **Problems Standing:** You become dizzy, light-headed, and fatigued after briefly standing.

➢ **Confused:** Your mind goes blank and you forget the simplest words, feel too confused to remember if you just brushed your teeth, and can't concentrate well enough to follow the movie on the TV.

➢ **Anxious & Depressed:** Anxiety and depression are constant.

Symptoms of Chronic Fatigue Syndrome	
Physical	**Thinking**
◆ Sore throat	◆ Short-term memory loss
◆ Cough	◆ Concentration problems
◆ Tender lymph nodes	◆ Disorientation
◆ Headaches	◆ Head fog
◆ GI problems	◆ Light-headedness
◆ Low-grade fever	**Sleep/wake Regulation**
◆ Palpitations	◆ Extreme fatigue after
◆ Chest pain	minor activities; lasting 6
◆ Low blood pressure	months or more
◆ Shortness of breath	◆ Sleep disorders
◆ Blurred or double vision	**Sensory**
Feelings	◆ Hypersensitivity to light,
◆ Anxiety	noise, sounds
◆ Irritability	◆ Chemical sensitivity
◆ Depression	◆ Hypersensitivity to heat &
	cold

Rain Barrel Effect

Chronic fatigue happens slowly. Here's a common scenario.

1. **Thyroid Dysfunction:** You have thyroid dysfunction and it doesn't get diagnosed.
2. **Infections:** Thyroid dysfunction leads to frequent infections.
3. **Antibiotics:** The doctors put you on antibiotics. These tear down the gut and yeast overgrow.
4. **Leaky Gut:** You don't adequately digest your food and develop leaky gut.
5. **Food Allergies:** The body starts to treat the food you eat as a foreign invader and puts out antibodies to the food and in addition to thyroiditis and the yeast problem you have food allergies -- all common mimickers of panic and anxiety.
6. **Epstein-Barr Virus:** Eventually unable to meet the total toxic load, your body becomes a host to the Epstein-Barr virus.
7. **CFS & Fibromyalgia:** All these conditions tax your immune system and eventually overwhelm it and you get not only CFS but, if you've had physical trauma, often fibromyalgia as well.
8. **Meds:** All these conditions -- and many others – elude doctors who, finding no apparent organic illness, easily misdiagnose your symptoms as "just stress" and put you on antidepressants and anti-anxiety medication.
9. **Further Depletion:** These medications further destabilize your system, particularly the gastro-intestinal system, further weakening your immune system.
10. **Overload:** Chronic fatigue gets worse and the slightest physical or emotional stress throws you into overload from which you can't recover easily.

It's the rain barrel effect. Each toxin that builds up adds one more drop until the water reaches the brim and the barrel over flows. Feeling better, Laura Hillenbrand and her boyfriend ventured to New York to visit the racetrack in Saratoga. The trip was more than her body could handle and she ended up too dizzy to sit upright for two years! That's the nature of the illness: you take one step forward; you feel better and take a giant step forward; you collapse and take two steps backward.

Causes

The origin of CFS is a mystery. Initially it was thought to be caused by a virus, such as Epstein-Barr or human herpes virus 6 (HHV6). But not all people with the syndrome test positive for these viruses. The new theory is that CFS, and its cousin, fibromyalgia are caused by a battered immune system. Implicated is a variety of triggers, alone or in combination.

CFS Triggers	
PHYSICAL	♦ Infections
♦ Anemia	♦ Surgery
♦ Arthritis	♦ Hormone imbalance
♦ Hypoglycemia	♦ Illness
♦ Hypothyroidism	
♦ Yeast overgrowth	**PSYCHOLOGICAL**
♦ Food sensitivities	♦ Stress
♦ Sleep problems	♦ Depression
♦ Environmental exposure-	♦ Substance abuse
mercury poisoning from	♦ Physical or emotional
amalgam fillings, e.g.	abuse

As CFS is becoming more accepted as a syndrome, researchers are making headway into the cause of many of the attending symptoms. For instance, neurological symptoms, such as the inability to remember, or think clearly may result from high cytokines, the messenger cell in the immune system that carries instructions to other cells. High cytokines may be responsible as well for the GI problems commonly experienced by the CFS patient, as the bowel has certain receptors for cytokines. Low body temperature, low blood pressure and cold intolerance may be from an imbalance in the hypothalamus, the master gland in the limbic system that controls autonomic functioning, temperature regulation, sleep, pulse, and blood flow.

Researchers at Johns Hopkins Hospital in Baltimore have also shed light on the dizziness, light-headedness and fatigue after standing. They discovered these symptoms to result from "neurally mediated hypotension," a specific kind of low blood pressure that causes blood pressure to drop swiftly when a person stands.

Detected by tilt-table testing, the researchers found the tilt-table to be abnormal in twenty-two of twenty-three CFS patients studied. Nineteen were treated with drugs commonly used to treat neurally mediated hypotension, such as fludrocortisone, disopyramide or a beta-blocker. Of these, sixteen showed dramatic improvement in their CFS symptoms, and nine had nearly complete recovery. Neurally mediated hypotension is frequently caused by salt (sodium) restriction and associated with adrenal exhaustion (see pages 83-84).

Diagnosis

Only recognized a decade ago as a syndrome, CFS is often difficult to officially diagnose. Often the tests that determine the presence of human herpes virus 6 (HHV6) or Epstein-Barr virus are abnormal but no definitive laboratory tests exist to prove CFS's existence. And the symptoms are similar to other illnesses, such as thyroid problems, anemia, infection, or depression, all of which may co-exist with CFS.

Without a definitive marker, some physicians still deny it as a syndrome and believe it to be "psychosomatic" – a euphemism for all in your head. To support their contention, more than two-thirds of patients with CFS appear to have an associated psychiatric disorder. Why would this be?

Coping with CFS alone creates anxiety and depression, even in people who were previously well adjusted. And the stress of not having your illness validated takes its toll. People often accuse you of dropping out of life or shirking your responsibilities because you're *demented*, not *ill*. Moreover, people with a battered immune system are often those vulnerable people who, born with a sensitive constitution, are more anxiety prone and more susceptible to illness. The histories of many CFS patients show stressful lives with the flight/fight stress response perpetually switched on, wearing down the body. Not surprisingly, CFS is most commonly diagnosed in previously healthy women between the ages of twenty and fifty, a time of high stress for many women.

Treatment Options

If you feel that you have CFS, persist in pursuing a diagnosis and explore all possible treatments. It's tough to beat but only a small percentage of sufferers actually get worse. Most have moderate to complete recovery though it takes several years and most will continue to have some symptoms. Expect improvement interrupted with relapses from overexertion, stress, or infection.

Conventional

Physicians tend to treat CFS with anti-inflammatory agents, antiviral and immunologically active drugs, and low doses of antidepressants. Commonly, your doctor will prescribe low doses of SSRIs like Prozac, Zoloft, or Paxil in the morning for energy, and the older tricyclic antidepressants in the evening to promote sleep.

Alternative

Alternative physicians take a holistic approach to healing CFS, as it involves many systems of the body, including the immune, digestive, hormonal, and central nervous system. They recommend nutritional changes, supplementation, detoxifying, rest, and moderate exercise. Homeopathy is often useful.

Nutritional Support

If you have CFS, you are likely under-nourished and especially if you are on the standard American diet. Not only is this diet low in nutrition but it takes up 60 percent of the body's internal energy to digest. As a CFS patient is operating at a low energy level, just digesting food eats up all available energy and more.

Basically you need a diet rich in antioxidants and essential vitamins, minerals, and fatty acids (see chapter 12), including:

➢ **B complex** vitamins, vitamin C, carotenes, selenium, zinc, copper, and, if low, iron.
➢ **Vitamin B$_{12}$** shots; if you don't digest your food well, you don't absorb the vitamin B$_{12}$ you need and this causes fatigue and other problems, including allergies
➢ **Folic acid**, necessary for anemia, fatigue, immune weakness, and infection (Food sources include green leafy vegetables such as spinach and kale, asparagus, broccoli, lima beans, greens peas,

sweet potatoes, bean sprouts, whole wheat, cantaloupe, strawberries, and brewer's yeast)

➤ **Magnesium** in your diet or supplement (oxygenated is best) as CFS sufferers are almost always low in magnesium (magnesium-rich foods include kelp, almonds, dulse, walnuts, filberts, sesame seeds, lima beans, white beans, red beans, and millet)

➤ **Licorice root**, a natural coricosteroid with activity resembling cortisone that raises low blood pressure and helps relieve neurally mediated hypotension

➤ **Glandular extracts** such as thymine, spleen, and liver to boost the immune system, and herbs such as golden seal, Echinacea, astragulus, or aloe vera, to name a few

➤ **Herbs** valerian and passion flower to help you sleep, and ginkgo biloba to enhance mental functioning

Detoxifying

Detoxifying your body of external toxins such as chemicals and drugs, as well as internal toxins such as *Candida* and free radicals, is a priority for CFS sufferers. New studies show that all CFS and fibromyalgia sufferers have a marked deficiency and depletion of glutathione, lypoic acid, and n-acetyl cysteine, the amino acids needed for the liver to detoxify heavy metals.

Load up on foods that contain glutathione, like avocado, asparagus, watermelon, squash, potato, and green vegetables like spinach and parsley. Chelate the aluminum out of your system using the guidelines explained in chapters 13 and 14, as aluminum affects memory, and avoid products that contain aluminum such as cookware, foil, certain medications, baking powder, table salt, and vanilla powder.

Homeopathy

To holistic practitioners, chronic fatigue indicates energy blockages in the system. If you correct that, many things fall into place. Homeopathy, a type of energy or vibrational medicine, is one method for opening up energy fields to stimulate innate healing forces. Acupuncture is another.

Here are some suggested homeopathic remedies for CFS. Take these remedies only for short periods, seldom more than two weeks. For best results, consult with a physician who specializes in homeopathy, such as a naturopath.

➢ *Gelsemium* for exhaustion

➢ *Arsenicum* for anxiety and restlessness

➢ *Kali phosphorica* for brain fog and memory problems

➢ *Anacardium* for brain fog and forgetfulness

➢ *Baryt carbonica* for poor focusing

➢ *Lycopodium* for brain fog and for poor digestion

➢ *Noxvomica* for poor liver function

Sleep and Rest

Some doctors recommend Aggressive Rest Therapy or ART to force rest for CFS and help build up your extremely debilitated immune system. Basically, you stay in bed all day, every day for a minimum of three months. The treatment is similar to that given for tuberculosis and rheumatic fever patients in the early half of the twentieth century that often proved effective.

Though you may stay in bed, you may not feel rested as many CFS sufferers suffer sleep disorders. See the next section on fibromyalgia for sleep strategies.

Exercise

For those who can manage it, a daily, low-level exercise program, preferably with the assistance of a physical therapist, can help greatly. Exercise helps build the immune system, promotes better digestion and thus more energy, and is a great stress buster.

Fibromyalgia

Imagine a sleepless night. You wake up exhausted, your mind is in a fog, and your body feels beaten up. Now imagine feeling this way all day, every day! Poor sleep, cold, humid weather, too much of the wrong type of activity may provoke a flare-up that could last for days, weeks, or even months. In constant pain, tense, tired, unwell, your activities severely limited and your relationships compromised, both anxiety and depression are pervasive. As anxiety intensifies, panic attacks frequently occur. Such is the fate of sufferers of *fibromyalgia*.

Though the name "fibromyalgia" might be new to you, it's been around for centuries as: chronic rheumatism, muscular rheumatism, fibrositis, myofibrositis, and spinal irritation. It has also been termed historically as "morbid affectation" and "Charcot's hysteria," reflecting a tendency for doctors to FMS as hypochondria or mental illness.

How Do You Know If You Have FM?

The chief characteristic of fibromyalgia is widespread body pain, which is at its worse generally in the morning. The pain varies between deep muscular aching, throbbing, burning, shooting, and stabbing pains. Sleep disturbances are common as chronic pain makes it hard to wind down to sleep. When you do finally nod off, you lack delta, the deepest, most restorative sleep. Apparently alpha waves, associated with the relaxed state when winding down into sleep intrudes and awakens you and you sleep shallowly throughout the night. Sleep deprivation exacerbates pain and causes a lot of "fibro fog" and memory problems. Occurring along with pain and sleep deprivation are many other physical symptoms and, commonly, anxiety and depression.

Symptoms of Fibromyalgia	
Physical	**Sleep/Wake Regulation**
♦ Body aching and pain	♦ Chronic fatigue
♦ Irritable bowel syndrome	♦ Sleep disorders
♦ Irritable bladder syndrome or interstitial cystitis	**Feelings**
	♦ Irritability
	♦ Anxiety
♦ Headaches	♦ Depression
♦ Dry eyes	**Thinking**
♦ Numbness	♦ Head fog
♦ Cold intolerance	♦ Poor concentration
♦ Allergies	**Sensory**
♦ Stiffness	♦ Hypersensitivity to smells, light
♦ Sinusitus	

Causes

The exact causes of fibromyalgia are unknown. Possible causes include:

➢ **Injury or Trauma**

➢ **Nervous System Disorders**: FM patients have reduced blood flow and energy production in the regions of the brain dealing with pain regulation, memory and concentration.

➢ **Chemical Toxicity:** Those exposed to chemical toxins, like pesticides, artificial fertilizers, petrochemical fumes, glue, varnish, aerosol sprays, some household cleaners, paints or perfumes often develop FM. Many with Gulf War Syndrome, who suffer multiple chemical sensitivity suffer FM.

➢ **Hormonal imbalance**

➢ **Gastrointestinal problems**

➢ **Immune system compromise:** As FM is commonly seen in conjunction with other diseases, like chronic fatigue, endocrine conditions, thyroid problems, infectious disease or Lyme disease, immune system compromise appears a precipitating factor.

➢ **Allergies**

➢ **Structural problems**

➢ **Genetics:** Some people appear to have genetic predisposition to FM. Under physical or emotional stress, their body breaks down. For instance, a whiplash from a car accident appears to lead some to develop FM, as tender points cause all-over aches.

Diagnosis

Long dismissed as arthritis or as psychosomatic, FM has finally been recognized by the medical establishment as a syndrome. Physicians diagnose FM by aching and pain at eleven of eighteen specific tender points on the body.

Treatment Options

Conventional

Small doses of antidepressants, such as Paxil, Zoloft, Wellbutrin, Prozac and Serzone help relieve symptoms. Anti-inflammatory medicines, such as ibuprofen or naproxen and muscle relaxants on a short-term basis help when pain flares up. Tender-point injections, which involve injecting a numbing agent like lidocaine into the body's tender points, help reduce pain for around three weeks.

Alternative

Exercise, hands-on therapy, such as myofascial release, along with chiropractic, osteopathy, and physical therapy all help ease fibromyalgia symptoms as do acupuncture, meditation, and proper belly breathing.

Proper nutrition and supplementation are a must to help balance the nervous system, as is detoxifying the body. Sleep aids make it easier to nod off at night.

Cranial Manipulation

If you have chronic aching muscles, the muscles are overworked indicating something amiss in your alignment. Cranial manipulation, such as neurocranial restructuring and biocranial work (see chapter eight) will help re-position the craniosacral system so the muscles need not strain to support your weight.

Nutrition

Most people with fibromyalgia are malnourished and deficient in certain vitamins and minerals, such as B_1, B_6, B_{12}, folic acid, and magnesium. Too little B_6 in the body has been linked to a low pain threshold. Sugar sensitivity is also a major factor as many FM patients are sensitive to carbohydrates. Eating the right foods, as outlined in chapter 12, helps reduce or eliminate abnormalities in the endocrine system, immune system, and nervous system that appear to trigger fibromyalgia, as well as the anxiety, panic and depression that accompany this dysfunction.

Supplements

Supplements that increase serotonin help with fibromyalgia as low serotonin levels are implicated in pain and fibromyalgia in particular. These include 5-HTP, St. John's Wort, GABA, and

Taurine (see pages 114-116). Zenbev, a natural source of the amino acid L-Tryptophan has become an extremely popular treatment. A precursor for melatonin in the evening, and serotonin during daylight, L-Tryptophan helps to reduce daytime anxiety and aid nighttime sleep. It only needs to be taken three or four days out of the week, as it has a cumulative effect.

Detoxifying

FM sufferers are overly toxic and therefore more susceptible to myofascial trigger points. Leaky gut is common and the gradual accumulation of toxic chemicals is one of the causes of pain. As toxins build up in the tissues, the blood becomes thicker and slows circulation and healing. Along with insufficient oxygenation, this leads to a sluggish lymph system and the lymph nodes swell and become sore and create pain. Apparently certain biochemicals, such as hyaluronic acid, quinolinic acid, and phosphoric acid, many of which are irritants, are higher in people with FM and detoxifying amino acids are low. Detoxifying is a high priority.

Exercise

Pain and fatigue make exercising hard for those with fibromyalgia and you tend to skip going to the gym. Don't. Not moving about actually exacerbates symptoms. Exercise helps balance endorphins and serotonin, making the brain function more effectively and relieves both painful physical and emotional distress. Yoga stretching, tai chi, and qi gong are especially good exercises for those with fibromyalgia.

Sleep Aids

Restorative sleep is critical for the FM sufferer as normal sleep patterns improve pain levels. And sleep is necessary to restore the body and nervous system, thereby improving thinking and reducing irritability and anxiety. Here are some suggestions for better sleep.

Develop Good Sleep Habits
➢ **Keep Sleep Schedule:** Maintain the same sleep schedule seven days a week, even weekends, to set your body's natural

circadian rhythm. Get up at the same time each day, seven days a week, regardless of how little you slept during the night.

➢ **Employ Wise Bedroom Use:** Use your bedroom for sleep and sex only.

➢ **Watch Eating Habits:** Eat a light evening meal and finish eating at least three hours before bedtime.

➢ **No Stimulating Substances:** Avoid stimulating substances like caffeine, including cola and chocolate, or smoking a cigarette in the evening, or spicy foods, high carbohydrate foods, and alcohol, which can disrupt sleep all night.

➢ **No Stimulating Activities:** Before retiring, don't watch TV, use the computer, or argue with your spouse.

➢ **No Drugs:** Don't take over-the-counter pain relievers and anti-anxiety drugs, like Valium or Xanax to help you sleep. They suppress melatonin and inhibit deep sleep.

➢ **Get Up if You Can't Sleep:** If unable to sleep, turn on the light, leave the bedroom, and read a boring book.

Create a Restful Bedroom Environment

➢ **Insulation:** Insulate your bedroom against sounds with carpeting, insulated curtains, closing the door, or white noise with a fan or air filter; ear plugs help some.

➢ **Cool and Uncluttered:** Keep air cool and bed uncluttered, but sleep with bedding that feels comfortably warm. Cold hands and feet are one reason for problems falling asleep. Research at the Psychiatric University Clinic in Basel, Switzerland found that warm extremities, a sign of dilated blood vessels and healthy blood flow, were linked to falling asleep quickly.

➢ **Negative Ions:** Use an air ionizer machine to increase relaxing negative ions in the air.

➢ **Darkness:** Keep bedroom very dark (fabric stores sell black-out material); night shades help. At the same time, exposure to outdoor or bright morning light will help you wake up.

Sleep & Noise

A quiet bedroom may not be as favorable to sleep as once thought. Anthropologist Carol Wurtman analyzed the sleep customs of hunter-gatherer groups like the Ache foragers in Paraguay. She found that sleep usually unfolds in shared spaces that feature constant background noise from other sleepers, various domestic animals, fires maintained for warmth and protection from predators, and other people's nearby nighttime activities. Noise appears more conducive to deep sleep -- remember the womb is noisy and babies often sleep better with white noise.

Natural Sleep Aids

➢ **Herbs:** Try sedative herbs like valerian or kava as a sleep aid, or melatonin supplementation which deepen sleep for many. In one study, people between the ages of sixty-eight and eighty who took melatonin fell asleep in half their usual time and felt more refreshed upon awakening. Be aware that melatonin is a hormone and without FDA approval as a medication. As the long-term effects of melatonin supplementation are unknown, some practitioners recommend taking it every other night and then only for a few months and then going off it.

➢ **Vitamins and Minerals:** Get enough B vitamins (particularly B_6) to regulate the body's use of the amino acid tryptophan which converts to melatonin. Vitamin B_{12} supplements help induce sleep as does taking calcium before bed. Taking the amino acid 5-HTP before going to sleep, which increases serotonin levels, reduces the time needed to fall asleep by half, and enhances sleep quality in some people.

➢ **Music:** To unwind before bed time, listen to relaxing music. Listening to a relaxation or meditation tape will naturally get your brain into the delta state of deep sleep (see Resources).

➢ **Breathing:** To ready you for sleep, do breathing exercises to help slow and deepen your breathing (see chapter seven).

➢ **Progressive relaxation:** Briefly tense and relax each muscle group -- hands, arms, legs, feet, back, stomach, face. Your body will relax quickly into an alpha state readying you for sleep.

➢ **Aromatherapy:** Rub a few drops of lavender oil on the bottom of your feet before nodding off, which will distribute the oil to every cell in your body in approximately 20 minutes. The most sedating scents are, in order of effectiveness are:

♦ Lavender   ♦ Sandalwood
♦ Bergamot   ♦ Lemon
♦ Marjoram   ♦ Chamomile

Lavender & Chamomile

A study at the Old Manor Hospital in Salisbury, Britain, found that diffused lavender essential oil could successfully replace medication to relieve insomnia. A cup of chamomile tea also helps to wind down to sleep.

➢ **Hot Bath:** Soak in a warm bath with soothing essential oils, like lavender, rose or geranium before retiring to bed. The hot water causes your body temperature to rise about 2°F. In response to a sudden rise in temperature, the pineal gland produces melatonin, which decreases and normalizes body temperature and lulls you to sleep.

➢ **Exercise:** Moving your body not only relaxes you but it elevates body temperature which then drops for improved sleep. Exercising regularly, preferably in the late afternoon or early evening, gives your body time to cool before going to bed.

➢ **Light:** Sleep difficulties intensify in the winter months when there is less sunlight. Strengthen your natural circadian sleep-wake rhythm by not wearing sun block or sunglasses when out in the sun as they block out UV light; Ott sunglasses are an exception (see chapter nine).

Quick Review

Chronic Fatigue

➢ *Chronic Fatigue Syndrome* is a disabling weakness, characterized by exhaustion, flu-like symptoms, mental disorganization and many other symptoms that may continue for months, or even years.

➢ **Doctors** often believe CFS is not an actual condition but a result of stress and all in the patient's head.

➢ **Initially** chronic fatigue syndrome was thought to be caused by a virus, such as Epstein-Barr or human herpes virus 6 (HHV6). The new theory is that CFS, and its cousin, fibromyalgia are caused by a battered immune system.

➢ **Diagnosing** CFS is often difficult. Often the tests that determine the presence of human herpes virus 6 (HHV6) or Epstein-Barr virus are abnormal but no definitive laboratory tests exist to prove CFS's existence. And the symptoms are similar to other illnesses, such as thyroid trouble, anemia, infection, or depression, all of which may co-exist with CFS.

➢ **Though** CFS is tough to beat, only a small percentage of sufferers get progressively worse. Most have moderate to complete recovery though it takes several years and most will continue to have some symptoms. Expect improvement interrupted with relapses from overexertion, stress, or infection.

➢ **Conventional** physicians tend to treat CFS with anti-inflammatory agents, antiviral and immunologically active drugs, and low doses of antidepressants. Commonly, your doctor will prescribe low doses of SSRI's like Prozac, Zoloft, or Paxil in the morning for energy, and the older tricyclic antidepressants in the evening to promote sleep.

➢ **Alternative** physicians take a holistic approach to healing CFS and recommend nutritional changes, supplementation, detoxifying, rest, and moderate exercise. Homeopathy is often useful.

Fibromyalgia

➢ **Fibromyalgia** involves widespread body pain, often at its worse in the morning. The pain varies between deep muscular aching, throbbing, burning, shooting, and stabbing pains. Occurring along with pain are many other physical symptoms and, commonly, anxiety and depression.

➢ **Physicians** often misdiagnose fibromyalgia as arthritis or as a psychosomatic complaint.

➢ **Exact** causes of fibromyalgia are unknown. FM can come from:

- Injury or trauma
- Nervous system disorders
- Exposure to chemical toxins
- Hormonal imbalance
- Immune system compromise
- GI problems
- Allergies
- Structural problems
- Genetic predisposition

➢ **Physicians** diagnose FM by aching and pain at eleven of eighteen specific tender points on the body.

➢ **Conventional** doctors treat FM with:

- Small doses of antidepressants, such as Paxil, Zoloft, Wellbutrin, Prozac and Serzone help relieve symptoms.
- Anti-inflammatory medicines, such as ibuprofen or naproxen and muscle relaxants on a short-term basis help when pain flares up.
- Tender-point injections, which involve injecting a numbing agent like lidocaine into the body's tender points, help reduce pain for around three weeks.

➢ **Alternative** practitioners focus on easing fibromyalgia symptoms through:

- Nutrition
- Acupuncture
- Meditation
- Belly breathing

➢ **Exercise,** hands-on therapy, such as myofascial release, along with chiropractic, osteopathy, and physical therapy all help ease FM symptoms.

➢ **Sleep** aids make it easier to nod off at night.

Resources

Suggested Books

> *Fibromyalgia, A Natural Approach*, by Christine Craggs-Hinton (Ulysses Press, 2004).
> *Hope and Help for Chronic Fatigue Syndrome: The Official Book of the CFIDS/CFS Network* by Karyn Feiden (Simon & Schuster, 1992).
> *A Clinician's Guide to Controversial Illnesses : Chronic Fatigue Syndrome, Fibromyalgia, and Multiple Chemical Sensitivities* by Renee R. Taylor, Fred Friedberg & A. Jason Leonard (Professional Resources Exchange, 2001).
> *The Doctor's Guide to Chronic Fatigue Syndrome: Understanding, Treating, and Living With Cfids* by David Sheffield Bell (Addison, 1995).

Websites

Fibromyalgia

www.fmetnews.com

Chronic Fatigue Syndrome

www.cfids.org

Meditative Tapes

www.centerpointe.com
www/neuroacoustics.com

Aromatherapy

www.younglivingessentialoils.com

Part Two

Neurological Compromise & Anxiety

Any trauma to the central nervous system, encompassing the brain and the spinal cord will impact thinking, emotions, memory and sensations and create neuropsychiatric symptoms such as anxiety, panic and depression.

Such trauma includes:

- Prenatal insult from drugs, maternal illness & stress
- Birth trauma or complications including asphyxia
- Post-birth trauma
- Prematurity
- Chemical abuse
- Chemical toxicity
- Acute or long-standing illness
- Head trauma
- Brain tumors
- Seizures

The next six chapters will cover specific insults to the nervous system, including:

- Concussions, seizures, brain tumor, Arnold Chiari Syndrome
- Hyperventilation
- Cranial/sacral misalignment
- Sensory processing disorder
- Vestibular dysfunction

♦ Photosensitivity

By the end of this section, you will have a good idea as to whether something neurological triggers your anxiety and panic.

6

★

Brain Misfiring

One week after she and her husband had resigned as motel managers, a 55-year old woman suffered severe anxiety, difficulty breathing, tight throat, a feeling of being unreal and impending doom. She had no previous history of psychiatric illness.

The "panic attacks" continued and lasted from a few minutes to an hour. During these episodes, her husband said she was difficult to understand, sometimes bit her tongue, and seemed unaware of what was going on around her. At times she became highly agitated and fell to the ground. Over the next 3 months, paramedics had taken her to the emergency room four times but nothing showed up but mild hypertension. During this time, she had gone from 280 pounds down to 220 pounds.

She sought help at an outpatient psychiatric clinic. During examination, she appeared anxious and had difficulty concentrating but was fully alert and coherent. She described a history of crying spells, low self-worth, and a fear of leaving her house. She was diagnosed with "agoraphobia with panic attacks and concurrent depression" and treated with imipramine 50 mg, increased to 150 mg over a 2-week period, and diazepam 5 mg four times a day. She responded well and her anxiety disappeared.

Three weeks later, she developed right-sided weakness. Again she went to the emergency room. They diagnosed her weakness as a "hysterical reaction." She deteriorated further and was admitted to a psychiatric unit. Two neurology residents concurred that her anxiety and weakness were psychological symptoms!

For legal reasons, they gave her an electroencephalogram (EEG) and CT scan. These tests revealed a left-sided frontoparietal mass. Following surgical removal, the panic attacks disappeared. Her panic attacks were not psychiatric but a result of complex partial seizures triggered by rapid tumor growth. Eight physicians had examined her before she was correctly diagnosed.

This case was published over twenty-years ago in the journal *Psychosomatics*. Yet such misdiagnoses continue to happen today as escalating health costs and busy doctors often prohibit seeing the whole picture. In this woman's case, fainting, biting her tongue, being unaware of her surroundings and being difficult to understand were a red flag for seizures. In this chapter, I will discuss why such misdiagnoses of seizures as psychiatric is more common than realized. I will discuss as well other common neurological anxiety mimickers: post-concussion syndrome, seizure disorders, brain tumor, and Arnold Chiari syndrome. I have eliminated traumatic brain injury as psychiatric symptoms are secondary to serious cognitive or motor deficits.

Post-Concussion Syndrome

When I was five, I fell and briefly lost consciousness. When I awoke, I felt dizzy and had a headache. I looked up and saw my concerned pediatrician peering down at me. The dim light in the bedroom felt overwhelmingly bright. The doctor told my parents that I had a head concussion but was all right. They had no reason to worry as long as I behaved normally. Until writing this book, it never occurred to me that the concussion could have anything to do with a lifetime of being anxious and spacey. Yet it could have.

If you've ever suffered a concussion, a minor brain injury that results in a temporary loss of consciousness (less than 20 minutes) or no loss of consciousness and no physical evidence of brain damage, you've had minor brain trauma. It could be causing or contributing to your anxiety or panic attack long after it happened.

After awakening from a concussion, people commonly experience delirium, disorientation, mental fog, restlessness and agitation but quickly return to normal. Physical symptoms such as headache, fatigue, dizziness and vertigo however may last for weeks or months then subside and disappear, along with temporary symptoms of learning disabilities, such as mental sluggishness, poor memory and concentration, diminished abstraction ability, poor calculation and reduced ability to process information, reason and plan.

Such symptoms happen because stopping suddenly jars the brain and causes microscopic damage to the blood vessels and nerve cell fibers in the cortex, the thinking part of the brain.

In general, symptoms improve markedly within three months and most people return to normal mental functioning. But some people experience *post-concussion syndrome* and symptoms persist for years.

POSTCONCUSSION SYNDROME SYMPTOMS	
Feelings	**Behavior**
♦ Irritability	♦ Personality changes
♦ Anxiety	**Physical**
♦ Tension	♦ Headache
♦ Panic	♦ Dizziness
♦ Mood swings	♦ Loss of balance
Thinking	**Sleep/Wake Regulation**
♦ Poor memory	♦ Insomnia
♦ Poor concentration	

Sufferers of post-concussion syndrome may also experience posttraumatic stress disorder (PTSD) and have repeated nightmares regarding the trauma, while cues related to the event can trigger intense fear. For instance, if you were driving down a ramp when you got into a car accident, even approaching a ramp can trigger panic.

Reasons for continuing symptoms remain a mystery. Doctors are miffed to explain these symptoms based on the brain injury, and especially as diagnostic tests, such as brain imaging, are often normal.

One possible explanation is that, even without losing consciousness, a blow or fall on the head will move cranial bones and upset the normal structural pattern that exists between the 22 interlocking bones of the head. This will upset the flow of the neurotransmitters that regulate emotions and mood and bring on anxiety symptoms (for more information, see chapter eight). Having been a victim twice in my life of head of post-concussion syndrome, I can attest that this happened in my case.

Treatment Options

Conventional

If traumatic brain injury has been ruled out by a brain scan, such as an MRI or CT, patients will generally be advised to see a neurologist for follow-up care. Generally neurologists prescribe various drugs to help post-concussion victims cope with symptoms such as dizziness, headache and head fog, and tranquilizers and antidepressants to cope with the psychiatric symptoms.

Alternative

Many alternative therapies can help the post-concussion victim cope with their symptoms, physical and psychological.

These include:

➤ **Acupuncture**
➤ **Structural work**: (see chapter eight)
  o Craniosacral therapy
  o Bio-cranial therapy
  o Neurocranial restructuring
➤ **Herbs**: Ginko biloba improves brain function by increasing cerebral blood flow and oxygenation.
➤ **Exercises**: Occupational and physical therapy can alleviate or eliminate vertigo and light-headedness (see chapter nine).

Complex Partial Seizure

When we think of a seizure, we picture a grand mal seizure with the person's whole body convulsing in "fits." In fact, there are many different kinds of seizures, some quite subtle and the person may momentarily stare off into space or stutter slightly.

In the normal adult, the cells of the brain communicate through tiny electrical signals at around 8 to 13 cycles per second (cps). These are called *alpha waves*. When the cells misfire and send signals that are too fast (more than 13 cps, or *beta waves)* or too slow (4-7 cps, or *theta waves)* a seizure ensues. This can be a grand mal seizure, when seizure activity spreads to the entire brain. Or it can be a partial seizure without convulsions, a mild seizure limited to a small number of nerve cells and the person may lose consciousness only for a fraction of a second. Afterward, you may feel groggy and be unaware anything happened and the seizure goes unnoticed. Other times, you experience such things as ritualized movements of the arms or legs, repetitive speech patterns, or altered sensations.

Between seizures, bizarre personality changes can take place and you may suddenly appear hyper-religious, antisocial or even psychotic as you begin to hallucinate. Anxiety and panic attacks can emerge out of nowhere. If *complex partial seizure* (previously called temporal lobe epilepsy) remains undiagnosed, you can easily be misdiagnosed as having an anxiety disorder, depression, hysteria, or schizophrenia. This is not a rare event. One study examining ten patients not responding to treatment and originally diagnosed as "borderline state" or "latent schizophrenia" suffering from "attacks of anxiety" found that all ten were actually suffering from temporal lobe seizure.

How to Know If You Have Complex Partial Seizures?

The hallmark of complex partial seizures is abrupt on-off behavior otherwise uncharacteristic of the person. For instance, out of nowhere you may suddenly feel overwhelming anxiety or fear or instant depression. And then the anxiety and depression quickly disappear and you feel "normal" again.

Another distinguishing characteristic is perceptual distortions. The temporal lobes, the area of the brain involved in perceptual integration, are the largest brain area implicated in complex partial seizures. As this part of the brain synthesizes and interprets sensory information, seizures result in distorted perceptions that feel eerily discomforting.

➢ **You** may feel déjà vu, an uncanny sense of having had an experience previously, or jamais vu, absence of an appropriate sense of familiarity, like feeling you've not slept in your bed before.

> **Sense** of odor may be distorted and you smell "rotting eggs" or "burning rubber."
> **Sizes** or colors may be distorted as if you are on a psychedelic drug, or as happened to Alice in Wonderland after nibbling the mushrooms and biscuits. And like Alice, your body may feel distorted –

> "What a curious feeling!... I must be opening up like a telescope! ... (she was now only 10" high)... Now I'm opening out like the largest telescope that ever was! Goodbye feet!" (For when she looked down at her feet, they seemed to be almost out of sight, they were getting so far away.")

Hallucinations may occur and you will see or hear things that aren't really there. You may feel confused, as if in a dreamlike state, and feel detached, not real or like yourself, a common event during a panic attack.

COMPLEX PARTIAL SEIZURE CHARACTERISTICS	
♦ Sudden automatic movement of lips ♦ Altered level of consciousness ♦ Hypergraphia (excessive writing) ♦ Hypersexuality ♦ Hyperreligiousity ♦ Hallucinations	♦ Uncontrollable rage followed by amnesia ♦ Profound mood changes ♦ Fugue states ♦ Drowsiness or sleep following seizure ♦ Déjà vu ♦ Jamais vu

Causes

> **Genetics:** Some people are genetically predisposed to seizure disorders.
> **Brain:** Problems that affect the brain will cause seizures, including
>   o Head trauma
>   o Brain tumors
>   o Meningitis and encephalitis
>   o Endocrine and metabolic diseases

- o Drug side effects and withdrawal
- o Birth trauma such as anoxia or forceps (temporal lobes are very sensitive and easily injured at birth)
- o Prolonged high fevers during infancy
- ➢ **Neurotransmitters:** Alterations in various neurotransmitter systems, including dopamine, serotonin, norepinephrine, and others likely account for the psychiatric symptoms associated with complex partial seizures.

Treatment Options

Seizure disorders are treated with various anticonvulsants. Anti-anxiety and antidepressant medications are generally counter-indicated, as they can lower the seizure threshold and increase the seizures. Such is the danger when symptoms of seizure are mistaken as psychiatric.

Brain Tumor

In the late 1930's George Gershwin, the great American composer, complained of fatigue and pounding headaches. Normally even tempered, he suddenly seemed uncharacteristically moody and critical. Friends and family attributed his symptoms to mounting stress in the composer's hectic life, including poor reviews of his Hollywood musical, *Shall We Dance*, and an affair with a woman considerably younger than himself with whom he contemplated marriage.

The symptoms progressively worsened and Gershwin went to the Cedars of Lebanon Hospital in Los Angeles where specialists subjected him to extensive medical testing. They found nothing and three and a half weeks later, he was discharged with the diagnosis of "most likely hysteria."

New symptoms emerged. Light was so painful to his eyes (photophobia) that he drew the blinds to keep out sunlight. He became unsteady on his feet and on one occasion fell while walking along a sidewalk. Convinced his problems were in his head, one of the women accompanying commented, "Leave him there. All he wants is attention." His brother Ira too felt that George suffered a "nervous disorder."

Gershwin's symptoms worsened. Headaches became unrelenting and he had trouble holding onto things. Readmitted to the hospital, he fell quickly into a coma. An x-ray revealed a mass compressing the right ventricle of the brain. Surgery was performed but the highly malignant tumor was inoperable. Gershwin died the following day at age 39.

Symptoms

Brain tumors are relatively common and, if undiagnosed, can mimic an anxiety disorder.

Location of the tumor within the brain, along with the type and size influence the kind of psychiatric symptoms, ranging from anxiety to depression to hallucinations and psychosis. Temporal lobe tumors – the thinking, higher order part of the brain – produce the most psychiatric symptoms, including anxiety, panic attacks, irritability, and personality changes.

BRAIN TUMOR SYMPTOMS		
PSYCHOLOGICAL	PHYSICAL	
♦ Anxiety ♦ Depression ♦ Irritabiity ♦ Panic attack ♦ Personality changes ♦ Hallucinations ♦ Psychosis	♦ Disk in eye ♦ Headache ♦ Nausea ♦ Vomiting ♦ Blurred vision or loss of sight	♦ Swelling of optic nerve ♦ Weakness ♦ Vertigo ♦ Confusion ♦ Seizure ♦ Excessive drowsiness

Treatment

Brain tumors are life threatening and require a medical diagnosis and generally medical treatment, although alternative methods of reducing and eliminating tumors are available. Generally the prognosis depends on early diagnosis.

Anyone who suffers anxiety or panic and also experiences the following should consult a doctor for an intense neurological workup to have a brain tumor ruled out:

➢ **Unusual** side effects from psychotropic medication
➢ **Cognitive** deficits
➢ **Personality** change
➢ **Soft neurological** signs like loss of balance, headaches or photophobia

Arnold Chiari Malformation

Monica was hard to be around. Highly anxious, she constantly darted her eyes, paced, wrung her hands, smoked cigarette after cigarette, chomped away at coffee hard candies or furiously chewed gum. She lost her temper in an instant, along with friends and lovers. She felt constant pain in her neck, lack of balance, TMJD, a feeling of being far away, and headaches. When she walked into a supermarket, the overhead fluorescent lights would make her feel extremely anxious. The world felt far away. Everything, including people's voices, seemed slowed down, as if a slow motion film.

For fourteen years, she went to numerous neurologists and neurosurgeons. They would do MRIs (Magnetic Resonance Imaging) and find nothing. They told her she suffered from stress and recommended Xanax and Zoloft. The Xanax made her sleepy and the Zoloft made her zonked. Neither medication alleviated her distress. Finally, a neurologist gave her a specific MRI that revealed the reason for her symptoms: Arnold Chiari syndrome, or herniation of the brainstem. Monica had neurosurgery for the condition. The surgery eliminated her balance problems, neck pain, and light sensitivity, and alleviated her feeling of being far away and her anxiety.

Chiari Malformation is a neurological disorder where the cerebellum, located in the brainstem, descends out of the skull into the spinal area. Compression of parts of the brain and spinal cord results, disrupting the normal flow of cerebrospinal fluid, a clear fluid which bathes the brain and spinal cord. Anxiety symptoms can result from this restricted flow, as well as from the stress of suffering in silence and being given ineffective treatments, or being told that your symptoms are in your head. Photosensitivity can trigger panic attack (see chapter 11). Some people develop symptoms as children, and some as adults.

Symptoms

The overriding symptom of Chiari malformation is **headache**, commonly described as an intense pressure in the back of the head and elicited or provoked by exercise, straining, coughing, sneezing, laughing, bending over, or similar activities. Balance problems, dizziness, and fullness in the ears are also common complaints. Very young children frequently have trouble swallowing.

ARNOLD CHIARI MALFORMATION SYMPTOMS	
NEUROLOGICAL	**PHYSICAL**
♦ Headaches	**Cardiovascular**
♦ Blackouts	♦ Palpitations
♦ Apnea	♦ Chest pain
♦ Vertigo & balance problems	♦ Hyper- or hypotension
♦ Loss of peripheral vision	♦ Tachycardia
♦ Double or blurred vision	♦ Shortness of breath
♦ Nystagmus	**GI**
♦ Abnormal gag reflex	♦ Abdominal pain
♦ Photophobia	♦ Nausea
♦ Waking up choking	♦ Vomiting
♦ Trouble hearing	**Ear, Nose & Throat**
♦ Tinnitus	♦ Earache
♦ Numbness/tingling in arm, hand, face	♦ Nosebleeds
♦ Weakness in arms, hands, legs or body	♦ Snoring
♦ Slurred speech	♦ Hoarse voice
♦ Word-finding problems	**PSYCHOLOGICAL**
♦ Memory problems	♦ Depression
	♦ Sleeping difficulty
	♦ Anxiety
	♦ Fatigue

Causes

Originally, Chiari malformation was thought to be a congenital condition - meaning you are born with it. But we know now that many cases are acquired and that these may even reverse if the source of the problem is removed. The problem is that what triggers the problem is ill understood. New research hypothesizes that Chiari may result from a bone in the skull base, the clivus, not developing properly. As the muscles of the larynx and pharynx attach to the clivus, this would help explain why Chiari patients have trouble swallowing.

Diagnosis

The varied, vague, and sometimes fleeting symptoms of Chiari malformation can indicate many different disorders and many patients, like Monica, go from doctor after doctor, sometimes suffering for years before the malformation is diagnosed. This can have dangerous consequences: the longer you are symptomatic, the less your chances of a good outcome.

If you suspect that you could have Chiari Syndrome, insist that you get a neurological exam and an MRI to show if the cerebellar tonsils are out of position. Unfortunately, though, no single, objective test exists that can clearly say if someone has a Chiari malformation that is causing problems.

Treatment Options

If symptoms aren't severe, doctors may recommend just monitoring the situation with regular MRI's and treating the symptoms individually. However, if symptoms are interfering with quality of life, or getting worse, or if the nervous system is being impaired, doctors may recommend surgery.

The most common surgical treatment, performed by a neurosurgeon, is known as decompression surgery. An alternative surgery involves placing a shunt (a tube like device) to channel the flow of CSF and relieve pressure. When trying to find a doctor, look for one with much experience in doing Chiari surgeries and check out their reputation among patients and the medical community.

Quick Review

Post-Concussion Syndrome

- ➤ *Post-Concussion Syndrome* is a minor brain injury that results in a temporary loss of consciousness (less than 20 minutes) or no loss of consciousness, and no physical evidence of brain damage.

- ➤ **Upon** awakening, you may experience delirium, disorientation, mental fog, restlessness and agitation but quickly return to normal.

- ➤ **Physical** symptoms such as headache, fatigue and vertigo may last for weeks or months than subside and disappear.

- ➤ **Likewise**, you may experience temporary symptoms of learning disabilities such as mental sluggishness, poor memory and concentration, diminished abstraction ability, poor calculation, and reduced ability to process information, reason and plan, but return to normal mental functioning.

- ➤ **In general**, symptoms improve markedly within three months. But in some patients symptoms such as irritability, anxiety, panic, mood swings, personality changes, headache or head pressure, dizziness, insomnia, poor memory and concentration, and sensitivity to noise or light persist for years.

- ➤ **Conventional** doctors treat symptoms largely with drugs.

- ➤ **Alternative** therapies include:
  - o Acupuncture
  - o Craniosacral therapy
  - o Neurocranial restructuring or bio-cranial if your skull was misaligned during the trauma (see chapter eight)
  - o Herbs that enhance brain function
  - o Exercises taught by occupational or physical therapists for vertigo (see chapter nine)

Complex Partial Seizure

- ➤ *Complex partial seizure* is a mild seizure where the person briefly loses consciousness for a fraction of a second and it may not be noticed. Afterward, you may feel groggy and be unaware anything happened. It is a common cause behind misdiagnoses of anxiety, depression, hysteria, and schizophrenia.

➢ **It** can be distinguished from a psychiatric disorder by the abrupt on-off behavior otherwise uncharacteristic of the person and other characteristic symptoms such as sudden movement of the lips, excessive writing, hyperreligiousity, hallucinations, fugue states, déjà vu and jamais vu.

➢ **Some** people are genetically predisposed to seizure disorders. Or seizures can occur from a wide variety of problems that affect the brain, such as birth trauma, head trauma, brain tumors, meningitis and encephalitis, endocrine and metabolic diseases and drug side effects.

➢ **Seizure** disorders are treated with various anticonvulsants. Anti-anxiety and antidepressant medications are generally counter-indicated, as they can lower the seizure threshold and increase the seizures.

Brain Tumor

➢ *Brain tumors* are relatively common and can be mistaken for a psychiatric disorder when undiagnosed. Location of the tumor within the brain, along with the type and size influence the kind of psychiatric symptoms, ranging from anxiety to depression to hallucinations and psychosis. Temporal lobe tumors – the thinking, higher order part of the brain – produce the most psychiatric symptoms, including anxiety, panic attacks, irritability, and personality changes.

➢ **Anyone** who suffers anxiety or panic and experiences unusual side effects from psychotropic medication, cognitive deficits, personality changes, soft neurological signs like loss of balance, headaches or photophobia should consult a doctor for an intense neurological workup to have a brain tumor ruled out.

➢ **Brain** tumors require immediate medical treatment.

Arnold Chiari Syndrome

➢ *Arnold Chiari Malformation* is a neurological disorder where the cerebellum, located in the brainstem descends out of the skull into the spinal area and disrupts the normal flow of cerebrospinal fluid. The primary symptoms are headache, balance problems and dizziness and fullness in the ears. Very young children frequently have trouble swallowing. Anxiety symptoms occur in some patients.

➢ **Some** people are born with it. Apparently the clivus bone in the skull base fails to properly develop. Other people acquire it.

➢ **Chiari** malformation can be diagnosed with an MRI and neurological exam.

➢ **If** symptoms are severe, decompression surgery is performed or surgery to implant a shunt.

Resources

Suggested Books

• *The Good News about Panic, Anxiety and Phobias* by Marc Gold (Villard, 1989).

• *Understanding Mental Disorders* by Ghazi Asaad (Brunner/Mazel, 1995).

• *Distinguishing Psychological from Organic Disorders, Screening for Psychological Masquerade* (2nd edition) by Robert L. Taylor (Springer, 2000).

• *Psychiatric Disorders with a Biochemical Basis* by David Donaldson, (Pantheon, 1998).

• *Preventing misdiagnosis of women: a guide to physical disorders that have psychiatric symptoms* by Elizabeth A. Klonoff, (Sage, 1997).

Websites

ncrdoctors.com
biocranial.com
conquerchiari.org

7

★

Overbreathing

How are you breathing at this moment? Deeply and slowly? Quickly and shallowly? If you are anxious, the answer will surely be the latter.

When relaxed, we take in and expel full and complete breaths, filling our body with oxygen and energy. When anxious, we breathe in quick spurts to get oxygen in quicker so we can run for our life.

Imagine feeling chronically tense, irritable, unwell, exhausted, nervous and anxious. Your habitual breathing pattern would be fast and shallow, with occasional breath holding and you would feel rushed, depleted and worn. You would never feel relaxed because your breathing pattern would lock you in "Danger!" In times of stress, breathing would be even harder and you may start to panic.

Chest Breathing

At the first sign of anxiety, breathing instantly changes and natural breathing is inhibited.

Here's what happens:
1. **Shallow Breathing**: You gasp, suck in your abdomen, and breathe high into your chest with short, shallow spurts.
2. **Diaphragm freezes:** You don't move air downward as you inhale and your lungs don't fully expand with air.
3. **Red Alert:** Lacking oxygen, your brain goes on red alert.
4. **PNS:** The stress passes and the parasympathetic nervous system kicks in to calm you.
5. **Calming Down:** The body quiets and returns to a baseline of relaxed, regular breathing.

If you are under continual stress, you remain in sympathetic arousal (flight/fight) and the following happens:

➤ **Failure to Recover:** You don't easily recover from distress and you may never return to a baseline of normal diaphragmatic "belly" breathing.'

➤ **Shallow Breathing:** You routinely breathe routinely quick, shallow breaths from your chest.

➤ **Not Enough Air:** As you are unable to get the air you need to breathe fully, you may fight even harder on the next breath to suck the air in and set up a vicious cycle: the harder you try the less air you get.

➤ **Hyperaroused:** This emergency breathing pattern typifies your breathing and keeps you overaroused and perpetuates chronic, free-floating anxiety and fatigue.

Once habitual, chest-breathing affects your whole body.

➤ **You** rely almost entirely on upper body muscles to breathe, weaker than the primary muscles that make up your diaphragm.

➤ **Chronic** tension in the neck, shoulders and upper back and chronically tightened abdominal muscles result and prevent the organs in your lower body from getting sufficient circulation, affecting digestion, assimilation and elimination.

➤ **As** your rib cage, diaphragm, and spine are stiff, physical constrictions reduce lung capacity, perpetuating shallow breathing.

➤ **You** may never know relaxation because anxiety leaves you breathless!

Hyperventilation and Panic Attack

If you are unable to breathe in fully, you can't breathe out fully. To compensate, you may breathe more quickly and breathe out too much carbon dioxide relative to the amount of oxygen in your bloodstream: you *overbreathe* or *hyperventilate.* This causes more carbon dioxide to be expelled at an even greater rate. The low levels of carbon dioxide cause the body to become more alkaline. This leads to even more hyperventilation and unleashes a chain of adverse events.

➤ **Less** oxygen is released to tissues, causing dizziness and breathlessness.

➤ **Diminished** blood flow to brain and other parts of the body causes headaches, lack of concentration.

➤ **Increase** in alkalinity creates excess calcium in muscles and nerves, making them hyperactive and causing muscle tension.

➤ **Reduced** blood flow to the extremities causes cold hands and feet.

➤ **Overexcitability** of the nervous system causes irritability, overreaction, rushed reactions, inappropriate responses.

➤ **Reduced** supply of glucose to the brain creates nervousness and shakiness.

HYPERVENTILATION SYMPTOMS	
Autonomic ♦ Rapid breathing ♦ Heart palpitations ♦ Rapid pulse ♦ Shortness of breath **Physical** ♦ Chest pain ♦ Faintness ♦ Tingling in limbs ♦ Distorted vision ♦ Ringing in ears (tinnitus) ♦ Yawning ♦ Lump in throat ♦ Burping ♦ Difficulty swallowing ♦ Stomach irritation ♦ Allergies ♦ Muscle spasms (muscles tense to prepare for flight but no action taken)	**Emotional** ♦ Anxiety ♦ Panic ♦ Feelings of unreality, depersonalization **Sleep/Wake** ♦ Insomnia ♦ Nightmares ♦ Exhaustion ♦ Anxiety ♦ Panic ♦ Feelings of unreality, depersonalization **Sensory** ♦ Increased sensitivity to light & sound

As breathing quickens to exchange more oxygen to prepare you to run you may experience breathlessness or "air hunger" as if smothering and grab for breath, along with other sympathetic arousal signs like lightheadedness, dizziness, palpitations, and disorientation.

Sounds like a panic attack. In fact, hyperventilation symptoms are not only nearly identical to those of panic attack, as you can see from the list on page 173 but they tend to co-exist: acute hyperventilation accompanies 60% of panic attacks. And like panic attack, hyperventilating has sent many running to the emergency room thinking that they are having a heart attack.

Acute vs. Chronic

Two kinds of hyperventilation exist: acute and chronic.

Acute: Hyperventilation   syndrome   occurs   from   acute hyperventilation and it is obvious when occurring – see symptoms.

Chronic: Less obvious is chronic and subtle hyperventilation that while not setting off panic attack, causes you to feel anxious and sets the stage for developing acute hyperventilation and panic attacks. You are probably breathing 18 or more breaths per minute (normal breathing is 12-14 BPM for men and 14-15 BPM for women), and you frequently sigh, gasp, yawn, cough, clear the throat, or moisten your lips.

Acute Hyperventilation Symptoms	Chronic Hyperventilation Symptoms
◆ Breaths erratic, noisy, rapid ◆ Chest heaving ◆ Abdomen barely moving ◆ Take occasional deep breath ◆ Difficulty breathing out ◆ Dizziness ◆ Sigh at intervals	◆ Upper chest breathing ◆ Breathe through mouth ◆ Breathe heavily

Who Invites Whom?

As hyperventilation and panic are frequent traveling partners who invites whom?   Researchers are unsure. Some believe that panic attack leads to hyperventilation in vulnerable individuals.

1.   **Some** threat sets off intense anxiety.

2.   **You** start to breathe faster.

3.   **You** begin to hyperventilate.

4. **Hyperventilation** sets off light-headedness, palpitations, chest tightening, loss of body awareness and impending doom.

5. **Once** the panic attack occurs, conditioned fear stimuli set in; the slightest sign of a racing heart or elevated blood pressure sets off hyperventilating and you have a panic attack.

Other researchers will argue the converse, that hyperventilation creates panic attack.

1. **You** overbreathe.

2. **You** become anxiously overaroused.

3. **You** start thinking catastrophic thoughts like "I'm losing control," "Something terrible is happening to me."

4. **These** thoughts set off genuine panic, eliciting the fear that you are having a panic attack and actually sets one off.

This scenario has gained support. According to psychologist Donald Klein, those who suffer panic disorder may have a *suffocation false alarm system* within the brain that is hypersensitive to an increase in carbon dioxide level. This produces sudden respiratory distress followed by hyperventilation, panic, and the urge to flee. Often this suffocation false alarm happens during sleep, when blood carbon dioxide (CO_2) levels rise significantly and you have a nocturnal panic attack.

Yet, the suffocation false alarm does not apply to all panic attack victims. For one, some panic attack patients who voluntarily hyperventilate don't necessarily have a panic attack. And not all who suffer panic attack demonstrate the respiratory abnormality. Further, hyperventilation that leads to panic attack can arise from a variety of organic reasons other than respiratory abnormality.

HYPERVENTILATION/PANIC ATTACK CAUSES	
◆ Drugs like cocaine, amphetamine, or LSD	◆ Head injuries
	◆ Hyperthyroidism
◆ Exposure to toxic chemicals in the workplace	◆ Hormones
	◆ Structural imbalance that prevents diaphragm from fully expanding
◆ Asthma	
◆ Exercise	

One study found that of 30 patients with hyperventilation symptoms, 7 had associated organic disorders. Hyperventilation also leads to imbalance in those suffering panic attack by creating abnormally high alkalinity.

Diagnosis

Hyperventilation syndrome can be assessed by measuring the "End Tidal CO2 (ETCO2)." This indirectly measures the blood level of CO2 and is easily done by sampling air from your nose or mouth.

Treatment Options

Both involuntary and voluntary, breathing can be consciously controlled. This power enables you to re-train yourself to breathe properly and change the chemical reaction that leads to panic attack. Breathing exercises, a breathing machine, chanting, blowing, singing and other exercises all increase lung power to deepen breathing and break the breath-catching habit. As you slow down your breathing, your heart rate, respiration and brain waves will match that rhythm, as all the bodies rhythms entrain to each other. Conversely, if you are able to slow down your brain waves, you can change your heart rate and respiration --the basis for the success of biofeedback.

Breath control may not come easily as it is hard to breathe properly when anxious. Shifting the center of your breathing from your chest to your abdomen will take time and effort. Remember, you haven't used these muscles in a long time. They need to be developed again.

Belly Breathing Exercises

Deep breathing exercises will help teach you to slow down your breathing and to breathe from your abdomen, or diaphragm. This will increase the amount of oxygen getting to your brain and muscles and stimulate the calming parasympathetic nervous system to override the arousing sympathetic nervous system.

If you spend three to ten minutes a day (10 to 40 breathing cycles), twice a day doing deep breathing, you will strengthen the muscles that support breathing and gradually enhance their flexibility and resilience. This will reset the rhythm and rate of your breathing and with regular practice of deep breathing, will increase lung capacity to enable you to breathe more deeply. Breathing exercises to increase lung power greatly help relax you as well because heart rate, respiration and brain waves all entrain to each other. Slow down your breath, for example, and you slow down your heartbeat and your brain waves. Conversely, if you slow down your brain waves through biofeedback, meditation or therapeutic listening, you can slow your heart rate and respiration.

How Deep Breathing Alleviates Anxiety

> **Increases** oxygen to the brain and muscles
> **Stimulates** parasympathetic nervous system to calm the body
> **Gets** you out of your head and grounds you in your whole body, increasing mind/body connectedness
> **Stops** your mind from racing and improves concentration
> **Act** of deep breathing alone creates a deep relaxed state

---

Urine pH

If you have panic disorder, testing the pH of your urine pH could be a simple way to evaluate your respiratory status and success of breathing retraining. If it is normal, slow breathing should help reduce symptoms of panic attack and return your system to homeostasis.

Pranayama

Pranayama, the ancient yogic means of breath control, offers formal breathing techniques to help teach you to slow down your breathing and to breathe from your diaphragm.

Doing these exercises will increase the amount of oxygen getting to your brain and muscles, nourish essential body organs, heighten energy levels and increase metabolic rate.

OCD & Yogic Breathing

Psychologist David Shannahoff-Khalsa of the University of California in San Diego has demonstrated that yoga breathing techniques significantly decrease symptoms of obsessive-compulsive disorder. Of eight adults who completed a one-year course of yogic breathing techniques, five were able to discontinue their medication (Prozac) and two others drastically reduced the dosage.

"Ujjayi" Breathing

A yoga breathing technique, *Ujjayi* breathing is deep-chest breathing that strengthens breath by slightly constricting the throat and producing a hissing sound – think Darth Vadar. Ujjayi breathing is employed throughout a yoga practice to energize the body.

Here's how to do it.

1. **Lie** down, so you're not fighting gravity.
2. **Close** your eyes and note the tension you're feeling and your breathing pattern.
3. **Place** one hand on the upper abdomen just below the base of the sternum, your power spot.
4. **Place** the other hand on your chest.
5. **Place** the tip of your tongue behind your bottom front teeth.
   a. Slightly pursing your lips, breathe out through your mouth and slowly push the stale air out of your lungs. (Though intuitively we take in a deep breath to breathe more fully, it is by exhaling fully that we prepare for deeper, spontaneous inhalations. The longer your exhalation, the more your eyes relax and facial muscles soften).
   b. Feel your navel collapse towards the floor, minimizing your upper chest motion. The hand on your chest should stay still.
   c. Squeeze all the air out of your lungs and let your whole body go, as if sinking into the floor.
   d. You can also breathe out though your mouth, emphasizing the exhalation by making a "hah" sound with your mouth open and relaxed.

6. **Place** the tip of your tongue against the back of top front teeth.
   a. Inhale slowly and deeply through your nose, creating a yawning sensation in the back of your nose and throat and expanding your abdomen like a balloon.
   b. Your hand should rise as you feel your navel rise.
   c. You should hear your breath filling your lungs – a "dragon" breath -- and rising up to where your throat and the back of your nose meet and you should feel your throat vibrating.
   d. Your chest should move only slightly while your abdomen expands.
   e. If you only feel your belly expand without the sensation of air rising up to where your throat and the back of your nose meet, you are breathing incorrectly.
7. **Pause** briefly at the end of the exhalation and let your next inhalation begin on its own, without "grabbing" for it. Pausing following exhalation extends parasympathetic arousal, which will prolong a feeling of calm and slows your breathing even further. (Holding your breath at the end of inhalation extends sympathetic arousal).
8. **Take** at least ten full abdominal breaths slowly and smoothly, prolonging exhale. Slowly increase to forty cycles a session.
9. **Take** a few regular breaths between each ten breath cycle.

Alternate Nostril Breathing (ANB)

Another excellent breathing exercise is Alternate Nostril Breathing (ANB)--breathing through one nostril at a time and alternating between sides.

Though unaware of it, we don't breathe evenly through both nostrils but, every couple of hours, alternate breathing between the right and left nostril. Which nostril we are breathing through links to brain function: when we breathe through our right nostril, the left, logical hemisphere dominates; when we breathe through our left nostril, the right, creative side of the brain dominates. By practicing ANB, you will oxygenate both sides of the brain equally to optimize creativity and logical thinking. Also, the right nostril is hypothesized to stimulate the arousal-producing sympathetic nervous system and left nostril the relaxation-producing parasympathetic system. ANB will help balance breathing so that neither nostril is dominant.

Here's how to do ANB.

1. **Sit** comfortably in a chair or cross-legged on a cushion.
2. **Clear** your nostrils by blowing each separately. (Even better clear your sinuses with a Neti Pot --Ayurvedic Sinus Relief).
3. **Close** the right nostril with your right thumb.
4. **Exhale** completely through the left nostril.
5. **Inhale** slowly and evenly through the left nostril.
6. **Hold** the air for a few seconds, closing the left nostril with the left thumb.
7. **Release** the right nostril and exhale slowly through it.
8. **Inhale** through the right nostril.

This completes one cycle. Continue for up to 20 cycles and finish by exhaling through the left nostril. Once you get the knack, try counting on each inhalation and exhalation with even counts. This will help your mind focus. Start with a low number, such as four, and gradually build it up.

Optional Positions

Though most recommend doing deep breathing while lying flat on your back, other yogic positions may better help open up your rib cage to allow for deeper breathing.

Extended child position: Start by kneeling and then gently fold forward until your head is resting on the floor in front of your knees and open your knees like frog legs. Extend your arms forward over your head, palms down, as if reaching for the wall in front. Can you feel your chest open and your breath deepen?

Lying on floor: Lie on the floor with a rolled up blanket under the small of the back, your knees bent and your backside pressing the floor. Close your eyes and begin deep breathing.

Catching Breath

If during deep breathing exercises, you need to catch your breath, this will subside. You want to breathe in quickly because your brain is telling you that you are suffocating. And, since it takes a few minutes for the symptoms associated with hyperventilating to subside, pausing after exhaling again triggers a perception of suffocating. Try to breathe slowly and deeply, but gently. Vigorous or forced breathing will create light-headedness -- an indication of a rapid lowering of carbon dioxide levels. If this happens, stop briefly and then start again.

Breathing Exercisers

If you find breathing exercises don't work for you, breathing exercise machines will enhance deep breathing (see resources).

Breathing Into a Paper Bag

The age-old of cure for hyperventilation is breathing into a paper bag in which you rebreathe in the same air, taking in higher levels of CO_2. But if you're panic prone, increased CO_2 can trigger panic.

Tap Your Energy Field

Our bodies are rhythmic energy fields. Like a Ouija board, moving our hands across our body creates a force that seems to carry us away by an energy outside ourselves. Tapping into this energy field is a tremendous power tool for deepening breath.

Try this qigong breathing exercise:
1. **Visualize** energy coming down from above and flowing through your body.
2. **Hold** the palms of your hand a few inches from your body, hands cupped.
3. **Sweep** them slowly from head to toe and back up.
4. **As** you slowly sweep your hands up, notice how you spontaneously deeply inhale, as if a force were pulling air into your body.
5. **As** you slowly sweep down, notice how you spontaneously deeply exhale, as if your hand is moving the breath down and out of your body.

You might be amazed at the pull of your energy field -- how breathing coordinates with the slow rhythmic movement of your hands and how it gets stuck in various places where you are imbalanced.

Suck, Swallow, Breathe

Stick out your tongue as far as you can and hold it there for a second. Did you start to take in a deep breath? Suck and swallow are our first organizers and depend on the tongue (try swallowing without using your tongue). If you don't breathe well, sucking and swallowing will increase respiratory effort and help get you organized, while blowing will increase exhalation and stimulate the mouth.

Activities to Deepen Breathing	
◆ Blowing through or into a straw	
◆ Playing wind instrument (flute, recorder, clarinet, saxophone)	
◆ Blowing a whistle	
◆ Blowing into respiratory breathing "whistle"	
◆ Blowing up balloon	
Activities to Increase Exhalation	
◆ Whistling	◆ Humming
◆ Chanting	◆ Singing

Also laugh, cry and giggle -- all change respiration, and help to balance and organize the nervous system as well as other systems in the body. Nervous people often giggle much as self-therapy.

When Nothing Works

If breathing exercises do not stop you from hyperventilating and you continue to feel anxious or have panic attacks, you may have medical or structural restrictions that interfere with the expansion and contraction of the diaphragm and inhibit deep breathing. In my own case, years of deep breathing did little because my shallow breathing resulted from a partially collapsed right lung and scoliosis. It wasn't until I received therapy for both issues that I was able to take in a full breath. *Now* deep breathing exercises worked!

Quick Review

➤ **Anxiety** triggers the flight/fight response and, breathing instantly changed you start to breathe in quick spurts to get in oxygen quicker so you can run for your life. If under continual stress, quick, shallow breathing becomes habitual and keeps you anxious.

➤ **If** unable to breathe in fully, you can't breathe out fully and to compensate, you start breathing more quickly and hyperventilate -- you breathe out too much carbon dioxide relative to the amount of oxygen in your bloodstream. This causes you to feel short of breath, light-headed, dizzy, disoriented, along with heart palpitations, chest pain, rapid pulse, trembling, tingling in the limbs, numbness, and a feeling of unreality.

➤ **These sy**mptoms are identical to those of panic attack and 60 percent of all panic attacks are accompanied by acute hyperventilation. It appears some vulnerable individuals have a false suffocation alarm which causes them to hyperventilate and triggers panic attack.

➤ **Hyperventilation** syndrome can be assessed by measuring the "End Tidal CO_2 (ETCO2)." This indirectly measures the blood level of CO_2 and is easily done by sampling air from your nose or mouth.

➤ **Both** involuntary and voluntary breathing can be consciously controlled. This power enables you to re-train yourself to breathe properly and change the chemical reaction that leads to panic attack. Breathing exercises, a breathing machine, chanting, blowing, singing and other exercises all increase lung power to deepen breathing and break the breath-catching habit.

Resources

Suggested Books

➤ *Hyperventilation Syndrome: A Handbook for Bad Breathers* by Dinah Bradley (Celestial Arts, 1992).

➤ *The Breathing Book* by Donna Farhi (Owl Books, Henry Holt, 1996).

➢ *Science of Breath* by Rudolph Ballantine, Alan Hymes (Himalayan Institute Press, 1998).

Audios & Videos

➢ *The Art of Breath and Relaxation* by Rodney Yee, 1999. (120 minutes on 2 audiocassettes with practice guide for $19.98). Available from: Living Arts 1-800-254-8464
➢ *The Art of Breathing Video: Six Simple Lessons to Improve Performance, Health and Well-Being* by Nanci Zi, 1997. Available from: Vivi Company, 1-800-INHALE-8.

Breathing Devices

Breathing Trainer v1.0 prompter, a simple visual prompting breathing display based on biofeedback. It is designed primarily for home – sierrabiotech.com**.**

Powerbreathe Inspirator

Websites:

Physiohypervent.org

8

★

In a Slump

If you want to cure the soul, cure the body.

- Aristotle

As an infant, Elaine was easy and outgoing. A delight. When she was four, a fall off the monkey bars broke her nose, damaged some teeth and rearranged her body so that her right side went down three inches. From that time she became fearful, clingy, and had difficulty separating from her parents. By adolescence, she began to have panic attacks in social situations, such as parties, football games, or going to the movies with a date.

Her concerned parents took her to see a psychiatrist who put her on Paxil to control her panic attacks. The drug helped reduce the frequency and intensity of the attacks but failed to eliminate them. She entered into cognitive-behavioral therapy with a psychologist who helped her learn to control her anticipatory anxiety about panicking in social situations. He gave her relaxation exercises to further reduce her symptoms once the attacks began. Nevertheless, she continued to experience anxiety in situations that created stress.

Exacerbating Elaine's anxiety was constant pain from slight scoliosis, an S curve of the spine. Chiropractic adjustments helped but only temporarily. A friend of her parents who suffered migraines had found great relief from a largely unknown treatment called neurocranial restructuring, or NCR. He felt NCR might alleviate Elaine's pain. She decided to try it.

The doctor put a small, inflatable endonasal balloon up her nostril, which inflated briefly into her throat. There was a very brief crack. Elaine took in a deep breath. For the first time since before her accident, Elaine could breathe fully! Her anxiety attacks abated.

She went off her Paxil and discontinued psychotherapy. Apparently, her broken nose had prevented her from breathing fully and caused her to hyperventilate and this set of her anxiety and panic attack. The procedure also straightened out some compression in her head that contributed to her anxiety. After eight series of NCR, Elaine breathed deeper, felt calmer and happier, slept more soundly, and her scoliosis disappeared, without surgery, along with years of excruciating pain!

Structural Imbalances

Your posture is your center pole supporting your whole being. The top of the pole is your skull (cranium) and extends down to your sacrum (bottom of your spine). Slouched, sagging, slumped, crooked, arched, posture indicates structural imbalances from structural misalignment as does body or facial asymmetry, and these may cause or contribute to your anxiety. How?

To start, poor posture prevents you from breathing three-dimensionally (expanding the abdomen, rib cage, and back) and relaxing into your body. If you don't breathe deeply and slowly, you will feel tense, nervous and anxious. Next, skull misalignment prevents the proper flow of neurotransmitters, your brain's messengers, through the cerebral spinal fluid that surrounds the craniosacral system. The result may be too much or too little serotonin, for instance, the neurotransmitter that governs mood. As the brain's messages get scrambled, you may also suffer sensory processing problems, learning disabilities, attention deficits, hyperactivity, and poor body awareness and feel disconnected from your body, a common symptom of anxiety and panic attack. Further, skull misalignment creates problems like headache, dizziness and vertigo (room spinning) that create irritability and tension.

Conversely, chronic anxiety and tension cause your posture to become rigid or slumped, causing or accentuating structural imbalances so that each feed the other in a vicious cycle. Chronic stress alone will lead to stiff neck, throat and jaw muscles that can throw off the musculoskeletal system and restrict breathing.

Subluxations

Stroll through the mall or supermarket and notice the bodies milling around: arched, bent, slouched, rounded. This is not what nature intended.

➢ **Vertical:** Our bodies are designed to be upright or vertical with gravity, not leaning or bending too far forward or backward. Pelvis should be upright rather than tilted forward or back.

➢ **In Line:** Shoulders, hips, knees, ankles, and feet should all line up.

➢ **Symmetrical:** Bodies should be symmetrical so that the right side equals the left and our weight is centered on both feet.

➢ **Spinal Curves:** Spinal cord, the backbone of all neurological functioning, should have three gentle curves to carry our weight:
  o a *slight* arch in the neck
  o a *slight* convex curve in our upper back
  o a *slight* arch in our lower back

SIGNS OF STRUCTURAL MISALIGNMENT	
♦ Head forward ♦ Shoulders rolled forward or not level ♦ Hunched upper back ♦ One shoulder higher or more forward than other ♦ Hips rotated ♦ Body leaning forward or backward ♦ Pelvis tilted too far forward or backward	♦ Knees turned out or in ♦ Feet pointed inward or outward ♦ Swayback (overly arched) ♦ Scoliosis (crooked back) ♦ Rounded neck or back ♦ Slouching ♦ Body Asymmetry ♦ Facial Asymmetry

When spinal injury, misalignment, stress, or illness cause the twenty-four bones or vertebrae that surround and protect our spinal cord to get out of alignment (subluxations), pressure is placed on the nerves in that area. The nerves function improperly and dysfunction, disharmony, and eventually disease result. Further, subluxations can imbalance the autonomic nervous system, resulting in sympathetic dominance, or constant anxiety.

Skull Misalignment

The integrity of the spine starts with the integrity of the bones of the skull, the cranium. Any number of events can tighten and throw the 22 cranial bone joints out of their optimal shape. The skull distorts and this puts pressure on the brain that interferes with the flow of cerebral spinal fluid and blood. When an imbalanced skull throws off the whole cranial sacral system, blockages prevent the neurotransmitters that regulate stress and mood from flowing properly through the cerebrospinal fluid, thereby altering mood and behavior and creating anxiety and depression.

Head trauma begins with birth trauma, including use of forceps, suctions, and even C-sections because the cranium needs pressure to open up or in essence pop open and get in the initial motion in the cranium as the fetus passes through the birth canal. So any abnormal delivery or trauma to the head can cause cranial imbalance. After birth, any fall or trauma whatsoever will affect cranial balance. Another large contributor to cranial bone imbalance is dental work. Orthodontics, TMJD, malocclusion, or any dental work at all can cause cranial imbalance. A study was done on 203 grade school children for proper cranial motion. There was a statistically significant correlation between poor motion and children having learning disabilities and behavioral problems.

How do you know if your skull is misaligned? Look for asymmetry in the face, such as:
♦ One eye larger than other or appearing lower than other
♦ One ear lower than other
♦ One nostril larger than other
♦ One side of face more creased or narrow
♦ One shoulder lower than other

Treatment Options

Structural imbalance can be corrected through structural repair of the body from a variety of treatments, including craniosacral therapy, neurocranial restructuring, biocranial, Rolfing, Feldenkrais, and Alexander technique. Many cranial problems occur at birth, so corrections early on can prevent years of suffering.

Though helpful, exercise alone, without changing body structure won't cure misalignments. When exercising we favor using our strong muscles and avoid using weak ones. As a result, our misalignments remain the same or become worse as stronger parts become stronger and weaker parts weaker. Though I took yoga for years, which works both sides of the body, the right side of my body remained shut down and the muscles weak until extensive biocranial therapy began to better align my skull and spine.

Craniosacral Therapy

In the 1900's osteopathic physician Dr. William Sutherland discovered cranial movement, dispelling the popular notion that the head is a solid, immovable skull. Twenty-two separate, movable bones join to one another by layers of tissue, or fascia.

The craniosacral system consists of the bones of the skull, face, and mouth (the "cranium") and extends to the lower end of the spine (the "sacrum"). It is connected by dura matter, the body's deepest fascia, which houses the brain and central nervous system. Cerebrospinal fluid bathes the brain and spinal cord and gets pumped through the dura in a distinct craniosacral rhythm (CSR) of 8 to 12 beats per minute, feeding the distant nerves all over the body. Stress will throw off this rhythm and interfere with the function of the craniosacral system.

The results in a variety of conditions including:

> Migraines
> TMJD dysfunction
> Hyperactivity
> Tension
> Agitation
> Chronic pain
> Depression

A craniosacral therapist will pick up subtle cues from the pulsing movement of fluids and detect discrepancies in the rate, amplitude, symmetry, and quality of the CSR. Using gentle compression, he helps realign the skull bones and stretch the underlying dura, freeing obstacles that inhibit the free flow of fluids and energies in the body. Your natural, self-adjusting system takes over and you may feel a tingling feeling through to the fingertips from increased circulation.

During a session, parts of the body that store trauma may begin to spasm, jerk, or gyrate as stored-up emotions release and some people shake, sweat, laugh, or cry. At the end of the session, many feel relaxed and grounded, with a greater ease of movement and of their bodies. For days, the body continues to shift and unwind and many feel lighter and more relaxed and integrated.

Still Point Inducer

Made of two soft foam globes, a "still point inducer" is a self help devise that can jump start your nervous system for the day. You place the device under your head, in the slight horizontal depression in your skull, about a third of the way up from the top of your neck. The gentle pressure of the inducer creates the "still point," a quiet pause in the rhythm of the craniosacral system. Used for around fifteen minutes a day, this device is a good "shotgun" technique for relaxing fascia, enhancing tissue and fluid motion, and slowing breathing and heart rate. You can purchase one from the Upledger Institute in West Palm Beach, Florida or from gaiam.com

---

Neurocranial Restructuring

For over twenty years, naturopathic physician Dean Howell has been developing a powerful manipulative therapy with profound mental and emotional effects: neurocranial restructuring.

NCR entails inserting small balloons through the nostril into the throat and inflating them, thereby precisely realigning the sphenoid, the deepest-positioned bone in the head. This releases the connective tissues of the skull, pushing the bones like a spring and creating permanent, cumulative changes in the skull alignment. It's like "banging out the bumps in a dented car from the inside," Howell explains. As the head becomes symmetrical, tension patterns relax and the body's reflexes push the head straighter on the spine, gradually optimizing the functions of the nervous system, spine and posture. Patients breathe deeper, feel calmer, think more clearly, feel happier and more confident, and sleep more soundly. Anxiety, depression, ADD, concentration difficulties, head fog, balance difficulties, vertigo, headaches, tremor, chronic fatigue and fibromyalgia all respond well to NCR. And the changes are permanent!

Anxiety is associated with the levels of neurotransmitters in the brain. The flow of cerebrospinal fluid and the flow of blood govern the distribution of neurotransmitters. The shape of the skull determines this. As skull shape changes with NCR, cerebrospinal fluid and blood flow more smoothly, explains Howell, and neurotransmitters are better distributed. Optimize skull shape and you optimize brain function and create a lasting change in anxiety and nervousness! Dr. Howell has treated thousands of patients who, after a lifetime of feeling anxious suddenly find tension, nervousness, irritability and worry to greatly dissipate, as well as aggression, OCD, learning disabilities and hyperactivity. More relaxed, people discover the entire quality of their life improves: relationships, learning, energy level, productivity, creativity.

Face Lift

Another bonus of NCR is changed facial appearance. Your face becomes more symmetrical, fuller and rounder. Facial muscles are less tight and you can better show emotions. This is significant. Tight muscles prevent your face from lighting up with a smile or showing clear sadness and you actually feel less joy or sadness and fail to convey accurate signals about your emotional state. When facial muscles relax, you express feelings fully and feel happier or sadder and therefore more in touch with your feelings.

Treatments are performed in a series of four daily treatments, generally repeated every six weeks to three months until treatment goals are achieved. Treatment can be started in the newborn period and continued into the late 90s without problems.

Biocranial

Pioneered by osteopath Robert Boyd, in Ireland, *biocranial* is another technique of manipulating the bones of the cranium to return them to a more natural position and relieve cranial (head) pressure and distortion. It has the same power and permanence as neurocranial restructuring but differs in procedure. While NCR is invasive, biocranial entails a gentle stretch sensation that lasts one to two minutes. It is safely performed on infants to geriatrics.

Rolfing

Working from the outer layers to deeper ones, "Rolfers" realign the body to work with, rather than against, gravity. Over a series of ten sessions, each focusing on a different part of the body with results building on each other, the Rolfer applies firm pressure to different areas of the body to slowly stretch and soften the body's connective tissue, allowing the body to right itself effortlessly in gravity.

Penetrating and powerful, the treatment can be painful. But once the head, shoulders, abdomen, pelvis, and legs align correctly, aches and pains alleviate. After, you feel lightness, freedom of movement, and greater self-awareness.

Feldenkrais

In the popular Feldenkrais method, you repeat a movement sequence correctly many times to develop "awareness through movement." New patterns of movement replace old ones and you learn greater body awareness, increased mobility and improved breathing and circulation.

The Alexander Technique

Every minute we sit, bend, stand, reach and walk automatically. Unknowingly, such unconscious movements cause posture limitations. The Alexander technique educates you to become aware of how you are misusing your body. By repeatedly experiencing correct movement, you learn to realign your body so that your head sits aligned on the tip of your spine. The spine lengthens and you move more fluidly.

Musculoskeletal Supports

Trauma to the body creates scar tissue that can lock the body into incorrect alignment. Cranial therapies go faster if you soften fascia and break down scar tissue. I utilized Yamuna's body rolling, foot wakers/savers, and face ball (yamunabodyrolling.com) to soften fascia and magnetic resonance therapy (MRT) to break down the scar tissue internally and externally.

Quick Review

➢ **Postural** imbalances indicate spinal or skull misalignment and may cause or contribute to anxiety. For instance, poor posture prevents proper breathing and you feel tense, nervous and anxious.

➢ **Spinal** injury, misalignment, stress, or illness causes your vertebrae to go out of alignment (subluxations) and pressure is placed on the nerves in that area. As a result, the nerves function improperly and lead to dysfunction, disharmony, and eventually disease. Further, subluxations can result in sympathetic dominance, or constant anxiety.

➢ **Birth** trauma, head trauma, falls and other events can tighten and throw the cranial bone joints out of their optimal shape and throw off the whole cranial sacral system. Skull misalignment prevents the proper flow of neurotransmitters through the cerebral spinal fluid that surrounds the craniosacral system and this affects mood. As the brain's messages get scrambled, you may also suffer sensory processing problems, learning disabilities, attention deficits, hyperactivity, and poor body awareness and feel disconnected from your body, a common symptom of anxiety and panic attack. Skull misalignment creates problems also like headache, dizziness and vertigo (room spinning) that create irritability and tension. Conversely, chronic anxiety and tension cause your posture to become rigid or slumped, causing or accentuating structural imbalances and each feed the other in a vicious cycle.

➢ **Treatments** that can help align your spine and skull include:
  o Craniosacral therapy
  o Neurocranial restructuring
  o Biocranial
  o Rolfing
  o Feldenkrais
  o Alexander technique
  o Somatics

Resources

Suggested Books

- *NeuroCranial Restructuring: Unleash Your Structural Power,* Third Edition by Dean Howell (Canyon Press, 2001).
- *Your Inner Physician and You: Craniosacral Therapy and Somatoemotional Release,* 2nd Ed. By John E. Upledger (North Atlantic Books, 1997).
- *Awareness through Movement* by Moshe Feldenkrais (Harper & Row, 1991).

Websites

www.Biocranial.com
www.Ncrdoctors.com
www.Feldenkrais.com

9

★

Sensory Havoc

Behavior is a reflection of the organization of your nervous system at that moment and under those conditions.

Patti Oetter, Occupational
Therapist

When Samuel was four, he fell off his bike and cracked his skull open. He was in a coma for a week. He recuperated and developed normally but his behavior changed: a formerly easy-going, happy child, Samuel became fearful and hypersensitive. He complained of every little noise, demanded that his mother remove the tags from his clothes, winced at the bright sun, and became fearful of the swing and roller coaster.

In his teens, he started to experience panic attacks when in an elevator and refused to fly in an airplane. By his twenties, the panic attacks extended to escalators and even stairways. A psychiatrist diagnosed him as having panic disorder and put him on Paxil. Taking the drug seemed to help take the edge off the panic but he still felt unsteady from elevators, escalators and stairs. He had problems dating because social situations overwhelmed him and he did not much like kissing or hugging which the psychiatrist attributed (falsely) to lack of maternal affection during childhood.

One day, a friend of Samuel's mentioned that her younger sister Dora had just been diagnosed with ***sensory processing disorder (SPD)*** and was being treated for the condition by a pediatric occupational therapist. Samuel knew that, like him Dora disliked being hugged and startled at loud noises. Could sensory processing disorder explain some of his fussy, quirky behavior? Indeed.

What is Sensory Processing Disorder?

Sensory processing disorder (SPD), previously known as *sensory integration dysfunction* is a common but relatively unknown condition in which sensory messages get scrambled in the brain and you cannot make sense of or respond appropriately to your world.

What does this mean? How does it affect well being? To answer these questions, let's briefly look at normal sensory processing.

All activities, whether figuring out what to wear, cooking a meal, washing the dishes, or hitting a hole in one require organization, planning, execution, muscle coordination and balance, and filtering out distractions. This process is referred to as *sensory integration,* a concept first recognized and researched in the 1960's by occupational therapist A. Jean Ayres whose theories and work with learning disabled children pioneered the field of sensory integration.

For the majority of people, sensory processing is organized and integrated enough so that routine actions like the above take place automatically and effortlessly, accurately and efficiently. But in anywhere from fifteen to thirty percent of normal functioning adults, *the focus of this book*, a "traffic jam" occurs in the brain that alters how sensation is received, perceived, organized and acted upon.

This faulty sensory processing plays out in different ways. People with SPD may experience extreme reactions to sensory input, from barely registering sensation – not hearing the phone ring -- to feeling overwhelmed by slight sensation – startling when the phone rings. You may have difficulties discriminating one sensation from another, for instance from the taste of lemon from lime, or the sound of a cat's meow from a bird chirp. You may have problems with movement and be clumsy, poorly coordinated and have a sloppy handwriting. Some people experience difficulties in one area of functioning, others in all three.

These difficulties make it hard for you to focus in on and act on your world efficiently, purposefully and in an organized way. Messages get scrambled, over- or under filtered and you feel confused by the input, or you feel starved for or flooded with sensory information, and what seems simple and automatic to the normal brain becomes perplexing, irritating, effortful or impossible.

Spontaneous, automatic behavior takes conscious effort and energy and, in spite of best efforts, is inefficient, excessive or useless. Consequently, the world swells with confusion and you feel off center, out of focus, missing a beat, detached, and innocently say and do things at the wrong time, in the wrong place, in the wrong way.

The following is an example.

1. **The** phone rings.
2. **Your** brain may not register exactly where the ring of the phone is coming from and you run around in circles trying to find your cell phone.
3. **You** see the phone on the table and walk to pick up the phone but have such poor body awareness that you knock over a chair in your path and almost miss the call.
4. **Stressed,** you pick up the phone which feels annoyingly hard against your face, further overloading you.
5. **The** unpleasant squeaky voice of your child's teacher adds to your already irritated state.
6. **Overloaded,** the words "Your child has a fever of 103" don't immediately register.
7. **You** foolishly blurt, "Is he sick?"
8. **The** teacher says, "yes" and, after telling her you'll be right there, you press the wrong button to turn off the phone.
9. **You** then run around in circles looking for your keys.

How does all this confusion impact your well being? Profoundly? Constant failure makes you feel stupid, clumsy, inept, embarrassed, self-conscious, humiliated, frustrated and guilty that you constantly disappoint. Reflecting your confused, disorganized state, your behavior appears frenetic, inappropriate, withdrawn, aggressive, self-absorbed, disorganized, or crazed. To function, you erect defenses, like avoidance, control, rigidity, and obsessive and compulsive behavior and people accuse you of being controlling, manipulative, and driving others crazy or *being* crazy.

How do you explain to them *or to yourself* that you are doing your best to adapt to the world as *your brain perceives it*? It's hard. How do you make sense of why life is a constant struggle when you don't know *what is wrong with you*? You can't.

Consequently, you feel deeply flawed: "I can't do it;" "I don't have fun like others;" "I'm not normal;" "People don't understand me;" "People don't like me." Psychotherapists try to convince you that these negative self-appraisals are unrealistic and can be changed through positive thinking and by changing your intentions to reflect greater competence. It's a tough sell. The negative self-appraisals are based on real neurophysiological deficits, not first and foremost on critical parenting or other causes of low self-esteem. As long as your senses keep betraying you, the deficits stubbornly persist.

The following is a list of the diverse ways that SPD manifests.

SPD SIGNS

OVERSENSITIVE TO SENSATION
♦ **Touchy** about light touch, textures, clothing, ordinary affection
♦ **Picky** about food
♦ **Bothered** easily by noise, odors, bright light
♦ **Fearful** from movement, like elevators, escalators, roller coasters, going fast, or spinning
♦ **Avoid** eye contact

UNDERSENSITIVE TO SENSATION
♦ **Slow** to get moving; tire easily
♦ **Seem** oblivious to environment
♦ **Seek** intense sensation, like loud noise, spicy food, strong perfumes
♦ **Crave** roller coasters and fast movement
♦ **May** not notice if cut or bruised
♦ **Hard** to get up in morning
♦ **Thrill** seeker, ignoring potential danger
♦ **Seek** stimulants -- caffeine, tobacco, cocaine
♦ **Hyperactive** & fidgety

COORDINATION PROBLEMS
♦ **Clumsy**, awkward, or accident-prone
♦ **Poor** balance
♦ **Rigid** & tense posture or floppy & slouching
♦ **Jerky** movements
♦ **Poor** fine motor coordination – sloppy handwriting

UNDERACHIEVER
+ **Fail** to work up to capacity
+ **Learning** problems but normal intelligence

POOR ATTENTION
+ **Distracted**
+ **Driven**
+ **Perseverate** on small detail
+ **Unaware**/spaced out
+ **Hyperalert**, not processing
+ **Turned** inward

POORLY ORGANIZED BEHAVIOR
+ **Disorganized**, distracted, spacey
+ **Problem** following directions or adapting to new situation
+ **Frustrated**, aggressive or withdrawn when encountering failure
+ **Compulsive**, obsessed
+ **Impulsive**
+ **Rigid,** controlling, short-tempered

POOR SELF-CONCEPT
+ **Feel** weird, crazy, different & inept
+ **Feel** you disappoint, anger & frustrate
+ **Feel** "lazy," bored, unmotivated, depressed

EMOTIONAL INSTABILITY
+ **Unable** to unwind & self-calm
+ **Emotionally** labile
+ **Emotionally** flat
+ **Withdrawn,** shy
+ **Explosive**
+ **Inappropriately** loud, silly, attention getting

How Common Is SPD?

SPD is common, though few people currently know about it. It afflicts in some degree anywhere from five to thirty percent of children and adults without disabilities. According to occupational therapist and researcher Lucy Jane Miller, however, only around 10% of children with SPD will likely be diagnosed and treated by occupational therapy, the profession involved with understanding, researching, evaluating and treating sensory processing problems. These are mostly children who have severe over- or under-responsiveness to sensory stimuli that interferes with daily life, including social skills, attention, self-regulation, and skills development, and in whom SPD co-exists along with other diagnoses, such as autism, pervasive development disorder, ADD and other learning disabilities (some estimate that many as 70% learning disabled children have sensory processing disorder). Many, like some on the autistic spectrum, suffer abnormal responses to sensation so severely that they live constantly traumatized by the condition. Recall in the film Rainman how the autistic savant Raymond, played by Dustin Hoffman screamed at the sound of the fire alarm or at being touched.

Undiagnosed & Untreated

What happens to the 15% to 20% of "normal" but "out of sync" difficult children with sensory processing problems? Most will remain undiagnosed and untreated. Few parents, teachers, caregivers, physicians, mental health workers or parents are aware of sensory processing disorder. Of those professionals familiar with the condition, many deny its existence as an actual and treatable condition, particularly psychologists and psychiatrists who will treat the child entirely from a psychiatric perspective. Consequently, many children grow into adults never having been identified with or treated for SPD.

This has dire consequences.

Missed Potential

Without appropriate treatment, you will not come near your potential. SPD truncates skills, robs you of stamina, causes spaciness, distractibility, disorganization and disorientation, restricts work choice and location, and creates extreme stress that ultimately leads to a barrage of stress related illnesses like headaches, GI problems, dizziness, and chronic fatigue, and psychiatric disorders ranging from anxiety to dissociation. All these conditions interfere with self-sufficiency and many flounder through life, and often a lonely one.

Loneliness

As few people understand or know of SPD and the problems it creates, family, friends and co-workers expect you to behave normally. When you don't, people become easily frustrated and disappointed in you and tend to attribute your behavior to a character flaw: you are difficult, fussy, stubborn, cranky, short-tempered, picky, unfriendly, disorganized, impulsive, lazy, depressed, attention getting or just spoiled. Such misunderstanding makes you feel weird and crazy and you believe your failings must be your fault, "Stupid me!" Feeling that you don't belong and not knowing how to help yourself be more "normal," many live isolated and lonely lives. This is especially so for the sensory defensive who feel overwhelmed and overstimulated by ordinary sensation, like noise, lights, crowds, and odors and sensations involved in social relations, such as making eye contact, closeness, sounds, smells, and touches.

Mis-Treated

If you turn to professionals for help, most assume your symptoms are psychological and treat you with tranquilizers and antidepressants or psychotherapy. Such treatment generally does mildly improve quality of life by helping you cope better and feel better about self but it has little to no impact on the sensory and regulatory issues underlying this dysfunction: sensory processing problems stem not from negative thinking or critical parenting but from miswiring in the primitive brainstem. Consequently, your functioning improves little and, still not knowing what is wrong with you, you feel invalidated and still anxious.

What are the causes of SPD?

SPD has numerous underlying causes:

➢ **Trauma**: SPD often appears in response to,
- Prenatal insult from drugs, illness and maternal stress
- Birth complications, such as asphyxia, post-birth trauma or prematurity

- Head trauma
- Physical, sexual or psychological abuse
- Chemical abuse
- Post-traumatic stress disorder

➢ **Genetics:** As other family members often show sensory processing problems, SPD appears to have a genetic component.

➢ **Allergies:** Virtually all people with sensory processing problems appear to suffer allergies and food sensitivities, linking the conditions.

➢ **Toxins:** Exposure to environmental toxins, such as air contaminants, creates hypersensitivity, confusion, disorientation, memory problems and other cognitive deficits.

How does SPD Manifest?

SPD presents as a problem in three different areas:

Sensory Modulation Disorder-SMD: inability to turn up or turn down volume of sensory input interferes with focusing in on and responding appropriately to relevant sensation. SMD can exist independent of other sensory issues.

Sensory Discrimination Disorder-SDD: difficulty determining source, pitch, and frequency of sensation and distinguishing one sensation from another makes it hard to accurately discern sensory information. SDD generally co-exists with motor & modulation problems.

Sensory-Based Motor Disorder-SBMD: difficulty navigating through space makes you clumsy, uncoordinated and often gravitationally insecure (over-responding to position changes). SBMD generally co-exists with discrimination & modulation problems.

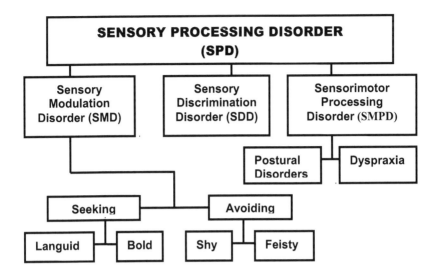

Sensory Modulation Disorder

An exquisitely sensitive physiological arousal system to detect and react to threat, our brain every second of our lives busily evaluates sensory input for potential danger. If something is *dangerous* – a loud noise in the dark -- we alert and prepare to fight or take flight. If it is *safe and interesting* – a baby's giggle -- we alert and engage. If it is safe and *we don't care* – a car diving by – we ignore it.

Sounds simple. Yet this ability relies heavily on how *accurately* you evaluate sensory input as dangerous, safe, or irrelevant and this varies from person to person. Imagine a smoke alarm going off. If it happened while you were boiling pasta for dinner, logically your brain would say, "safe/ignore," and you would calmly turn off the boiling water and switch to preparing salad until the alarm stopped. If the alarm sounded off in the middle of the night, your brain would scream "danger!" and you would jump out of bed.

Wouldn't everyone behave this way? Not exactly.

Each of our brains turns up or turns down the volume of sensory input at a different rate and with a different intensity based on individual sensory threshold or arousability -- how quickly our brain notices and responds to sensation -- and how quickly we return to baseline or homeostasis. This process is called *sensory modulation*.

Seekers (resilients) possess a high sensory threshold: experiencing sensation slowly and mildly, you require much sensory input to alert to and tune into the world and, once aroused, quickly return to baseline. Quickly bored and disinterested, you need more and more to feel "just right." Unless posed with a charging tiger, you evaluate the world as safe – precisely how our brain is designed to function -- and ignore the noxious sound of the smoke alarm, calmly turn off the boiling water and continue preparing dinner.

Avoiders (sensitives) possess a low sensory threshold: you experience sensation quickly and intensely, requiring little sensation to become alert and tuned in and, easily aroused, take long to return to baseline. Quickly over-stimulated, you need less and less to feel just right. You evaluate noxious but safe sensation as a threat and feel disturbed by the smoke alarm, though not enough to discontinue preparing dinner. Nevertheless, you feel distress and distracted to some extent until the sound ceases.

The average person falls somewhere in the middle of the continuum and you neither strongly avoid nor strongly seek sensation.

You likely have a good idea where you hang out most of the time. This is because differences in how you respond to a threat underlie basic inborn temperament patterns, based on sensory threshold, emotional regulation and the speed with which you can change from one state to another. This basic modus operandi remains stable throughout life.

Infant Temperament Patterns & Sensory Processing

Seekers—the Resilient:

➢ **Languid**: happy, easy, undemanding, inactive; unbothered by sensation or changes in routine; adapt easily, cry little, play contentedly alone.

➢ **Bold**: happy, social, curious and active; quest constant new and different sensation; get fidgety if restricted or not given enough new stimulation, like if forced to be in the house too long or play alone.

Avoiders – the Sensitives:

➢ **Shy**: quiet, inactive, and quickly alert to sensation; adapt slowly to change and cling to mommy but don't overly fret.
➢ **Feisty**: fussy, difficult crybabies; easily overstimulated; quickly thrown from change in place or routine; hard to calm.

These patterns are normal and typical. Some people, though, strongly under- or over-react to sensation to where it guides behavior and interferes with normal functioning and they are unable to easily alert to and focus on a task or wind down. They have a sensory modulation disorder, or SMD.

➢ **High Sensory Threshold/Seekers** quest extreme sensory input and evaluate dangerous sensation as exciting, compromising personal safety, or they fail to tune into a danger signal. You might dismiss the smoke alarm going off in the middle of the night as a false alarm, if you don't actually smell fire, and go back to sleep, or you may not even hear it. If you got burned from the scalding water you may not treat it as you barely feel pain.
➢ **Low Sensory Threshold/Avoiders** over-react to what should be evaluated as "don't care" as dangerous. Upon hearing the smoke alarm, you smack your hands over your ears and run out the room. The water boils out and the pasta and pot are ruined.

Such constant misinterpretation of sensation gives rise to extreme behavior to get to the comfort zone where you feel neither anxious/threatened nor bored/oblivious. The result is a slew of psychopathological conditions, from anxiety and depression to mania and substance abuse that SMD mimics, exaggerates, or results in.

Sensory Seekers

Under-reactive to sensation, seekers require intense sensation to register "pay attention!" and it takes longer for you to tune into the world -- think of the "daredevils" who swallow fire or lie on nails. You love thumping music, spicy food, bright lights, and stimulants like coffee, coke or nicotine, for instance. If strong sensation is unavailable, dopamine, the pleasure seeking neurotransmitter drops too low and you zone out or run around frantically seeking something to perk interest.

Sensation seekers fall into two categories based on: energy level (high/low); muscle tone (firm/floppy); and self-regulation --control of under-stimulation (active/passive):

> **Languid**: low energy/low muscle tone/passive sensation seeking
> **Bold**:   high energy/firm muscle tone/active sensation seeking

Low-Passive/Languid

The languid easily tunes out the world, unbothered by sensations that most find disturbing, like a passing siren, the smell of rancid milk, or the pain of a cut or bruise. This makes you easy going and able to go with the flow. At the same time, tuning out much sensation around you makes you unaware of what's going on and you may appear dull and out of it. Possessing low energy, you passively seek the intense sensation you need to become alert through intense tastes, strong perfumes, bold colors, tattoos, TV watching or video games (couch/mouse potatoes), sex, self-stimming like giggling, addictive behavior like over-eating, gambling and substance abuse, and physical activity like rocking or repeatedly riding the roller coaster.

In most languids, low responsivity goes hand in hand with low muscle tone and weak muscles, evident by slumping, that makes it hard to get your system going and moving through the world takes effort and concentration (see motor problems on page 218). Consequently, you fatigue easily and, getting little done, appear lethargic, "lazy," disorganized, and depressed. Frustrated and feeling a failure as a result, many experience learned helplessness and fearful that you won't succeed give up trying, seemingly unmotivated to help yourself.

How languids cope with under-responsivity relies on intelligence. The less intelligent are withdrawn, dull and disengaged. Those with higher intelligence are artistic dreamers who, turning inward for self-stimulation, live in their own world where they weave fantasies from which they derive intense pleasure. Kind, knowing, spiritual and psychic, some fit the profile of the "indigo child," while others that of the computer geek.

The need for unusually intense sensation to tune into the world, along with low muscle tone that makes action effortful can create a range of mental health issues.

Generalized Anxiety: Because so much information is missed, the world often doesn't make sense and, easily confused and frustrated, you get quickly anxious.

ADD: Needing much sensation to tune in, you appear unfocused and out of it.

Addictions/Substance Abuse: You rely on stimulants to rev up enough to tune into the world.

Depression: Under-responsivity to sensation, low muscle tone that makes moving effortful and low energy creates lethargy and depression.

Overeating & Inability to Lose Weight: Passively seeking sensation, you overeat and, as moving takes effort, don't exercise. As a result, many languids are overweight and fail at dieting. Added weight also feels oddly comforting as it makes you feed more grounded and therefore more secure.

Bulimia: Over-eating and lack of control over your weight may lead to gorging and purging, which provide intense sensory input.

Sexual Acting Out: You engage in frequent sex as intense odors, sounds and movement, as well as heavy pressure into the skin, which increases body awareness, provides intense sensory stimulation. Some women will become frequently pregnant as pregnancy adds weight, enhancing bodily sensation and body awareness.

Cutting: Emotionally frozen and out of touch with your body, cutting your skin provides at once intense sensation into the skin for body awareness and distraction from intense emotional pain.

Dependent Personality: You become dependent on others to force you out of lethargy and organize you.

Depersonalization: Underresponsivity to both touch and proprioception (sense of body awareness) makes it hard for you to figure out your edges and, out of touch with your body, you may feel unreal and the world distant.

Low/Active Bold

The bold are easily bored and need constant newness, intensity, uncertainty, challenge or thrills for life to sizzle. You love chilé peppers, sequins and bangles, fast cars and are always on the go, stay up late at night and multi-task. You may be overly affectionate and intrude on the other's personal space but, at the same time, charming and upbeat, exciting to be around. A leader, you think divergently and come up with innovative ideas.

If you are unable to get sufficient sensation, you will create it and might doodle, jiggle your foot, crack gum, giggle loudly, or act silly and attention getting. With your high energy level, you may dance around and nudge others and appear hyperactive -- as a child, you may have crashed into walls, people, beds and the like to get weight, pressure and traction into your body.

This constant need for new, different and interesting sensation interferes with focusing on relevant information needed for everyday functioning and you forget your wife's birthday, look away and fidget when people talk to you or change the subject, and finish late the dull report your boss has requested. As such, many seekers are irresponsible, undependable and self-serving who, focused on sensation seeking, miss social cues and are insensitive in social interactions.

If your time is not sufficiently filled with challenge, you engage in sensation seeking behaviors that compromise personal safety regardless of the consequences to yourself or your family: addictive behavior, such as gambling and risky sex; aggression and you may harm others or yourself; extreme sports; substance abuse. You lack motivation to change these patterns as self-help strategies, like therapy, meditation, journaling – anything that requires quiet focus – offer too little sensation to engage you and, needing instant feedback, you get quickly bored. Fortunately, risk taking diminishes as you grow older and by middle age you calm down and are more capable of healthy relationships and greater productivity.

Driven to sensation seeking, regardless of the task-at-hand or the consequences, sensation seekers may experience the following mental health issues:

ADHD: If you don't get enough sensation to feed your nervous system, you become frenetic and appear hyperactive and distracted.

Mania: Constant sensation seeking makes you appear manic and you may be misdiagnosed bipolar. Psychologist Martin Zuckerman found that bipolar disorder and sensation seeking are highly correlated (see resources).

Bulimia: You engage in gorging and purging to control weight as this provides intense sensory input.

Addictions/Substance Abuse: You use stimulants to rev up and tune in.

Sexual Acting Out: You engage in promiscuity and risky sexual behavior for intense sensation and thrills.

Overeating: You overeat as food with intense taste revs you up and chomping provides input into the jaws, which quickly modulates.

Cutting: Emotionally frozen and out of touch with your body, cutting your skin provides at once intense sensation into the skin for body awareness and distraction from intense emotional pain.

Sociopathology: Insensitive and poor at reading social skills and hell-bent on sensation seeking irregardless of the other's needs, you exhibit sociopathic behavior.

Sensory Avoiders – Sensory Defensiveness

The avoiders – the sensory defensive -- feel *too* much, *too* soon and for *too* long, and, experiencing the world as *too loud, too bright, too fast and too tight,* become easily distressed by everyday sensation. For instance, you may interpret a light stroke on the shoulder as an attack and become anxious, hostile, or aggressive and spontaneously flinch, withdraw or lash out.

Remaining on red alert after the irritation has passed, you fail to return to baseline and feel constantly hyped, stressed and agitated. To manage overwhelming sensation, you minimize unpleasant sensation and control your world through order, structure, sameness, and predictability: familiarity breeds contentment. At the same time, your hypersensitivity allows you to pick up more information than others, particularly social cues, and this makes you more aware and sensitive than others.

Shy/Feisty

Avoiders fall into two categories two categories depending on energy level (high/low) and self-regulation, which is control of over-stimulation (active/passive):

➤ **Shy:** low energy/passive sensation avoiding
➤ **Feisty:** high energy/active sensation avoiding

High/Passive Shy

Some avoiders are shy/introverted and fearful who, wishing to not make waves and draw attention, passively avoid sensation. You make an excuse to not go to a noisy restaurant and opt to stay home. You avoid eye contact, need much personal space, cry easily, and have difficulty making friends. At the same time, needing to carefully monitor your world, you read faces well, making you highly tuned into others, and you are sensitive, empathic and kind.

Energy is often low, evident by a body that seems caved in, though inside you may be jumping. Nervousness, along with sensation avoiding and a natural cautiousness that enables you to delay gratification gives you the patience to engage in self-development and you may learn more active ways of coping and overcome shyness and inhibition. For instance, you may become a teacher, public speaker, or actor/actress.

This change in strategies was first noted by developmental psychologist Jerome Kagan, who was the first to identify the two temperamental extremes -- shy children that cling to mommy, and bold ones that easily explore. Kagan found that when parents actively encourage shy children to explore and play with other children many switch to a more active pattern of controlling overstimulation and overcome their shyness – assertiveness training!

High/Active Feisty

Other avoiders are temperamental, edgy and, possessing high energy, hyper and you actively avoid sensation. You will complain in a restaurant, for instance, that the music is too loud and the lights too bright and demand to sit somewhere quieter and dimmer. Things have to be just so and, fussy, stubborn, negative, intense and uncooperative you are difficult and hard to be around. If not over-stimulated, however, you can be upbeat and engaged.

SENSORY DEFENSIVENESS SYMPTOMS

➢ **Feeling** annoyed when certain textures touch your skin
➢ **Recoiling** to light, ticklish touch or when someone, particularly a stranger, unexpectedly touches you
➢ **Shunning** crowds
➢ **Startling** to loud, sudden, or piercing sounds; being unable to shut out constant noise
➢ **Wincing** at bright lights; becoming disorganized by excessive visual stimulation
➢ **Grimacing** at odors others don't notice
➢ **Feeling** light-headed and sick from chemicals in the environment
➢ **Avoiding** foods of a certain taste or texture
➢ **Feeling** anxious when:
  o Experiencing sudden or fast movement
  o Leaning forward or backward
  o Confronted with heights, unstable surfaces, swings, or roller coasters

---

The need to design a world highly specific to your needs makes some feisty avoiders artsy and creative, while high energy and the need for order and predictability makes you productive and you get much done. Highly aware of your world, you perceive more than others and often have great insight into human nature.

Like your shy counterpart, constant jumpiness and an ability to delay of gratification motivates you to relieve inner tension and you engage in self-development, enabling you to grow and evolve throughout life.

Anxiety, Panic ......

As avoiders feel constantly hyperaroused, you experience life as a constant emergency and anxiety is omnipresent. By adolescence, you were likely referred to as anxious, phobic, depressed, compulsive, hostile, aggressive or controlling. By adulthood you will have been in therapy for anxiety, fears or depression, and have taken tranquilizers, antidepressants, and beta-blockers for panic and, also, likely engaged in alcohol and recreational drugs to self-calm.

Here are the many psychiatric conditions that sensory defensiveness mimics, exaggerates, or results in:

Generalized Anxiety Disorder (GAD): As the world feels constantly overwhelming, the sensory defensive feel hyped and stressed and you experience muscle tension, fidgeting and restlessness, irritability and perhaps angry outbursts, sleep difficulties, concentration difficulties and fatigue – the symptoms generally used to describe people with GAD.

Phobias & Panic Attack: Easily destabilized from movement experiences, like elevators, escalators, roller coasters, going fast, or spinning, which create gravitational insecurity and nausea, dizziness and light-headedness, the sensory defensive may panic and display space related phobias like fear of heights, claustrophobia, fear of flying, and so forth.

Agoraphobia: Continually overwhelmed by sensation, some sufferers will experience panic on an ongoing basis and bury themselves in their homes and appear agoraphobic. The sensory defensive can also become reclusive because the home is the only place where they can reasonably control sensory input.

Obsessive-Compulsive Personality: As the sensory defensive feel victimized by sensations they cannot control, they go overboard trying to control what they can and behave rigidly. To self-calm, they will indulge in compulsive eating, shopping, and in some sexual activity predisposing them to obsessive/compulsive behavior.

Obsessive-Compulsive Disorder (OCD): Acutely bothered by certain sensations on their hands, some SDs will wash them constantly, wear gloves when preparing meals, and obsess over getting dirty, leading therapists to believe they have OCD. Other behavior as well can mock OCD. For instance, the sensory defensive might engage in rituals, like repetitive rocking or counting as a distraction.

Addictions: To create a steady flow of pleasurable vibes and blunt feelings of tension, anxiety, and frustration, as well as to blunt the senses, the SD might develop an addiction to controlled substances, like alcohol or tranquilizers.

Anorexia: If you are oral defensive, certain food textures or temperatures irritate, as do some taste sensations and the SD develops many food fetishes. Some also have a strong gag reflex. Eating may feel unpleasant and the oral defensive will snack rather than sit down and eat a meal. By adolescence, some will starve themselves and appear anorexic.

Depression: Loneliness, anxiety, extreme fatigue and sleep problems, and lack of human affection set up passive resignation and depression. Adding fuel to the too hot fire, lack of control in your life leads to learned helplessness and you drag through life.

Post-Traumatic Stress Disorder: After someone experiences extreme trauma, their body gets stuck in the "fight or flight" mode and, when they can bear no more, shut down or freeze. For the severely sensory defensive, ordinary sensation like a fire alarm will send them into a numbing, traumatized state and, hypervigilant and constantly on guard, many live their lives in constant PTSD.

Borderline Personality: Marked shifts in mood, impulsive and unpredictable behavior and great difficulty in personal relationships, often transitory, along with addictive behavior, like substance abuse for self-calming make the SD appear a borderline personality.

Bipolar Disorder: Sensory overload causes impulsive, frantic, aggressive, and even violent behavior, and the SD appear manic. At the same time, the SD will shut down when too overloaded and seem depressed. As such, some SDs get misdiagnosed as bipolar.

Depersonalization/Dissociation: When life inside one's body becomes intolerable, the sensory defensive shut out the world and depersonalize, losing sense of self as real. Some dissociate and lose memory, as in amnesia or multiple personality disorder.

Suicide: If anxiety and tension becomes unrelenting and maddening and you constantly want to jump out of your skin, a psychiatric condition called akathisia, some SDs will attempt suicide.

SENSORY MODULATION DISORDER & BEHAVIOR

ENERGY LEVEL	SENSORY THRESHOLD	
	LOW ⟸⟹ HIGH	
	Avoider **Increased Sensitivity** **(Over-Responsive)**	**Seeker** **Decreased Sensitivity** **(Under-Responsive)**

LOW	**Shy/Inhibited (flight)**
	Passive Self-Regulation
	♦ Fearful/anxious
	♦ Quiet/introverted
	♦ Cautious/wary
	♦ Compliant
	♦ Socially phobic
	♦ Dependent
	♦ Rigidly structured
	♦ Overly serious
		Languid (oblivious)
		Passive Self-Regulation
		♦ Disinterested/bored
		♦ Easily fatigued,
		♦ lethargic, "lazy"
		♦ Sedentary-- couch/
		  mouse potato
		♦ Unmotivated
		♦ Shy, withdrawn,
		♦ depressed
		♦ Low muscle tone
		♦ Unstructured,
		  undisciplined
		♦ Unaware, dreamer,
		  "Indigo" child

HIGH	**Feisty (fight)** Active Self-Regulation ♦ Difficult/fussy ♦ Willful ♦ Angry ♦ Defiant/rude ♦ Edgy, explosive ♦ Impulsive ♦ Hyped ♦ Rigidly structured ♦ Intense/serious ♦ Aware	**Bold (charged)** Active Self-Regulation ♦ Extroverted ♦ Risk taker/thrill seeker ♦ Impulsive ♦ Hyperactive/manic ♦ Uninhibited ♦ Insensitive ♦ Bored/distracted ♦ Undisciplined ♦ Cross boundaries/in your face

(Sharon Heller, PhD, 2010)

See-Sawing

Some of you will think that you fit into more than one category, for instance that you may be touchy but love roller coasters; shy with some people but feisty with others; laid back and placid but freaked out by a roaring truck or the odor of bleach. This is not unusual. Some people commonly seesaw between seeking and avoiding, constantly needing to rev up or calm down, even to where, emotionally labile and disorganized, you get mistakenly diagnosed as bipolar. This is because, though the quadrant helps us to categorize our behavior, it's "too simplistic," says Lucy Jane Miller, founder of the nationwide SPD research program and recipient of an NIH grant to study the disorder. "Things are along a continuum, not divided into dichotomous boxes."

At any moment behavior is colored by many variables, including context, trauma and parenting.

Context: The basic fabric of our temperament creates a baseline of response that defines our modus operandi. From baseline, arousability moves up or down according to sensory input, which can be external (like bright/dim lights) or internal (like heartbeat or thoughts) and which interacts with conditions such as time of day, health, emotional state, activity, fatigue, hunger, previous pain/ pleasure, expectations, motivation, task-at-hand, and environment, all of which will vary according to our body rhythms that orchestrate behavior, such as cranial-sacral rhythm and brainwaves.

If you are in a good place, everyone can more easily tune out noxious stimulation. If you are in a bad place, everyone is capable of becoming "touchy."

Trauma: Any trauma to the nervous system can create sensory defensiveness. For instance, a bold seeker who experiences head trauma from a car accident may still dye her hair red, smoke, drink coffee all day, and blast the radio but startle if lightly touched.

Hyperarousal and a low sensory threshold is one of the three criteria to define post-traumatic stress disorder. Stated D. Jeffrey Newport and Charles B. Nemeroff in an APA article entitled *Neurobiology of Posttraumatic Stress Disorder*, "disturbances in sensory processing are believed to play a prominent role in the hyperarousal symptoms of PTSD such as the exaggerated startle response" (p.315).

Birth trauma may alter basic temperamental patterns, modifying inborn tendencies. Feisty avoiders may be temperamentally bold but, from birth trauma, emerge as hypersensitive and fussy which would help explain why they will both avoid and seek sensation. As such, I suggest that temperament, as Kagan first proposed, falls into two extremes, bold and shy, and languid and feisty are variations: languids passively seek sensation because of low muscle tone; feisty avoiders are seekers with a damaged nervous system from birth that results in hypersensitivity to sensation and inability to modulate emotion.

Early experiences: Parenting greatly influences behavior. Warm, sensitive parents calm their babies when they are over-stimulated and rev them up when they need sensation and this helps the infant develop strategies for self-organization that help tone down sensory modulation problems. At the same time, insensitive parents amplify sensory modulation problems and an active child may become hyperactive, a languid child depressed, a feisty child highly anxious and insecure, and a shy child more inhibited and fearful. Coupled with sensitivity in reading a child's cues, parents who offer firm guidance and limits, along with gentling pushing the child into new territory create a safe haven for exploring and socializing. As noted, shy children can become more social when parents encourage them to develop more active social skills.

Behavior is also modified by cultural expectations. For instance, American culture is more likely to encourage bold behavior than many Asian cultures.

Self-development: As adults, we have many strategies for better organizing our nervous system, from exercise and meditation and modifying our diet and detoxifying to learning positive thinking and gratitude.

Sensory Discrimination

Sensory discrimination refers to the ability to distinguish one sensation from another. It enables you to pluck out the salient characteristics of a sensation and correctly interpret its meaning – gritty, smooth, silky, gooey – and to place sensations correctly in time and space.

➢ **Characteristics:** You recognize that something you just put in your mouth tastes bitter rather than sour. Fine tuning further, you can distinguish the taste of a tangerine from an orange, the sound of the violin in the orchestra from the flute.

➢ **Time:** You know that you just cut your finger tip and that the pain is on the inside tip of your index finger not on the side.

➢ **Space:** You perceive that a car is coming toward you rather than away from you; you can tie your shoes in the dark and zip up your pants without looking at them as you know where you are touching things without having to see them.

With the ability to quickly distinguish one sensation from another, you immediately evaluate if something is safe, dangerous, or if you care:

➢ **You** ignore the sound of a child screaming on the TV but alert to the sound of your child screaming in pain.

➢ **You** ignore smoke from the barbecue peeling into the house but alert to smoke from your toast burning in the oven.

➢ **You** ignore the tag in your blouse but immediately flick off an ant crawling up your arm.

➢ **You** ignore indifference in a face but quickly discern anger and back off. an angry face from an indifferent one and discontinue il to pick up differences in facial expression and don't discern anger at a remark you made and continue to expound on the subject.

If you cannot easily discriminate sensations, you do not respond to signals from the environment accurately and may fail to:

➢ **Find** your glasses that are on your face and you run around looking for them (touch);

➢ **Make** the correct while driving and you get lost;

➢ **Figure** out that the announcement of a blue Honda Civic blocking the driveway is yours and fail to move it (auditory);

➢ **Easily** distinguish the smell of milk turning sour and drink it (smell);

➢ **Recognize** that a tick just bit you and may have put you at risk for Lime's disease and you don't seek medical help (touch);

➢ **Perceive** that the dead animal in your driveway is a possum, not your cat and you panic (vision);

➢ **Know** that a remark you just made annoyed your boss and continue in the same vein, increasing his anger (vision).

Such lack of sensory discrimination makes the world feel confusing, frustrating, taxing, and dangerous, interfering with how easily you can meet the ordinary challenges of everyday life, and you worry constantly about doing what you need to do to get your needs met. In other words, you feel constantly anxious.

The following typifies sensory discrimination challenges.

➢ **Fear of dark:** Disoriented in the dark, you become fearful.

➢ **OCD:** Confused and easily thrown, you need everything in place and, not trusting it is still there without seeing it, keep checking.

➢ **Learned helplessness/depression:** Easily confused and disorganized, you often feel inept and unable to meet your wants and this creates learned helplessness and depression.

➢ **Dependent personality:** Needing to rely on input from others to glean appropriate information from the environment and to help you get organized, you appear helpless and dependent.

➢ **Depersonalization:** Out of touch with your body, you may at times feel unreal and the world distant.

These feelings are greatly compounded by motor issues that commonly accompany discrimination problems.

Motor Problems (Dyspraxia & Postural Issues)

Motor problems occur from the inability to translate sensory input into organized, purposeful motor output and result in clumsiness and lack of coordination. They generally co-exist with low muscle tone and weak muscles and you lack sufficient voluntary control over your body to move easily and gracefully. This presents numerous problems. As you don't maneuver space well, doing everyday automatic tasks requires exertion and you feel incompetent, dependent, and lacking control. Such effort, along with the passive under-responsivity to sensation that generally accompanies motor problems, interferes with the alertness needed to tune into the world and you may appear and be depressed.

Children with this difficulty may be labeled dyspraxic (unable to plan or execute movement well) or as having developmental co-ordination disorder (DCD). After following a group of these children into adolescence and adulthood, a study in the UK confirmed that they were likely to have emotional and other behavioral difficulties, especially depression. If taking certain drugs, like steroids, MAO inhibitors, tricyclic antidepressants, or L-dopa, or if they have infections, metabolic disturbances, or tumors, all of which can create mania, they appear bipolar and may get misdiagnosed and mistreated as such.

Winston Churchill stands as an example of depression, mania and low muscle tone. Fleshy Churchill felt hounded by depression -- his "black dog." He hated sports but preferred horseback riding, a powerful means of vestibular and tactile-proprioceptive input, and swimming, which permits easier mobility and provides water pressure to hug the body. Quick tempered and easily bored in school, he was an abominable student and a discipline problem, indicating a problem with emotional modulation. And he showed signs of reckless sensation seeking – mania -- indicating a problem with sensory modulation. In a well told anecdote, he flew off a bridge and landed in a tree when he was eighteen, to prevent his two cousins – hunters flanked on either side of the bridge – to catch him, the deer. He woke up with a concussion and ruptured kidney.

In addition to depression, fears and phobias are common in those with low muscle tone who often experience gravitational insecurity, a severe reaction from change in head position, especially sudden, that creates dizziness, vertigo, light-headedness, or nausea and fear and anxiety about falling. Everyday activities like bending forward to change a sheet, bending backward to get your hair washed or turning your head while driving can feel traumatic. Unsteady on your feet, you are also accident prone, further increasing spatial insecurity and fear.

The following are examples of common fears and phobias:

➤ **Sports:** Afraid of getting hit by a ball that you misjudge, or tripping and falling while running, as well as other realistic mishaps, you dislike sports.

➤ **School:** Worried you would be ridiculed for your clumsiness, as a child you dreaded school.

➤ **Socializing:** Concerned that you will look awkward when writing or signing your name in front of others, or eating and drinking in public, you avoid social situations. You may refuse to go dancing, nervous that others will laugh at your two left feet.

➤ **Space:** Easily losing your place in space, you fear flying, heights and wide, open spaces.

➤ **Elevators/Escalators:** Afraid of not being able to get on or off the escalator on time or without tripping, you fear escalators; worried you will be unable to get in or out of an elevator before the door closes, you fear taking elevators.

➤ **Tunnels:** Nervous that you will be unable to keep your car within its lane in the dark, you fear tunnels.

➤ **Hitting/Getting Hit:** Unable to determine the speed, position, or direction of moving vehicles, you fear getting hit while crossing a street or hitting someone while driving.

➤ **Crowds:** Afraid of getting knocked over, you fear being in a crowd.

➤ **Choking:** Worried you will choke (vestibular dysfunction may un-coordinate normal reflexes), you fear swallowing pills.

➤ **Agoraphobia:** Afraid of jelly legs because of floppy muscle tone, you fear falling, fainting, getting injured or losing control and may panic in situations from which you can't easily escape, like being in a theatre or church.

The list goes on. For instance, inability to lose weight may relate to gravitational insecurity, suggests Kathryn Smith, an occupational therapist in England. If we feel grounded, we feel secure moving through space and having our body leave the ground, as when jumping, diving, trampolining, riding elevators. "But without gravitational security about our body's relationship to gravity, we are

unable to free ourselves from being stuck down to earth," says Smith, and to feel grounded, you need to keep your feet firmly planted to the earth. The heavier you are, the more gravity has to work on and the more firm is your grip to the earth. When you lose weight, you feel an uncomfortable lightness of being and unknowingly overeat to feel more grounded. Some who fit this profile, Smith hypothesizes may have fearful dreams of flying off in space.

Diagnosis & Treatment of SMD

If you have SPD, you will need to incorporate sensorimotor activities into your life. In addition, you must alleviate all possible causes of neurological dysfunction: nutritional (chapter 12); toxicity (chapters 13 and 14); food sensitivities, yeast overgrowth, and other GI problems (chapter one); adrenal exhaustion (chapter two); structural misalignment (chapter eight); chemical sensitivity (chapter 14); breathing restrictions (chapter seven); neurological issues (chapter six); illness (chapters two and five); hormonal issues (chapter four); and so forth.

Occupational Therapy

If you suspect SPD, ideally you should get a proper evaluation and diagnosis from an occupational therapist who will give you a battery of tests to evaluate your specific sensory processing problems. She will then set up a "sensory diet" for you to follow consisting of sensorimotor activities tailored to your specific needs. These will consist largely of activities that tap into the different sensory systems:

> **Tactile system** (sense of touch), such as brushing and massaging your skin;
> **Vestibular system** (sense of balance), such as swinging or jumping on a trampoline;
> **Proprioceptive system** (sense of body awareness) such as weight lifting, pushing against a wall, or moving furniture;
> **Auditory system** (sense of hearing) such as therapeutic listening;
> **Visual system** (sense of sight) such as eye exercises to increase binocularity or long arm swinging.

You will need to see a pediatric occupational therapist, as these are the OTs trained in sensory integration therapy. Though they work primarily with children, pediatric OTs can accommodate adult clients as sensory integration therapy is easily adapted for adults. Find an OT trained in sensory integration; the more training, the better (see Resources).

Self-Treating

If you are unable to see a pediatric OT, you can self-evaluate and self-treat SPD to some extent (see my books *Uptight & Off Center* and *Too Loud, Too Bright, Too Fast, Too Tight*) depending on what sensory processing issues you suffer and to what extent you can create and adhere to your own sensory diet. Sensory modulation problems are at once the easiest to self-treat and those that create the most mental health issues in adults.

Here are some general suggestions for a sensory diet.

TOUCH:
➢ **Have** a massage once or twice a week
➢ **Use** a high powered massager at home.
➢ **Brush** your skin.
➢ **Learn** the Wilbarger deep pressure touch protocol.
➢ **Do** body rolling for deep pressure touch.

PROPRIOCEPTIVE & VESTIBULAR:
➢ **Do** daily physical activity that offers strong tactile, proprioceptive and vestibular input, such as: jumping and crashing on a trampoline; swimming underwater or scuba or deep sea diving; walking upstairs or walking or biking uphill (preferably carrying weights); horseback riding; play wrestling.
➢ **Make** yoga, Tai Chi, or martial arts part of your life.

LIGHTS:
➢ **Use** full spectrum lighting.
➢ **Use** therapeutic colored lights and color therapy eyewear.
➢ **Get** out in the sun during safe hours.

SOUND:
➢ **Surround** yourself with healing music.
➢ **Do** therapeutic listening: Tomatis, Berard, SAMONAS cd's.

➢ **Use** earplugs under headphones that cover the whole ear and listen to calming music. The earplugs will block out some sounds and the music will mask other uncontrollable sounds.

DRIVING:

➢ **Infuse** essential oils.

➢ **Play** a relaxing CD.

➢ **Sing**, hum, chant or sing loudly to music.

➢ **Use** an electric back massager on your car seat and hand massagers for deep pressure.

➢ **Take** a deep breath at a red light.

➢ **Blow** a kazoo.

➢ **Chomp**, chew, suck (preferably whole organic food!).

➢ **Wear** colored therapy glasses, if it doesn't interfere with visual alertness. (More than an hour at a time is not recommended.)

➢ **Do** qi-gong or reiki breathing using only one hand (pull the energy out, pull it back in (see chapter seven, p. 181).

RELAXATION TECHNIQUES:

➢ **Do** progressive relaxation.

➢ **Practice** visualization.

➢ **Meditate** (meditation tapes work well).

➢ **Do** daily deep breathing exercises.

BODY WORK:

➢ **Get** deep cranial/sacral work such as biocranial, neurocranial restructuring, craniosacral therapy, or dental manipulation .

➢ **Get** myofascial release, Trager, Feldenkrais, Rolfing, or somatics.

HEALTH:

➢ **Eat** primarily whole, organic fresh vegetables, fruits, grains, nuts and beans.

➢ **Reduce** indoor toxins.

➢ **Stop** smoking, drinking alcohol or using recreational drugs.

➢ **Get** plenty of fresh air and sunshine.

➢ **Detox** your colon and liver and get the heavy metals, particularly mercury out of your system

LIFESTYLE:

➢ **Simplify** your lifestyle.

➢ **Structure** your day to help stay on track.

➢ **Take** on less responsibility.

➢ **Sleep** as much as you need to feel alert and productive.

➢ **Avoid** feeling rushed and pressured.

➢ **Take** a walk, run, bike, roller skate, ski outside in nature whenever possible.

For a complete treatment overview, see my books *Uptight and Off Center* and, specifically for sensory defensiveness *Too Loud, Too Bright, Too Fast, Too Tight* (www.sharonheller.net).

Psychological Intervention

Drugs like anti-depressants and anti-anxiety medication can reduce the panic associated with SPD, as well the often accompanying underlying depression that accompanies the dysfunction. You can however achieve similar results with natural supplements (see pages 112-116).

Sensory defensiveness especially creates chronic, ongoing agitation, anxiety, and hyperarousal -- essentially post-traumatic stress disorder (PTSD) in those who suffer SD severely -- and you cannot tolerate even minor stress. As the brain of those diagnosed with PTSD is low in GABA and serotonin, you may need to supplement these important brain chemicals. For PTSD sufferers, Julia Ross, author of *The Mood Solution* recommends a combination of GABA, 5-HTP, and tyrosine to raise depleted brain levels, reduce excess stimulation, and restore energy.

These substances, however, are limited in what they can do to alleviate the distress associated with sensory processing disorder. Boosting brain chemicals will take the edge off your anxiety but it will not eliminate hypersensitivity as this is a knee-jerk survival reflex that originates in the primitive brain stem, not the mind. You need sensorimotor activities tailored for your particular dysfunction. Research conducted in 2003 by occupational therapists Beth Pfeiffer and Moya Kinnealey showed sensorimotor activities to reduce both sensory defensiveness and anxiety. These findings are confirmed by English OT Kathryn Smith, who treats and researches sensorimotor interventions in adults with sensory defensiveness, many of whom are hospitalized with borderline personality disorder.

As for psychotherapy, talking things out will help you feel less emotionally fragile and better about the self and this is good. But it will not produce any understanding or change of the underlying cause of your anxiety – sensory processing. Consequently, unless you get specific therapy for this dysfunction you will continue to feel invalidated, confused … and anxious.

Nutrition/Supplementing

Healthy nutrition is essential for those with SPD. To start, the on-going stress accompanying SPD eats up vitamins and minerals that need to be replenished or you become malnourished.

EFA's & the Brain

Sufficient essential fatty acids (EFA's) are crucial for brain function. That many SPD sufferers are spacey may relate in part to a brain starved of EFA's. A diet high in EFA's or supplementing improves the reading ability and behavior of adults with dyslexia, as well as dyspraxia, or poor motor planning. See chapter one.

Second, many problems relating to sensory processing disorder interferes with proper digestion and elimination, and malabsorption is common. The following are a partial list of such problems:

➢ **Sensation** seekers need caffeine and nicotine to get their system going, depleting minerals, as well as much fat and intense taste and you eat much junk food. Such habits result in vitamin and mineral deficiencies.

➢ **Sensation** seeking can lead to addictions and substance abuse. Feeding your body the nutrition it needs, including getting enough B and C vitamins, as well as minerals such as magnesium and calcium, will reduce addictive behavior. Also, blue-green algae produce an amino acid called phenyl ethylamine (PEA) that boosts dopamine, the feel good hormone that drives seeking behavior. Thus supplementing with blue-green algae may reduce seeking.

➢ **Sensory** defensiveness creates on-going stress that affects digestion and can lead to malabsorption and you need to eat food high in nutrition.

➤ **Oral defensiveness** makes certain food textures feel irritating and, a picky eater, you confine your eating to specific textures such as chips or crackers, or soft food, like a banana, spaghetti, or ice cream, or cold or hot food. Consequently, you may have nutritional and vitamin deficiencies that affect your behavior and development. In adolescence, this can present as anorexic like starving and be misdiagnosed and mistreated as such. This will need treatment.

➤ **Problems** with tactile discrimination may not cue you that you are hungry or satiated and you may eat too much or too little. This will need treatment.

➤ **Poor** proprioception may interfere with signal reception for urination and defecation. This will need treatment.

➤ **As** you get ill more often, you may have been given long-term antibiotics which upset the natural flora in the intestine and you suffer in Candida overgrowth and leaky gut as a result. This will need the interventions presented in chapter one.

Detoxifying

Detoxifying is a must for anyone with SPD (see chapters 13 and 14). People with sensory processing disorders and particularly sensory defensiveness frequently suffer disorders that indicate overtoxicity and poor immune system functioning, such as the following:

➤ **Allergies** -- Allergies such as reacting to dust, pollen, grass, fur, medicines like penicillin, or toxins like bee venom commonly coexist with SPD.

➤ **Yeast Overgrowth:** If you've had SPD since childhood, you likely have compromised immune functioning and may have taken long-term antibiotics. This leads to yeast overgrowth, a condition that in and of itself will create hypersensitivity.

➤ **Food sensitivities:** Often you have food sensitivities, such as for wheat, milk, sugar, eggs, soy or corn. Symptoms lessen when eliminating triggers such as dairy and wheat from diet, along with artificial or processed ingredients.

➤ **Drug Side Effects:** Frequent reactions to medication are common and indicate that the liver is not expelling toxins from drugs. The liver's inability to eliminate heavy metals from the body is implicated as the cause in some cases of autism.

> **Multiple Chemical Sensitivity:** MCS is common in people with sensory defensiveness. If you suffer it, you may have been exposed to CO fumes. MUSES Syndrome, or severe sensory defensiveness is a symptom of CO poisoning. See p. 302.

Postural Alignment

Postural misalignment and poor posture are rampant in those with sensory processing disorder and likely one of the primary causes of the condition. Therapies like craniosacral therapy, or the more powerful and permanent neurocranial restructuring and biocranial are crucial for neurological integrity, and especially if you have pronounced body or facial asymmetry (see chapter eight). If you have an S curved spine, shuffling gait, weak grip or flattened thenar (ball of thumb), common in those with low muscle tone, you have underactive vestibular functioning and will also need to work on your balance system (see next chapter).

Better Breathing

If your posture is off, it's a bet you're a belly breather and breathing exercises to increase lung power and to self-calming are essential. For more information, see chapter seven.

Alternate Nostril Breathing

In a research study using the yogic technique of alternate nostril breathing to deepen and slow breathing, spatial memory was increased in 10 to 17 year olds. Increased spatial awareness relates to field independence, the ability to be relatively independent of the physical environment and still accurately orient and maneuver in space. As the field independent are more centered and grounded in space, this exercise offers an important opportunity for better body awareness for those with SPD.

This chapter has presented an overview of sensory processing disorders and their treatments. The next two chapters look at two particular problems of sensory defensiveness that create panic attack and get easily misdiagnosed as psychological: balance issues or gravitational insecurity, and photophobia or light sensitivity.

Quick Review

> **Sensory processing disorder (SPD)** is a condition in which poor processing of sensory messages makes you unable to easily focus in on and act on your world efficiently, purposefully and in an organized way.

> **Signs** of SPD include: overlysensitive to sensations; undersensitive to sensation; unusually high or low activity level; coordination problems; underachiever;poorly organized behavior.

> **As** many as 30% of children suffer SPD to some degree. But only around 10% of these children will likely be diagnosed and treated by occupational therapy. Generally these are children in whom SPD co-exists along with other diagnoses, such as autism, pervasive development disorder, ADD and other learning disabilities. Normal but difficult children with SPD remain undiagnosed and untreated and grow up with this dysfunction.

> **As** few professionals know of the dysfunction, they generally assume the symptoms to be psychological and treat it with drugs and psychotherapy. Neither greatly impacts SPD.

> **Sensory** processing disorder entails problems with:
> - Sensory modulation, the ability turn up or turn down the volume of sensory input to respond to relevant sensory input and ignore the irrelevant
> - Sensory discrimination, the ability to distinguish one sensation from another
> - Motor planning or praxis, the ability to translate sensory input into organized, purposeful motor output.

> **Sensory** processing problems are often inherited or acquired through trauma that disrupts the nervous system.

> **SPD** is evaluated, diagnosed and treated by occupational therapy.

Resources

Suggested Books

- *Too Loud, Too Bright, Too Fast, Too Tight, What to do if you are sensory defensive in an overstimulating world* by Sharon Heller (HarperCollins, 2002).

- *Uptight & Off Center, How sensory processing disorder creates anxiety, confusion & other mental health issues,* by Sharon Heller, PhD (Symmetry, 2010)
- *Living sensationally: Understanding your senses,* by Winnie Dunn (Jessica Kingsley Publishers, 2008).
- *The Sensory-Sensitive Child* by Karen A. Smith & Karen R. Grouze (HarperCollins, 2004).
- *The Out-of-Sync Child. Recognizing and Coping with Sensory Integration Dysfunction* by Carol Stock Kranowitz (Skylight/Perigee, 1998).
- *Sensational Kids,* by Lucy Jane Miller (Putnam Adult, 2006).
- *Sensory Integration and Learning Disorders* by A. Jean Ayres (Western Psychological Services, 1972).
- *Sensory Integration and the Child* by A. Jean Ayres (Western Psychological Services, 1998).
- *Behavioral Expressions and Biosocial Bases of Sensation Seeking* by Martin Zuckerman, (NY: Cambridge University Press, 1994).

Websites

- sharonheller.net (adults)
- adultsid@yahoogroups.com (adults)
- spdlife.org (adults)
- spdfoundation.net (information, research, all ages)
- sensory-processing-disorder.com (all ages)
- out-of-sync-child.com (children)
- sensoryproject.com (adults)
- sifocus.org (magazine-all ages)

Products
- www.Southpawenterprises.com

Finding an occupational therapist, see

- www.Sensory-processing-disorder.com (all ages)
- www/Spdnetwork.org (research)

10

★

Shaky Place in Space

A happily married father of two, Michael is warm, friendly, cheerful and pleasant, adoring of his children and close to his parents -- *not* a candidate for an anxiety disorder. Yet for over two years Michael has suffered debilitating panic attacks.

The first one began while standing outside on his balcony. The room began to spin and he felt ringing and pressure in his ears. Anxious and shaky, he sat down and leaned against a wall for support but continued to feel dizzy for hours. A week later, he had a similar attack which exploded into a full blown panic attack, with pounding heart, sweaty hands, a floating sensation, and a feeling of dread and unreality. He thought he would pass out. Having never been a fearful person, he was clueless as to what was happening. He must be stressed from over-working, he thought, as he had just opened a restaurant and worked long hours.

For two years, doctors could find no reason for his vertigo and sent him to psychiatrics to treat him for panic disorder. He was put on Paxil and the panic attacks abated for over a year. But three months later, he had another full-blown panic attack, again starting with vertigo. After having "every test from every doctor," he went to an otolaryngologist at the University of Miami Medical Center. He was diagnosed with Ménièré's disease, a disturbance of the inner-ear balance system in which the fluid-filled chambers swell and cause periodic attacks of vertigo. It was Ménièré's disease that set off his first panic attack. After that frightening event, Michael feared a recurrence. The slightest feeling of dizziness generated a full-blown panic attack: anticipatory anxiety or the fear of a panic attack turned a physical condition to a psychological one.

Inner Ear Dysfunction & Phobias

Does your panic attack involve?

➢ Disorientation

➢ Dizziness

➢ Lightheadedness

➢ Vertigo

➢ Depersonalization

➢ Floating sensations

➢ Imbalance

➢ Falling

➢ Nausea

If so, your panic attack is space related and likely comes from *vestibular dysfunction*. The vestibular system is located in the inner ear and controls sense of balance and direction, coordinates and sequences movement in time and space, and fine tunes all sensory input. Damage to this system can impair these functions, and you feel dizzy, disoriented, lightheaded, floating, faint, or nauseated -- the symptoms of panic attack!

Symptoms of Inner-Ear Dysfunction	
◆ Vertigo	◆ Disorientation
◆ Dizziness	◆ Disassociation
◆ Loss of balance	◆ Panic attack

The poorer the vestibular functioning, the greater the likelihood of having a panic attack in situations that challenge balance, orientation and movement and panic attack quickly escalates into a phobia, a deep, primal persistent fear of physical harm from a situation or a thing. In his practice, psychoanalyst Harold Levinson, author of *Phobia Free*, has found that some *90 percent of specific space related phobias and panic attacks are the result of an underlying malfunction within the inner-ear balance system.* For instance:

➢ **Fear of elevators** or planes might result from an inner-ear failure to handle motion input

➢ **Fear of heights** might result from a sense of imbalance – a broken gyroscope

➢ **Fear of tunnels** might result from a problem with orientation in space – a broken compass

> **Fear of driving** might result from movement defensiveness, hypersensitivity to change in direction and inability to process disturbing visual input.

Levinson happened upon this startling discovery in the 1960's when treating dyslexic children. Dyslexia was believed caused by a disturbance in the cerebrum, or thinking brain. But after examining 1,000 patients, Levinson found only 1% showed evidence of cerebral dysfunction, but 750 of the children exhibited problems with balance and coordination. He concluded that dyslexia correlated with problems related to inner-ear, or vestibular dysfunction. At the same time, occupational therapist A. Jean Ayres, the mother of sensory integration theory, discovered most learning disabilities and hyperactivity were characterized by tactile and vestibular processing problems and therefore a byproduct of sensory processing disorder.

Levinson believes that vestibular dysfunction may account as well for learned phobias in some cases. Explains Levinson, an integral part of the anxiety-control network is mediated in the vestibular system in the inner ear. If the inner-ear system is impaired, the entire anxiety-control network may be affected. Under stress, your system may be unable to properly dampen or regulate anxiety. You quickly reach your sensory threshold and mild to moderate anxiety erupts into panic. This may help explain why, after being robbed, some people become terrified of being home alone while others don't. Thus, even if actual trauma sets off your phobia, inner-ear malfunction predisposes you to react excessively, and for the panic attacks and phobias to persist. What starts out as physiological becomes psychological.

Causes of Space Related Phobias

> **Balance & coordination problems (broken gyroscope):**
  - Triggers fear of heights, bridges, stairs, escalators, wide-open spaces;
  - Provokes anxiety, dizziness, light-headedness, feeling off balance, floating sensations, spinning, falling fainting, tipping or swaying.

> **Disorientation in space (broken compass):**
  - Triggers fear of tunnels, shopping malls; other disorienting situations

- Provokes anxiety, disorientation, confusion, floating sensations, spaciness, light-headedness, depersonalization, dizziness

➢ **Motion sensitivity to change in direction, speed of movement or sudden movement:**
  - Triggers fear of riding in vehicle, elevator, escalator, roller coasters, boats, rocking chair;
  - Provokes anxiety, dizziness, light-headedness, nausea, vomiting

Common Causes of Dizziness

How do you get inner ear dysfunction? It comes from a variety of infectious, metabolic, toxic, allergic, or physical traumas to the nervous system. These include:

➢ **Pregnancy:** Infections; malnutrition; drug use
➢ **Delivery:**
  - Asphyxia
  - Traumatic use or forceps resulting in fetal concussion state
  - Torqueing of head and neck resulting in fetal whiplash
➢ **Pre-mature** birth which arrests the development of the inner ear system
➢ **Severe** or repeated ear infections
➢ **Sinus** infections
➢ **Illness** like:
  - Mononucleosis
  - Hypothyroidism
  - Hypoglycemia
  - Diabetes
  - Degenerative disorders
➢ **Drugs** like:
  - Antibiotics
  - Tranquilizers
  - Blood pressure medications
  - Heart medications
  - Anti-seizure medications
➢ **Drug** abuse, especially alcohol and barbiturates
➢ **Malnutrition**
➢ **Allergies**
➢ **Motion sickness**
➢ **Hyperventilation**

> **Low** blood pressure (you feel dizzy when getting up or sitting down quickly)
> **Prolonged** or turbulent air travel
> **TMJD:** the temporomandibular joint is the center of the vestibular network and acts as the reference point to the entire proprioceptive system; a tight jaw can throw off balance
> **Chemical** changes in the brain due to a variety of factors including:

- Female hormonal changes
- Aging
- Anesthesia
- Stress

> **Concussion** due to:

- Head trauma
- Temporal bone fracture (fracture of bone that contains inner ear balance organs)
- Penetrating trauma to ear drum (even a cotton swab can do quite a bit of damage)
- Barotrauma (ear trauma related to sudden pressure changes, like deep sea diving)
- Traumatic injury of the neck or back (such as whiplash)
- Traumatic injury of the eyes

> **Chemical** sensitivity
> **Toxicity** due to chemical exposure

Phobias & Toxicity

Edgar Allen Poe suffered claustrophobia and MUSES SYNDROME, a specific kind of toxic poisoning characterized by multiple chemical sensitivity and acute hypersensitivity to stimuli (sensory defensiveness) that comes from carbon dioxide (CO) poisoning. As toxicity will affect balance, it's likely that his claustrophobia, which inspired tales like "The Premature Burial" and "The Black Cat," was tied to the CO poisoning.

Let's look closely at the common causes of dizziness: *BPPV* and *Ménière's disease.*

BPPV: *Benign Paroxysmal Positional Vertigo (BPPV)* is a condition in which changes in head position causes the small crystals (otoconia) in the inner ear to get loose and bang against nerve endings, resulting in brief vertigo that usually lasts a few seconds. It happens commonly following even mild head trauma and is easily treated through a procedure called Canalith Repositioning Procedure that takes only about 10 minutes, and that the patient can do at home.

Ménièré's Disease: Ménièré's disease is characterized by ear pressure, ear noise – ringing (tinnitus) or roaring -- decreased hearing, and vertigo that typically last for hours. The attacks come out of nowhere. Suddenly, the room spins and you lose balance. You may eventually lose hearing. Over-abundance of fluid (endolymph) in the inner ear is the cause of the symptoms. The cause of the disease is still unknown though in some cases it appears genetic. Autoimmune disease and allergies may be implicated. Ménièré's can be diagnosed with hearing tests, balance assessments or an MRI.

For treatment, doctors generally recommend a low salt-diet and diuretics to control fluid retention, and avoiding alcohol and caffeine which affect how the fluids move through canals, where balance is controlled. Watermelon or celery juice are natural diuretics.

If these remedies fail to control the symptoms, you may be given a Meniett device. Self-administered, it delivers low-pressure air pulses through a tube to "shake up" inner ear fluid.

If this fails, more invasive procedures might be necessary, such as inserting a shunt into the endolymphatic sac to drain fluid, severing a nerve in the inner ear, or even removing part of the inner ear.

Double-Jointedness

Those with "hypermobility syndrome" or double-jointedness, an inherited trait, commonly experience panic attacks. Apparently, they appear to inherit a fear gene. At the same time, people with hyper-mobility syndrome have wobbly ankles and feet and therefore poor balance. Their panic may be set off by this instability as well as a faulty gene sequence.

Treatment Options

If you feel that dizziness, light-headedness, vertigo, or balance problems may be tied to your experience of anxiety, panic attacks or phobias consult an otolaryngologist (ENT) for a complete neurological and physical examination. If nothing comes up, explore further by getting evaluated by an audiologist. If you are diagnosed as having inner ear dysfunction, treatment includes:

➢ **Anti-motion** sickness medications, antihistamines and other drugs useful in treating inner-ear problems or natural alternatives

➢ **Specific** exercises

➢ **Neurocranial** restructuring; biocranial therapy; osteopathy

➢ **Auditory** Integration Listening Therapy

Psychological intervention may be inappropriate and entirely unnecessary or phobias may be deeply entrenched and you will require psychiatric intervention along with physical treatments.

Drugs

Harold Levinson has had much success in treating inner ear dysfunction with medication specifically targeting the inner-ear system. These include a variety of antimotion-sickness medications, antihistamines, vitamins, and stimulants known to improve vestibular functioning. These medications should be taken under the supervision of a physician.

Be aware of the drawbacks of medication. They often create unpleasant side effects (see chapter three). You will have to take them for a long time, generally one to four years, before going off them. And they treat the symptoms, not the cause. Natural supplements are a better option and include the following:

➢ **Essential Oils**: basil (most recommended), cypress, lavender, ginger, rose, rosemary, sage and tangerine; for quick relief, dab a drop of lavender on temples

➢ **Ginger** for motion sickness and nausea – tea or capsules

➢ **Gingko** for vertigo (popular remedy in Europe) as it increases circulation

➢ **Cayenne** pepper to enhance blood circulation

➢ **Apple** cider vinegar mixed with honey

> **Homeopathy** – specific remedies for specific problems

Cawthorne Exercises

For many decades, Cawthorne exercises, a form of physical therapy, have successfully alleviated dizziness. The exercises are each repeated 10 times. Here is one complete set:

1. **Sit** in an arm chair. Hold your upper body and head still and move only your eyes. Look up, then down. Look left, then right.
2. **Moving** your head, look up, then down. Rotate your head to the left, then right.
3. **Remain** seated, and bend forward from the waist and then back. Bend to the left from the waist and then to the right.

These exercises may cause dizziness; if so, try to continue the exercises despite the dizziness. Do one set of exercises in the morning, and one set in the evening. Begin at 5 minutes per set, and over several days extend this time to 10 minutes by increasing the number of repetitions.

Physical or Occupational Therapy

Trained physical or occupational therapists employ specific exercises to help the brain learn to adapt to disordered sensory data. These may include exercises like walking across a foam pad, or walking while moving the head from side to side. A variety of Eastern disciplines, such as T'ai Chi, yoga and Aikido, can be equally effective for vestibular rehabilitation.

NCR/Biocranial

Look at your face in the mirror. Cover the right side of your face with your hand and then do the same to your left. Is your face asymmetrical? If so, your skull is misaligned. If your head is even slightly imbalanced, or your ears not symmetrical, your inner ear system will be thrown out of balance and you may feel easily dizzy or experience vertigo, common triggers of panic attacks.

In treating people with poor balance, dizziness and vertigo, Dean Howell, naturopath and developer of neurocranial restructuring has found that they generally have ears that are not uniform or symmetrical. "When this happens," explains Howell in *Neurocranial Restructuring: Unleash Your Structural Power,* "the brain is using two groups of sensors placed at different angles and heights to determine the position of the ground." Consequently, you will be dependent on vision to maintain balance. "I have examined people whose ear positions differ more than three centimeters (1.2 inches). No wonder that they are clumsy!" says Howell. Even if the ears differed in position by only a centimeter (0.4 inches) in vertical position, the signal from the inner ears would have a five-degree/ one-centimeter difference in figuring out where the ground is. Ordinarily, this may not make much difference. But if you are walking on uneven terrain, like grass, or moving in the dark, or standing on one leg, this small discrepancy would throw you.

What might your experience be if your ears are not positioned symmetrically? Howell compares it to a feeling of walking blindfolded with two persons at each ear, whispering walking conditions to you. If you get different information, your brain doesn't know which to believe. What confusion! NCR or biocranial can correct this asymmetry and balance and coordination improves (see chapter eight).

Therapeutic Listening

Sound vibrates the inner ear and stimulates the vestibular sense, making listening to music a powerful means of impacting the vestibular system. To release all this power from sound requires special electronically altered music that filters in and muffles certain sounds, creating dissonance. As you listen to specifically selected compact discs through headphones, the unexpected sounds wake up the brain and force it to listen and process the music.

The alteration also causes the stapedius muscle in the middle ear to contract and then relax, teaching the brain how to tune out aversive sound and help attenuate auditory defensiveness and gravitational insecurity. Each CD is modified for different purposes, such as for self-regulation, body awareness, auditory processing, and cognitive skills. To lightly draw the listener in, the music is generally played softly.

If your therapeutic listening program is right, you experience greater internal harmony: breathing slows; sleep is more restful; focus and concentration improve, along with coordination and balance and you feel less hypersensitivity to sound, touch, movement and so on.   Even handwriting is better. An audiologist or occupational therapist trained in auditory integration can set you up with a listening program individualized for your special needs.

Nutrition

Nutritional factors can be implicated in vestibular dysfunction and should be addressed and attended to.

➢ **Patients** with vestibular dysfunction commonly have hypoglycemia, or low blood sugar. In one study, nearly 75% of Ménièré's patients had an abnormal glucose tolerance test. When placed on a low carbohydrate, high protein diet, nearly all controlled their vertigo.

➢ **The** cochlea has a high concentration of vitamin A and deficiency may be associated with inner-ear dysfunction.

➢ **Deficiency** of the enzyme lipase is a possible cause of Ménièré's disease.

➢ **The** minerals calcium and magnesium are implicated in vestibular problems, as well as potassium and sodium as electrolyte imbalances may affect the inner ear.

Systematic Desensitization

In cases where phobias have both a physiological and psychological cause, systematic desensitization, along with physical interventions, may be useful. Systematic desensitization begins with first relaxing through breathing techniques, meditation, muscle control, and so on. Next, you imagine or literally go through a hierarchically ranked series of fearful situations. For instance, if you fear heights, you go start by looking down at your feet; next you look down from a step stool; you then look down from the top of a staircase and, lastly, you look down from a thirty-story building. Any time you become too fearful, you stop and relax and then start again. This technique is highly successful for learned phobias.

Let's now look at how faulty vestibular processing can also provoke light sensitivity that can produce anxiety and panic in some people.

Quick Review

➢ **The** vestibular system in the inner ear controls sense of balance and direction, coordinates and sequences movement in time and space, and fine tunes all sensory input. If this balance system is damaged in some way, any one of these functions, or all, can be impaired and you can feel dizzy, disoriented, lightheaded, floating, faint or nauseated -- the symptoms that sufferers of panic attacks report.

➢ **In** situations where balance, orientation and movement are challenged, panic attack quickly escalates into a phobia, a deep, primal persistent fear of physical harm from a situation or a thing. In his practice, psychoanalyst Harold Levinson, author of *Phobia Free*, has found that some *90 percent of specific space related phobias and panic attacks are the result of an underlying malfunction within the inner-ear balance system.*

  • Fear of elevators or planes might result from an inner-ear failure to handle motion input.

  • Fear of heights might result from a sense of imbalance – a broken gyroscope.

  • Fear of tunnels might result from a problem with orientation in space – a broken compass.

  • Fear of driving might result from movement defensiveness, hypersensitivity to change in direction and inability to process disturbing visual input.

➢ **Though** psychiatrists assume phobias are emotional and learned following a trauma, many phobias pop out of nowhere without apparent cause. Or they are held in check and then suddenly intensify, or randomly come and go. Sensory based phobias fall into this category. As psychiatrists generally don't look at possible physical causes for phobias, most don't know associate faulty vestibular processing as a cause of sensory based phobias and those who do don't buy into it.

➢ **Psychoanalyst** Harold Levinson has been successfully treating sensory phobias with medication that acts on the vestibular system for over 40 years. Sensory based phobias can be treated as well with specific exercises that work on the balance system, with auditory listening programs and with neurocranial restructuring. At times, phobias have both a physical and an emotional cause and systematic desensitization may need to be included in the treatment protocol.

Resources

Suggested Books

- *Phobia Free* by Harold Levinson (MJF, 1986).
- *NeuroCranial Restructuring: Unleash Your Structural Power,* Third Edition by Dean Howell (Canyon Press, 2001).

Websites
- sharonheller.net (adults)
- levinsonmedical.com

Products

- Southpawenterprises.com

11

★

Assaulted by Light

Growing up, Teresa was molested by both her grandfather and her stepfather. Just short of graduating high school, her stepfather turned violent, wielding an ax, and beat up her mother and her. Neither Teresa nor her mother was seriously hurt but both felt extremely traumatized and Teresa feared leaving her mother alone.

Her mother insisted that Teresa get on with her life and in the fall, Teresa reluctantly left to attend a state college two hours from her home. Soon after starting classes, she began to have uncontrollable crying spells, depression, appetite loss, anxiety, and helplessness, along with frequent headaches, light-headedness and cold sweats that forced her to wear sweaters in the summer heat.

A month into the term, while studying in her brightly lit dorm room, she suddenly felt claustrophobic, dizzy, short of breath, trembly and disoriented. Filled with terror, she feared she was going crazy or dying and ran to the student mental health building. The psychologist diagnosed her with panic attack triggered by post-traumatic stress disorder (PTSD) and started her on the anti-anxiety drug BuSpar. But that made her dizzy and caused her moods to fluctuate wildly and she stopped taking it. Unable to concentrate in her classes, she quit school and returned home.

Once home, she was too terrified to leave the house or her mother and they clung to each other. A psychologist diagnosed her as depressed and put her on 20 mg of Prozac. Within three weeks, Teresa felt normal and registered for two night classes at a local junior college.

The first night of classes was a lecture held in a dimly lit classroom and she made it through the hour and a half class with little trepidation. The second night was in a lab, brightly lit with overhead fluorescent lights. She had her second panic attack. "I felt my blood pressure drop and all of a sudden I felt dizzy. I felt my anxiety rushing back. I tried to control myself and my tears. But I freaked out and stormed out of the classroom."

PTSD accounted for Teresa's anxiety, agoraphobia and depression. But bright lighting, which Teresa had always disliked – she wore sunglasses outside even on rainy days -- apparently triggered panic attack the first time in her overly lit dorm room and again in the college lab.

Light, explains light therapy pioneer and photobiologist John Ott, is a nutrient much like food. The right kind, specifically sunlight, is medicine and helps regulate our internal biological clock, which controls most body functions, including heart rate, breathing, digestion and brain waves. The wrong kind, specifically artificial incandescent and fluorescent light, is poison and disrupts our daily, monthly and annual rhythms, creating irritability, eyestrain, headaches, allergies, hyperactivity and depression, and a compromised immune system. Everyone will experience these problems to some degree. For instance, even those not consciously bothered by light will report burnout and fatigue at the end of a day at the office under fluorescent lights. But those with vestibular processing problems suffer *photosensitivity* and experience these problems in the extreme.

Photosensitivity

Photosensitivity is a condition in which you find it difficult to tolerate bright light and visual patterns, a common affliction of the sensory defensive.

The following visual signals are implicated:
- **Sunlight**
- **Bright** incandescent lights & fluorescent, especially older ones that buzz & flicker
- **Color** distortions
- **Various** hypnotic patterns
  - Tiled floors
  - Moving cars
  - Oncoming headlights
  - Wallpaper patterns

> **Flickering** lights
> **Blurred** images
> **Darkness**
> **Various** visual and color patterns created by stationary or moving crowds

Photosensitivity comes primarily from the inability of the vestibular system to properly filter incoming visual signals and this provokes dizziness and severe anxiety.

Under stress, the pupils of the eye dilate to admit more light and increase peripheral vision to scan for danger and sensitivity to bright light and visual disturbance commonly occur. When the stress passes, vision returns to normal. But if vestibular processing is off, the alarm system doesn't completely turn off. Your eyes easily dilate in response to light and you become photosensitive: a 100-watt bulb looks like a 1000-watt beacon and feels glaring and irritating. If inner-ear dysfunction is severe, the sun or bright lights sets off an alarm system in the brain that creates anxiety and, under extreme stress, you panic and become *photophobic*.

Unaware of the profound role between sensory processing and anxiety, few photophobics make the connection between bright lighting and panic. Nor will psychiatrists or physicians likely *enlighten* them, as these professionals rarely take sensory issues into account as an anxiety trigger.

In fact, light may be a common hidden and undiagnosed anxiety trigger.
> **Anxiety:** Fluorescent lights contain certain colors or color distortions, as well as pulsing vibrations that make older lights start to buzz and flicker and this stresses the body's nerve endings, confusing and overwhelming the nervous system. As a result, fluorescent lights in the work place, gym, classrooms and supermarkets may unknowingly cause you to quickly feel drained, spacey, agitated and often acutely anxious.
> **Social Phobia:** In social settings, bright lighting will render you unable to make eye contact and you seem social phobic.
> **Agoraphobia:** In public places bright lights may also be the fear finger that pushes the panic button for many agoraphobics who are commonly photophobic.

➢ **Fear of Dark:** Driving at night for the photophobic is a nightmare as the bright street headlights of oncoming cars scream at you, and the sensation of the flickering, blurring, or hypnotic effects created by objects that pass in front of or next to you overload your visual circuits. The faster you are driving, the worse is the effect. Highway driving is worse than driving on slower, local roads and under stress fear may escalate to panic while you are cruising I95.

➢ **Hyperactivity:** Bright lighting and fluorescent lighting in classrooms causes or contributes to hyperactivity, something that has been documented for over thirty years with time-lapse cinematography studies. In 1973, light therapy pioneer and photobiologist John Ott, and the Environmental Health Research Institute compared the performance of four first-grade, windowless classrooms in Sarasota, Florida, under full spectrum, radiation-shielded fluorescent light fixtures, which emit the full range of the sun's colors, or the standard cool-white fluorescents. Under the cool-white fluorescent lighting, some students demonstrated hyperactivity, fatigue, irritability, and attention deficits. Under exposure to full-spectrum lighting for one month, their behavior, classroom performance and overall academic achievement improved markedly. Several learning-disabled children with extreme hyperactivity calmed down and seemed to overcome some of their learning and reading problems. Since then, other studies of the same nature have found similar results.

What are the causes of photosensitivity?

Any insult to the nervous system can impact vestibular processing and cause photosensitivity and photosensitivity commonly accompanies many neurophysiological problems, including migraine headache, *Candidiasis*, brain tumor, and Arnold Chiari Syndrome. Photosensitivity to both sunlight and fluorescent lights is also a symptom of the autoimmune disease lupus.

Treatment Options

If you suffer anxiety or panic in the presence of bright or unnatural lights, the answer the life force: the sun's full spectrum of light. You can do this directly through:

> Sunlight
> Full-spectrum lighting
> Color lighting

> Syntonic light therapy
> Sensory integration therapy

Natural Light

Sunlight is the purest healing force for life on this earth. As light enters through the eyes, it travels through the hypothalamus in the limbic system, the master controller of the stress response. The hypothalamus controls:

> **Endocrine** systems
> **Timing** of biological clocks
> **Immunologic** responsiveness
> **Sexual** development

> **Control** of infections
> **Regulation** of stress and fatigue
> **Functioning** of the nervous system

For these systems to function optimally and optimize nervous system functioning, we require the sun's full spectrum of solar radiation:

> **Visible** color spectrum (red, orange, yellow, green, blue, indigo, violet;
> **Infrared** (heat just beyond red that we feel when sunburned)
> **Ultraviolet** (UV) wavelengths (just beyond violet)

If you don't get it, you feel agitated, fatigued, drained, spacey, depressed, and prone to viral and bacterial infections and *increased* photosensitivity. Insufficient light can also create anxiety and depression in a syndrome called seasonal affective disorder which I'll soon discuss.

Unfortunately, the photosensitive for obvious reasons avoid the sun. But there are ways around this. To start, you do not you need direct sunlight to get its benefits. You can be outside and stay in the shade. Also, you can block the sunlight by wearing Ott full-spectrum sunglasses, which, unlike regular sunglasses, allow all the color wavelengths of natural light to come through, while eliminating glare and distortion.

In general, our nervous system needs daily at least 30 minutes of exposure to natural spring or summer sun without sunscreens or sunglasses to function optimally. This is the bare minimum to produce adequate daily levels of vitamin D, necessary for healthy teeth and bones, and for the functioning of the brain and the immune system. Ideally, some experts believe we should be getting two hours of daylight, while avoiding direct sunlight between 10:00 A.M. and 2:00 P.M., to minimize burning and the risk for skin cancer.

Here are other ways to maximize natural sunlight and rely less on artificial lighting:

➢ **Increase** outdoor activities, and take greater advantage of backyards and porches.
➢ **Keep** windows clean and open when possible, unobstructed by drawn curtains or blinds.
➢ **Use** full-spectrum lights in place of incandescent and fluorescent.
➢ **Install** non-tinted skylights, and create atriums and sunrooms where you can.
➢ **Dress** bedroom windows with sheer or semi-sheer curtains or blinds to let in early morning light.

Healthy Artificial Light

Another way to get the sun's benefits is to use full-spectrum light bulbs which are the nearest thing to sunlight in terms of spectral distribution and brightness, and without heat and glare. Unnatural lighting, like incandescent and fluorescent, in contrast, offers only a portion of the full spectrum of the sun's light. Even on a rainy morning, it is brighter outside than inside with the lights on.

➢ **Incandescent bulbs,** or ordinary household bulbs, give off more red light than normal daylight and give a yellow tone to objects: blues look green; reds look orange. They actually produce more infrared heat than they do light.
➢ **Fluorescent bulbs** give off ultraviolet and blue light that gives a cold, stark appearance to a room and creates glare.
➢ **UV light** is virtually absent from incandescent lighting (lightbulbs), shielded in standard fluorescent bulbs, and virtually

blocked by normal window glass, including that on our automobiles and eyeglasses.

Such distortion from incandescent, fluorescent, and also by halogen lights creates eyestrain within twenty minutes of exposure, even if you have normal vision. Full-spectrum lighting in contrast is far easier on the eyes, eliminating glare and color distortion and colors are more accurately and easily perceived. Further, exposure to full spectrum lighting feeds your nervous system benefits similar to sunlight.

Full spectrum lights do emit slightly higher levels of UV than ordinary bulbs and tubes but the manufacturers deem them safe. They are available in most lighting stores both in a light bulb and in fluorescent lighting, and are widely available on the internet (see resources).

Here are some suggestions:

➢ **Replace** overhead fluorescent lights with full spectrum fluorescents or an Ott floor lamp.

➢ **Replace** all incandescent bulbs with full-spectrum bulbs.

➢ **Use** a bright Ott bulb for computer work, reading, artwork or drafting. It emits an uplifting white light, without glare or heat, that enables you to see the screen or objects more clearly and accurately, and provides the benefit of sunlight while working.

➢ **Replace** bathroom lights with full spectrum bulbs as it will help wake you up in the morning, and your body will receive the same effect as natural sunlight. And the whiteness of the light makes you look more natural, as you do in sunlight.

Colored Light

Another way to get the sun's full spectrum of colors is to use colored light. A much underused mood changer, colored light, strategically placed, profoundly affects our emotional state. Each color of light is a different wavelength or frequency and sends a different vibration into the energy system: one color excites, another calms.

> ➢ **Red, Yellow, Orange.** The red end of the light spectrum has the longest wavelength and slowest frequency of vibration. Red, yellow and orange are warm and uplifting, while pink is calming.
> ➢ **Green:** In the middle of the spectrum, green relaxes and speeds up the body's own healing mechanisms, making it good for recuperation.
> ➢ **Blue:** On the cool end of the spectrum, blue calms the mind and helps you sleep. In a study in which hospital patients with tremors watched blue light, their tremors lessened.
> ➢ **Violet.** With the shortest wavelength and the quickest vibration, violet is the most cooling. It helps balance both sides of the brain, harmonizing your thoughts and emotions, and induce a deep, relaxed sleep. Leonardo de Vinci said, "The power of meditation can be ten times greater under violet light falling through the stained glass windows of a quiet church."

You can utilize different color light frequencies in different ways:

1. **Illumination** of natural light through color
   a.   through glass -- think of the impact of the light streaming through stained glass windows in a cathedral
   b.   through a colored blind or curtain of a sheer fabric
   c.   using a colored lampshade with a white light bulb
2. **Colored** light bulbs
3. **Colored** therapy eyewear
4. **Voyager** program (see resources)

As the photosensitive react to some colors, you may need to experiment with your emotional response to different colored light. As someone easily overaroused and extremely photosensitive, I have never been able to have red in my environment or wear red apparel. But I love an orange wall!

Light Therapy

Syntonic (from "syntony" which means to bring into balance) light therapy flashes different portions of intense colored light into your eyes, each with a specific effect on the brain and the nervous system that helps reestablish the body's rhythms and balance the body.

Syntonic light therapy is done under the care of an optometrist, physician, psychiatrist, psychologist, or chiropractor who determines the appropriate colors for each patient. Incorrectly used, red can produce tension, while blue can produce depression. Thus, deciding the best color or colors takes clinical experience by a trained professional.

SYNTONIC LIGHT THERAPY	
Effects	**Conditions Improved**
♦ Raises endorphin levels ♦ Stabilizes brain waves ♦ Lowers heart rate, respiration & blood pressure ♦ Strengthens immune system ♦ Expands visual field	♦ Anxiety ♦ Clinical depression ♦ Stress ♦ Light sensitivity ♦ Visual problems ♦ Premenstrual syndrome ♦ Sexual dysfunction ♦ Chronic fatigue ♦ Thyroid problems ♦ Migraines ♦ Jet lag

A typical protocol of light therapy involves twenty 20-minute daily sessions of exposure to colored lenses. Some clinicians treat with the light flickering at varying rates, to better wake up the brain, though not everyone can tolerate flickering. Though light therapy is most intense with a light therapy device, less expensive home devices create a milder therapeutic effect, physically and emotionally. *Let There Be Light* by Darius Dinshah outlines how to use different colored filters directly on the body to alleviate disease.

Sensory Integration Therapy

As faulty vestibular functioning sets off photophobia, sensorimotor activities that work on improving vestibular functioning help improve visual processing and this will help reduce photosensitivity. An occupational therapist trained in sensory integration will set up a sensory diet based on your individual sensory needs.

Deprived of Light: SAD

> *His body, he said, was like an aneroid barometer-thermometer*
> *reacting violently to every oscillation of atmospheric pressure,*
> *temperature, or altitude. Gray skies depressed him, leaden clouds*
> *or rain enervated him, drought invigorated him, winter*
> *represented a form of mental "lockjaw," the sun opened him up*
> *again... His nervous system cried out for sun and dry, still air.*
>   -*When Nietzsche Wept,* by Irvin Yalom

Do you get grumpy, lethargic and down in the dumps in October as
the days start to get short and the sky gray?   Lack of light causes
winter doldrums in many people and as winter approaches, you start
to hibernate: you eat more; store more fat; become listless; sleep
more; and, as dark approaches, return quickly to your cave. In some,
sadness becomes depression and irritability becomes anxiety until
spring when the sun starts to light up the world again. If you are one,
you suffer some degree of Seasonal Affective Disorder (SAD). And
though SAD is called "winter blues," anxiety may actually be the
primary symptom, according to some experts. One study found that
9 of 22 panic attack patients had panic attacks more frequently in
winter.

Though SAD was not recognized as an actual disorder until the
1980s, it's been around throughout human history. "Lethargics are
to be laid in the light and exposed to the rays of the sun, for the
disease is gloom," observed Artaeus in the second century A.D.

SEASONAL AFFECTIVE DISORDER SYMPTOMS	
Feelings/Thoughts	**Sleep/Wake Activity**
♦ Anxiety	♦ Increased sleep
♦ Hopelessness	♦ Feeling unrefreshed
♦ Despair	after sleep
♦ Irritability	♦ Lethargy
♦ Depression	♦ Hypersomnia
♦ Spaciness	(oversleeping as much as
Physical	4 hours per night)
♦ Weight gain	
♦ Craving carbs & sugar	

What Causes SAD?

SAD is brought on by the decrease in sunlight, and believed to result from an increase at night of the sedating hormone melatonin, which gets turned on as lights gets turned off, as well as from a lack of sufficient light to regulate emotions. We need light to produce the neurotransmitter serotonin, which governs mood. As light decreases, serotonin levels in the brain drop and people get depressed and may also get anxious. As such, SAD can occur anytime a person lacks sufficient sunlight, not just in winter. In other words, if you're depressed and stay in your room with the shades down, you will become more depressed. Get out in the sun!

The opposite of winter blues happens as well. Some people get depressed in the hot, muggy summer months, and endure spells of anxiety, including panic attacks. Implicated is the hypothalamus of the limbic system, the part of the brain which helps the body adjust to outside conditions, including both light and temperature.

Who Gets SAD?

The hormones involved in SAD are closely related to the female hormones, making women four times more likely to suffer it than men and particularly during childbearing years. So many women suffer SAD that initially some discounted it as only the stress of raising children and balancing home and career. Half or more of women with SAD also suffer PMS.

Treatment Options

Light Up Your Life

If lack of light makes you anxious and depressed, the solution is obvious: light, lots and lots of light. First, get as much sunlight as you can. Morning sunlight with its higher concentration of ultraviolet rays is best as long as you avoid sun exposure after 10 a.m. And remember that light enters through the eyes, not the skin, so don't defeat the purpose by wearing sunglasses, as they block UV light. If sunlight is too bright and you need to wear sunglasses, wear Ott full-spectrum sunglasses.

You may also greatly benefit from phototherapy with a full spectrum light box screen designed by John Ott. This will expose you to light equal to the full-spectrum of the sun, including a small amount of ultra violet (UV) radiation. Generally, SAD sufferers sit in front of a light that delivers between 2,500 and 10,000 lux (unit of illumination) of light energy, twenty times brighter than that of average indoor lighting, for about a half hour each morning sitting about three feet from the lamp. Such exposure alleviates the symptoms of SAD in 80 percent of sufferers. Amount of exposure needed however need varies individually and should be determined and monitored by a trained health professional. Light stronger than 2,500 lux has potential side effects including anxiety, nervousness and even eye damage. In some susceptible people, light therapy can generate mania.

Under full spectrum lighting, symptoms generally reduce significantly within two to four days but it takes around a week to fourteen days to begin to see the full effects of light therapy. Taking B_{12} supplements will enhance the effects of light therapy.

Balance Brain Messengers

SAD sufferers are not only light deprived but also serotonin deprived as serotonin lowers as melatonin rises. You can regulate serotonin with SSRIs or naturally with herbs and amino acids as outlined in chapter three, pages 112-116.

Try Yoga

Yoga moves involving the top of the head, such as headstands, may stimulate the pineal gland. The pineal gland produces serotonin and melatonin and helps regulate circadian and seasonal rhythms.

Quick Review

> **Photophobia** comes from faulty vestibular functioning. As visual input is improperly processed, bright lights and fluorescent lights, flickering lights, blurred images, the dark, various hypnotic patterns (tiled floors, moving cars, oncoming headlights, wallpaper patterns and so), various visual and color patterns created by stationary or moving crowds can provoke dizziness and severe anxiety, and even panic.

> **Artificial** lighting contributes to photosensitivity because it distorts the natural color spectrum of sunlight.

> **The** lengthening of light from electricity confuses our natural twenty-four night/day cycles and throws off internal rhythms, further disorganizing those who are anxious, mentally confused or ill.

> **Any** insult to the nervous system can impact vestibular processing and photosensitivity accompanies many neurophysiological problems, including migraine headache, Candidiasis, and Arnold Chiari Syndrome.

> **Photosensitivity** can be treated by getting more sunlight, using full-spectrum lighting, experimenting with color lighting and syntonic light therapy, and exploring sensory integration therapy.

> **Lack** of light causes winter doldrums and anxiety in many people who suffer Seasonal Affective Disorder (SAD), or "winter blues. SAD is believed to result from an increase at night of the sedating hormone melatonin, which gets turned on as lights gets turned off, as well as from a lack of sufficient light to regulate emotions.

> **SAD** is easily controlled through full-spectrum lighting devices.

Resources

Suggested Books

- *Let There Be Light* by Dinshah Darius (Dinshah Health Society, 1985).
- *Light, Medicine of the Future* by Jacob Liberman (Bear & Co., 1991).
- *Health and Light: The Effects of Natural and Artificial Light on Man and Other Living Things* by John Ott (Pocket Books, 1973).

- *Light Years Ahead, the Illustrated Guide to Full Spectrum and Colored Light in Mindbody Healing.* Berkeley, CA: Celestial Arts, 1996.
- *Winter Blues: Seasonal Affective Disorder: What It Is and How to Overcome It* by Rosenthal, Norman (Guilford Press, 1993).

Websites

- sharonheller.net (adults)
- Syntonic Phototherapy.com
- Wj.net/dinshah.com (colored lights for medical problems)

Products

- Light Energy Company.com
- Lumiram.com
- Full Spectrum Solutions.com
- Ott-lite.com (Ott Technology Products)
- Tools for Wellness.com (offers several light therapy devises)
- Vitaminpills.com – Voyager computer colored light program (download)

Part III

Toxicity & Anxiety

We have learned that illness, digestive disorders, neurological insults, drug reactions, hormonal imbalance, sensory processing issues and cranial/sacral misalignment all create anxiety symptoms that can be misinterpreted as primarily psychiatric. In this section, we will look at one of the most common underlying causes of many of these other conditions – an overly toxic system.

The next four chapters will show you how to detoxify body and brain by taking in life, cleaning out poisons, and blocking further invasion.

1. **Taking in life:**
   - Eating raw, living foods
   - Taking natural, whole food supplements
   - Drinking purified water

2. **Cleaning out poison:**
   - Colon cleansing
   - Liver cleansing
   - Fasts
   - Enemas/colonics
   - Skin brushing
   - Infra-red saunas
   - Lymphatic drainage
   - Sun
   - Exercise

3. Blocking further invasion:
- Natural hygiene
- Natural cleansers
- Natural furnishings
- Natural wardrobes
- Clean air
- Clean alkaline water
- Natural cookware
- Alleviating EMF's

By the end of this section, you will know to what extent toxicity has caused or contributed to your anxiety and panic and what to do about it.

12

★

Toxic Food, Toxic Brain

Imagine living in the Stone Age. If hungry, you picked an apple off a tree, or dug a potato root from the ground and sat down to eat quietly with the clan. You ate highly nutritious raw and fresh food in season: in the spring it may have been apples; in the summer strawberries; in the fall squash. As you were unlikely to find a banana tree next to a strawberry bush or a tomato plant next to a pecan nut tree, you ate one food at a time, as do wild animals. Occasionally, you found a bit of honey and so ate very little pure sugar. You ate no milk products and hardly any grains.

What a huge leap to the modern diet of processed, pasteurized, salted, sugared, colored, artificial, overly cooked and toxic food that we eat hurriedly and with dozens of foods combined together at one sitting. The average store bought cake mix contains 28 ingredients and most are *not food*. Some 3,000 chemicals get added to the food supply, while processing and storage of food involves as many as 10,000 chemicals in the form of solvents, emulsifiers and preservatives that can remain in the body for years. And our diet is heavy in allergens, like wheat and milk that we eat virtually at every meal.

Does it affect how we think and feel? You bet. Our physiology and anatomy has changed little since antiquity: we are cave people dressed in business suits and still digest our food the same way. Unfortunately, food nutritionally deficient of vitamins, minerals, amino acids and fatty acids, loaded with artificial ingredients, toxins, and so forth, and with many ingredients combined is hard to digest and assimilate and the brain fails to get sufficient nutrition needed for production and communication of neurotransmitters, the brain's messengers. In this chapter, you will learn how to eat to replenish and restore your brain.

Feeding the Brain

The first step in achieving optimal physical and mental well being is to avoid food toxic to the brain. This includes virtually all of the processed, refined, chemical laden, fatty, salty, sugary foods that comprise the Standard American Diet (SAD).

BRAIN TOXIC FOOD	

♦ Sugar
♦ Caffeine
♦ Nicotine
♦ Alcohol
♦ Food with:
  • Food additives
  • Preservatives
  • Coloring
  • Artificial flavoring
  • Artificial sweetener -especially aspartame
  • Anything cured
♦ Refined flours:
  • White unbleached, bleached
  • Enriched flour
♦ Common food allergens:
  • Cow's milk (creates
  • mucus)
  • Gluten grains (wheat, rye, barley, oats)
	• Eggs
	• Peanuts (very acidic)
	• Soy (creates mucus)
	♦ High saturated fats
	  • Meats
	  • Butter
	  • Palm oil
	♦ Commercial red meat & poultry
	♦ Foods containing yeast
	♦ Fish containing high levels of mercury:
	  • Tuna
	  • Swordfish
	  • Sea bass
	♦ Products with aluminum (link with Alzheimers)
	  • Antacids
	  • Deodorants
	  • Baking powder

If you've been on the SAD, avoiding these foods may sound daunting. If so, arrange a plan to cut back gradually.

➢ **Reduce** and gradually eliminate white sugar which makes you feel anxious, tired, and melancholic, even depressed.

➢ **Reduce** and gradually eliminate white flour, and dairy which are common allergens that compromise the nervous system.

➢ **Reduce** and gradually eliminate all products with artificial ingredients which can be neurotoxic.

> ➢ **Eat** less meat, especially red meat which is highly acidic and hard to digest, affecting mineral absorption and stressing the body.

What should you eat instead? Whole, natural and preferably organic food.

Eating Healthy

The best diet for optimal physical and mental health is:
> ➢ **Nutrient** dense and calorie low
> ➢ **High** in antioxidants, omega-3 fatty acids, and fiber
> ➢ **Rich** in enzymes to make the food quick and easy to digest, assimilate and eliminate
> ➢ **Producing** the least amount of waste/waist in your body
> ➢ **Balancing** pH to 80% alkaline and 20% acid
> ➢ **Containing** solar energy in an easily digestible form:
>   - **Sprouts** (living as you bite into them)
>   - **Fresh** water algae & phyloplankton
>   - **Sea** vegetables (dulse, kelp, nori, wakame etc.)
>   - **Chlorophyll** rich greens, and especially wheatgrass which strengthens the immune system, detoxifies the body, and oxygenates the blood
>   - **Vegetables** and fruits high in phytonutrients, the organic components of plants that:
>   - ✓ Serve as antioxidants
>   - ✓ Enhance the immune system
>   - ✓ Enhance cellular communication
>   - ✓ Kill cancer cells
>   - ✓ Repair DNA damage

The "diet" that best satisfies that equation is one in which you eat primarily raw, organic vegetables and fruits, whole sprouted grains, seeds, nuts and beans. This may be *very* different from how you are accustomed to eating. But the payoff for eating nutrient rich, living food happens quickly: within weeks, you will feel more energetic, upbeat, emotionally stable, and clear-headed and experience better relationships, greater productivity, and creativity.

NUTRIENT DENSE, BRAIN HEALTHY FOODS

- **Fruits & vegetables;** fresh, organic, in season
- **Sprouted beans:**
  - Chickpea
  - Lentil
  - Mung
  - Adzuki
  - Fenugreek
- **Sea Veggies:**
  - Dulse
  - Kelp
  - Nori
  - Arame
  - Laver
  - Alaria
  - Wakame
  - Kombu
  - Hiziki
- **Non-gluten, whole grains:**
  - Kamut
  - Buckwheat
  - Amaranth
  - Millet
  - Quinoa
  - Spelt

- **Sprouted seeds:**
  - Sunflower
  - Buckwheat
  - Pea
  - Clover
  - Alfalfa
  - Radish
  - Broccoli
  - Fenugreek
  - Mustard
  - Hemp
  - Flax
  - Sesame
- **Raw, unsalted nuts:**
  - Almonds
  - Walnuts
  - Filberts
  - Pine
  - Macadamia
- **Superfoods:**
  - Goji berry
  - Camu berry
  - Açai (ah-sigh-eee)
  - Blueberries
  - Pomegranate
  - Maca Root
  - Bee pollen
- Himalayan or Celtic sea salt

- **Unsaturated cold-pressed oils:**
  - Grapeseed
  - Olive
  - Hemp
  - Flax
  - Cod liver oil
- **Natural sweeteners**
  - Stevia
  - Agave
  - Dates
  - Honey
  - Yacon
- Coconut water, meat, oil
- Organic raw apple cider vinegar
- Goat's milk
- Organic eggs, free-range chickens
- Organic lamb, beef, free-range poultry
- Fish from non-polluted waters (no shellfish)

Few people quickly make a transition from the Standard American Diet to that of organic living foods as you may not feel as full or satisfied. But as you begin to eat complex carbohydrates, healthy fats and proteins, your taste buds and smell will return to their natural sensitivity and you will lose your taste and desire for creamy, sugary, fried, oily and rich food. Also, the reward of feeling better and more upbeat, having more energy and being more productive will motivate you to do what is best for your body and brain. To boot, eating whole foods generally results in weight loss without having to consciously diet! And when we reduce body fat, we reduce toxic overload as toxins are stored in fat.

Sprouting and Soaking

The road to the fountain of youth is paved with green sprouts. Literally growing as you bite into them, sprouts are the most nutritious food you can put into your stomach. They abound with antioxidants, are loaded with protein, chlorophyll, vitamins, minerals and amino acids and contain **200% percent the nutrients of their non-sprouted counterparts.** Well documented to kill breast cancer cells, broccoli sprouts contain 50 times the antioxidant sulfurophane as mature broccoli. Packed with enzymes, sprouts also give your body a rest as they digest themselves. As an added bonus, sunflower, buckwheat and grain sprouts help regulate insulin level and will get you off the sugar seesaw that so affects thinking and productivity.

Before sprouting, soak all grains, seeds, legumes and nuts in water to remove enzyme inhibitors and make the seeds more digestible and easier to assimilate. For information on what and how to sprout, see resources.

Juicing

Want to jumpstart your day? Skip the heavy cereal breakfast for fresh, raw organic vegetable juice first thing in the morning and preferably again in the afternoon. It will fill you with vibrantly alive food that feeds body and brain at the cellular level, allowing cells to regenerate. High in enzymes and nutrients, pure green juice is pre-digested and gets absorbed into the bloodstream within 30 minutes.

Green Juices Benefits:

➤ **Fills** the body with live enzymes, alkaline minerals, and electrolytes and all nine linked amino acids required for building protein.

> ➢ **Purifies** the blood, builds red blood cells, and detoxifies, heals and energizes the body.
> ➢ **Alkalizes** and rejuvenates the body.
> ➢ **Hydrates** the body with highly mineralized water.
> ➢ **Gets** absorbed in the body in 20 to 30 minutes.

Green juices can be made with cucumber, celery, sunflower and pea sprouts, cabbage, kale, dandelion greens, spinach, and other green vegetables, including wheatgrass. Make green juices fresh daily and consume immediately as they will start to lose enzymes and other nutrients within 15 minutes or so. Carrot and beet juice are also great detoxifiers but high in sugar.

To get the most nutrition from juicing, invest in a quality juicer (Green Power Kempro, Green Star, Omega or Champion) as inexpensive juicers do not extract nutrients efficiently.

Phytonutrients & High-Power Blenders

If you aspire to longevity and good health, pack your body with phytonutrients, the medicine inside fruits and vegetables. One apple alone has about 385 different phytochemicals.

The problem is getting to them: just munching on an apple or chewing a carrot won't do it. To start, phytonutrients are not located primarily inside the part we eat, the fruit, but inside the parts we throw away--the seed, the skin and stem—and who wants to chew on these. Yet, when we spit out the apricot seed, for instance, we discard mega life-giving phytonutrients and antioxidants.

Next, it is hard to get all the phytonutrients out of the parts of the plant that we *do* chew. Plants are covered with cellulose, a protective cell wall. To release the enzyme cellulose in the plant, which we need for pre-digestion as we do not have this enzyme in our systems, we must first break down the cellulose. But to do so requires that we chew our food to a creamy consistency and swallow liquid, as we are meant to do. But most people chew once or twice per mouthful and woof their food down. And even if we chew the requisite 100 times a mouthful, we won't get to the plant's fiber as our jaw muscles are too weak from having been brought up eating mostly soft, cooked food. And many people have fillings, and false and missing teeth. Further, even if you chew vigorously, you could not chew each seed in a grape long enough to break it down.

Another problem in absorbing plant nutrients is deficient hydrochloric acid in the stomach. Stomach acid has to be a pH between 1 and 2 to digest the released minerals and vitamins. But for many it is not and especially as you age. If you suffer the following signs, you could have low stomach acid.

LOW STOMACH ACID SIGNS	

◆ Digestive problems
  ○ Chronic Candida
  ○ Parasites
  ○ Flatulence
  ○ Stomach carcinoma
  ○ Gastric polyps
  ○ Ulcerative colitis
◆ Auto immune disease
  ○ Celiac disease
  ○ Multiple sclerosis
  ○ Myasthemia gravis
◆ Osteoporosis
◆ Asthma
	◆ Diabetes
	◆ Hyperthyroidism
	◆ Addison's disease
	◆ Skin disorders
	  ○ Dermatitis
	  ○ Acne
	  ○ Eczema
	  ○ Psoriasis
	  ○ Rosacea
	◆ Arthritis
	◆ Gall bladder disease
	◆ Hepatitis
	◆ Depression

Stomach Acid Test

According to Russian doctors, a good way to test your own level of hydrochloric acid is to drink a quarter cup of beet juice. If the color of your urine or stool changes even slightly to the red of a beet, you are low in stomach acid.

Enter the 3HP blender (Blendtec and Vita-Mix both make them). High-powered blenders pulverize fibers of the vegetable, fruit, or herb down to a micro, easily digestible level without destroying nutrients. The result is perfect chewing.

According to Victoria Bountenko, author of *Green for Life*, is green smoothies also appear to increase stomach acid. Boutenko informally had 24 people drink green smoothies (one or two pieces of fruit and greens) for a month. After one month, level of hydrochloric acid vastly improved in more than half of the 24 participants. If you have low stomach acid, you may nevertheless wish to supplement with HCL. See resources for betaine HCL supplements.

High Powered Blending Advantages:

➤ **Superior absorption** and assimilation of vitamins, minerals and proteins, which are absorbed within 30 minutes.
➤ **Maximum nutrition** as you can eat three times the quantity of greens blended than in a salad.
➤ **Easier digestion** as blending increases the surface area for digestive enzymes to work on.
➤ **Increased stomach acid**, necessary for digestion.
➤ **Bypass** of all digestive problems like sore teeth, peptic ulcer, colitis, and a sick pancreas.
➤ **Nutrient loading** as you can easily mix in some healthy ingredients whose taste or texture you may not savor in a smoothie—for instance, dandelion greens, ginger, or bitter herbs—and barely taste them in the cornucopia of phytonutrients.

My daily power smoothie (makes around 6 cups):

♦ 1 cup sunflower sprouts -- phytonutrients
♦ 1 cup pea sprouts -- phytonutrients
♦ ½ stalk celery – for hydration
♦ Handful beet greens (blood purifier, anti-depressant), kale (antioxidant, anti-inflammatory), dandelion greens (digestion), parsley (glutathione booster), or watercress (memory & thinking enhancer)
♦ ½ whole lemon -- taste, vitamin C
♦ ½ lime outer skin (green) peeled – taste, vitamin C, antibiotic

- 1 granny smith apple – taste, phytonutrients
- 1 tablespoon Maca root powder – endocrine enhancer; antidepressant
- Handful goji berries (if you can handle the sugar & don't have candida) – antioxidant superfood; antidepressant
- 1 tablespoon Acai powder – antioxidant superfood
- 8-10 raw cacao beans – antioxidant superfood; mood booster
- ½ inch ginger -- anti-inflammatory
- 1 scoop Sun Warrior raw protein
- 1 scoop hemp powder protein or 1 tablespoon chia seeds (preferably Mila) – omega 3s
- Teaspoon bee pollen (start with a few granules) – energy booster
- Teaspoon cinnamon – sugar balancer
- ½ avocado (optional) – healthy fat; thickener
- 4 cups filtered water with Adya Clarity added (decalcification and heavy metal release, see www.therawfoodworld.com)

For the most amount of nutrition, drink 2-3 cups immediately. Refrigerate the rest and drink within four to six hours or it will have lost too many enzymes.

You may include all the ingredients in one smoothie, make two smoothies with half the ingredients in each, or vary the ingredients daily. Warning – this smoothie is quickly habit forming and hard to go a day without!

Choose Organic

People often complain that organic food costs too much. What about disease caused by toxicity? In reality, we can't afford to *not* eat organic!

Organic food:
- ➤ **contains** less pesticides, chemicals, hormones, antibiotics, health hazards, etc..
- ➤ **has** more vitamins, minerals, and health benefits than non-organic.
- ➤ **is** grown in richer soil and therefore contains more nutrients. At Tufts University, researchers found organic produce to

have a nutrient content around 88% higher than commercially grown produce.

➢ **promotes** farming practices that encourage ecological harmony and environmental responsibility. Organic farmers are rebuilding the soil. The more organic we buy, the less organic produce will eventually cost.

➢ **tastes** better.

Do your health and your family a favor and invest an extra $20 a week in organic produce and food. If you eat animal products, buy free range and grass fed which are not raised with growth hormones and antibiotics.

If you cannot always eat organic, at least buy organic of the most pesticide-laden -- the dirty dozen fruits and vegetables:

DIRTY DOZEN	
1. Peaches	7. Nectarines
2. Apples	8. Sweet bell peppers
3. Cherries	9. Lettuce
4. Strawberries,	10. Celery
5. Grapes (from chili)	11. Spinach
6. Pears	12. Potatoes
ALSO SUSPECT	
1. Cantaloupe (from Mexico)	4. Cucumbers
2. Red raspberries	5. Green beans
3. Apricots	6. Winter squash
	7. Tomatoes
LOWEST LEVELS OF PESTICIDES	
1. Onions	7. Asparagus
2. Avocados	8. Frozen peas
3. Frozen sweet corn	9. Kiwi
4. Pineapple	10. Cabbage
5. Bananas	11. Broccoli
6. Mangoes	12. Papaya

(This information was found and published by the Environmental Working Group at ew.org)

Some feel it is better to buy fresh from a local farmer, and in season than organic from out of state or out of the country as the longer it takes for fruits and vegetables to reach your plate, the more nutrition lost. In other words, food with some pesticides might be better from time to time than food with little nutrients. On the other hand, if you choose to do your own organic gardening and you eat food that is in season, you can generally avoid this problem altogether.

Rainbow Diet

When choosing your daily fruits and vegetables, think of the colors of the rainbow and fill your salad plate with lots of color -- the more color, the higher the phytonutrients to act as antioxidants and protect you from harmful oxidants. First fill your plate with lots of GREEN, which detoxifies, followed by the rest of the colors of the rainbow, and especially RED, which rejuvenates. The deeper the color, the greater is the punch. So choose red pepper vs. green pepper; butternut squash vs. zucchini; red cabbage vs. white; pink grapefruit vs. white; and so on. Think of how your teeth turn color after eating blueberries or how you could die a dress with the red that seeps from beets.

What makes food so colorful? The different color frequencies bestowed by condensed sunlight. Each specific frequency nourishes different energy centers, glands, organs, and the nervous system. So feast on red (tomato), orange (carrot), yellow (squash), green (lettuce), blue (berries), and purple (kale).

Maintain pH Balance

If you want to feel your best, physically and mentally, alkalize your body so it's slightly more alkaline than acidic – an acid environment promotes disease; an alkaline environment prevents it.

To create greater alkalinity:

➢ **Avoid acid foods:**   Reduce your intake of acid-forming foods, like animal-based foods, sugar, and refined flour products, and most nuts except for almonds.

➢ **Eat alkaline:**   Consume about 80 percent of your calories in alkaline-forming foods:

  • **Vegetables,**   especially parsley, red pepper and asparagus

  • **Fruits**, especially lemon and watermelon; plums and prunes are acidic

  • **Whole grains** such as millet, amaranth, brown rice, and buckwheat

  • **Sprouts**

  • **Sea veggies**

  • **Wheatgrass**

  • **Apple cider vinegar** (raw and organic)

➢ **Get Your Minerals:**   Eat foods high in calcium, magnesium, sodium, potassium and iron, the primary alkalizing minerals that your body needs to balance pH and nourish the nervous system.   When lacking, the body draws them from nerve cells to help buffer the blood.   Get them from whole foods like wheatgrass, algae and phyloplankton.

➢ **Do a Morning Flush:**   To set up your pH, drink warm water squeezed with lemon upon awakening, and follow it with green juice or a green smoothie.

➢ **Supplement:**   Take a pH supplement.

If you are overly acidic, it's easy to find out.   In the morning before eating anything, test your urine and saliva with a pH strip (easily available in health food stores).   The color determines your acid/alkaline balance.   Your body is more acidic in the early morning and becomes more alkaline as the day goes by.   If it does not, pay special attention to the above recommendations.

Sitting Down to Eat

➢ **Eat** all meals sitting at a table and in a relaxed atmosphere.

➢ **Eat** slowly and savor the varying textures and varying tastes as you pass the food over your tongue.   Woofing down your food makes you unaware of the sensory pleasures of your food and strains your stomach and intestines, creating indigestion, bloating or cramps.

> **Drink** no more than 4 oz. of liquids with your meals or you will dilute stomach acid and digestive enzymes and not digest your food well. Hydrate 30 minutes before meals.

> **Eat** when you feel relaxed. If you are tired, upset or stressed, your sympathetic nervous system takes over and blood gets shunted away from the stomach to the muscles. This happens to ready you to flee or fight imaginary enemies, like a grouchy child or bossy co-worker.

> **Swallow** liquid! To enhance digestion, chew slowly and at least 40-100 times per mouthful to partially predigest the food in your mouth so you will better digest and assimilate your food.

> **Eat** your heaviest meal early in the day and a light meal for dinner, three to four hours before retiring to bed. In this way, you won't waste sleep time on digestion but maximize down time for restorative cellular cleansing and rebuilding.

Nutritional Support

Enzymes

As we grow older, we lose our ability to produce concentrated digestive enzymes and we do not digest and assimilate our food as well. Consequently, even if we eat raw, organic veggies as our mainstay, we can still be malnourished. *It's not what you eat but what you assimilate!*

To better insure proper digestion, take *digestive* enzymes thirty minutes before a meal to empty the stomach and activate digestion. Take digestive enzymes especially when eating any cooked meal which lacks naturally occurring enzymes. To slow the aging process, take *systemic* enzymes as well as they build up enzymes and destroy free radicals. Take systemic enzymes one hour before or two hours after a meal so the enzymes will absorb quickly into the body to boost the immune system.

ENZYME DEFICIENCY SYMPTOMS	
♦ Bloating	♦ Obesity
♦ Belching	♦ Food sensitivities
♦ Gas	♦ Endocrine disorders
♦ Heartburn	♦ Diabetes
♦ Irritable bowel syndrome	♦ High cholesterol
♦ Cramps	♦ Arthritis
	♦ High stress

Probiotics

Though we've been taught that bacteria are bad, in fact, we need "good" bacteria in our intestinal tract for healthy digestion and to consume bad bacteria and other invaders.

In the healthy gut, over 100 trillion microorganisms from some 400 different species flourish and act as your immune system's first defense against disease, as well as helping to prevent gastrointestinal problems such as irritable bowel syndrome, lactose intolerance, food sensitivities and Candida overgrowth--all major anxiety mimickers.

Unfortunately, if you eat much meat and bad fat, suffer constipation, and live a stressful life, or smoke cigarettes and drink alcohol, your gut likely contains more harmful, putrefying bacteria than the necessary good bacteria. This imbalance weakens your immune system and encourages chronic degenerative disease. The imbalance will be even more extreme if you over-take antibiotics which indiscriminately destroy both bad and good bacteria. Taken over the long-run, antibiotics, like the commonly long-term use of tetracycline for acne, create virulent, mutant strains of harmful microorganisms that run rampant inside the body.

Fortunately, you can greatly increase the good bacteria in your gut by taking probiotics. Probiotics naturally occur in certain yogurts, and fermented foods such as veggie sauerkraut, kefir, and kombochu tea, or you can get take probiotic supplements that contain acidophilis, bifidus and other friendly bacteria. HSO, homeostatic soil based organisms are the most powerful.

Supplementing

As toxins release, you need to protect yourself from nutrient deficiency by supplementing. As mentioned earlier, it's best to do so with a whole food nutritional supplement, like blue-green algae and chlorella which provide necessary vitamins and minerals synergistically so your body can best absorb them. In addition to converting toxic waste material into harmless substances, providing free radical protection, and supplying a balanced profile of vitamins, minerals, and essential and non-essential fatty acids, the single-cell blue-green algae appears to rebuild the brain-center and will even, studies show, re-activate the unhealthy cells in Alzheimer's patients.

Blue-green algae also improves mood – highly so! When euphoric, extremely happy and excited, your brain produces an amino acid called phenyl ethylamine (PEA) which boosts dopamine (the 'feel good' hormone). PEA is found in high concentration in blue-green algae.

Blue-Green Algae Power & Children

Several studies with children have shown amazing improvements in behavior, learning, and emotional stability when given blue-green algae. In a study at Harvard's Center for Family Wellness, 142 children given between 0.5 gm and 1 gm of Blue-Green Algae a day for ten weeks got along better with their peers, were less anxious and depressed, argumentative, controlling and demanding, and better able to follow directions and focus. A similar study conducted at The Stillwell Learning Center in Sierra Vista, Arizona showed the children who had the blue-green algae supplements to improve 40% in memory recall, 20% in concentration, and to have better behavior and less illness. They also had reduced levels of toxic levels of aluminum, correlated with learning problems and ADD.

Mineral baths, consisting of sodium, potassium, and magnesium, which seep into our bodies through the pores of the skin, also help add important minerals to our bodies.

Quick Review

➢ **Our** modern diet of processed, pasteurized, salted, sugared, colored, artificial, overly cooked and toxic food makes us sick and affects how our brain functions.

➢ **Feed** your brain by eating organic, healthful vegetables, fruits, grains, nuts, seeds, and legumes, rich in color.

➢ **Enhance** nutrition by soaking and sprouting vegetables, grains, beans, seeds and nuts, along with juicing and blending smoothies.

➢ **Eat** according to the rainbow as each food color contains different phytonutrients.

➢ **Take** digestive enzymes with your meals, probiotics and whole food supplements.

➢ **Practice** healthy eating habits by chewing your food well, eating slowly, not drinking with your meals, eating your heaviest meal for lunch and not eating for three to four hours before going to bed.

Resources

Suggested Books

Diet

• *Diet for a New America*, by John Robbins (H. G. Kramer, 1998).

• *Conscious Eating,* by Gabriel Cousens (North Atlantic Books, 2000).

• *Living Foods for Optimum Health*, by Brian Clement (Three Rivers Press, 1998).

• *The Brain Wellness Plan: Breakthrough Medical, Nutritional and Immune-Boosting Therapies*, by Jay Lombard (Kensington, 1998).

• *The China Study,* by T. Colin Campbell (Benbella books, 2006).

Acid/Alkaline Balance

• *The pH Miracle: Balance Your Diet, Reclaim Your Health* by Robert O. Young (Warner Wellness, 2003).

Herbs
- *Herbal Prescriptions for Health and Healing* by DJ Brown (Prima, 2000).
Oxygenated Supplements
- *Flood Your Body with Oxygen*, by Ed McCabe (Energy Publications, 2002).
- *Cellfood* by David S. Dyer (Feedback Books 2000)
Magnesium
- *Natural Calm* by Peter Gillham

Products

3Hp Blender
- Blendtec
- Vita-Mix
Algae/Phyloplankton
- E3Live/Brain On
- FrequenSea
- Umac-Core Marine Phytoplankton
Other
- Betaine HCL
- Phpure.com
- Adya Clarity

Websites:

Raw Food Lifestyle
- Hippocratesinst.org
- Therawfoodworld.com
Sprouting Chart
- Livingfoods.com
- Veggiewave.com

13

★

Toxic Gut, Toxic Brain

With every inhale and exhale, every drop of sweat emitted from our pores, every ounce of waste released from our bladders and bowels, our body is detoxifying to keep us healthy. This job gets harder every day: our modern lifestyle confronts us with toxins unparalleled in human history.

Toxicity from drugs, junk food diets, smoking, drinking, yeasts and parasites, environmental poisons, and electromagnetic radiation accumulate dangerously in our system daily. The liver, lymph, kidneys, skin, and other detoxifying organs must work overtime to process the daily assault. If your system detoxifies poorly or if your lifestyle overly exposes you to toxins, eventually all your organs may become toxic to some extent, including the brain, and psychiatric symptoms emerge. Anxiety, nervousness, insomnia, anorexia, dizziness, moodiness, depression, fatigue, brain fog, confusion, and disorientation – all could be your body crying out that it is too congested for your brain to function efficiently.

If this information resonates with you, view your symptoms as a wake up call begging you to cleanse your body of years of accumulated sludge. If you do, numerous studies document remarkable changes, physically and mentally, including less anxiety, greater energy, clearer thinking, and more upbeat mood.

How Toxic Are You?

To get started, gauge your level of toxicity by checking off the symptoms below that apply to you.

SYMPTOMS OF TOXICITY

PHYSICAL

Digestive
__Indigestion; bloating
__Constipation; nausea; diarrhea
__Stomach pains/cramps
__Heartburn
__Less than 1 b.m. a day
__Reacting to foods containing MSG
& sulfites (wine, dried fruit,
sodium benzoate preservative)

Urinary
__Burning when urinating
__Strange urinary odor after eating
asparagus

Heart
__Palpitations
__Irregular heartbeat

Nose, Eyes, Mouth, Throat
__Sinus congestion
__Itchy, runny or stuffed nose
__Bad breath
__Allergies
__Frequent colds & infections
__Sinus congestion
__Excess mucous
__Metallic taste
__Irritated eyes
__Coated tongue

Joints & Muscles
__Muscle aches/pains
__Tight or stiff neck

Weight
__Water retention
__Binge eating or drinking
__Food cravings
__Anorexia
__Insomnia

Skin
__Body odor
__Skin rashes
__Acne

Arousability
__Fatigue
__Restlessness
__Fatigue
__Sluggishness
__Hyperactivity

Sensory
__Sensitivity to chemicals,
pollution, cigarette smoke,
perfumes

Other
__Anemia
__High cholesterol
__PMS
__Allergies
__Frequent colds & infections
__Genital itch or discharge

PSYCHOLOGICAL

Feelings
__Anxiety
__Moodiness
__Irritability
__Anger
__Depression
__Apathy

Thinking
__Difficulty concentrating
__Memory lapses
__Brain fog

Behavior
__Anorexia
__Binge eating
__Volatility
__Substance abuse & addiction

The more symptoms you checked off, the more toxic your body and brain and the greater the need to cleanse and detoxify. Here's what's involved.

Cleansing Lifestyle

Cleansing entails on-going detoxifying as well as an occasional deep cleanse to really get down and dirty. On-going detoxifying will happen automatically if you eat whole, organic vegetables and fruits, juice or blend, drink herbal teas, and take blue-green algae, as well as following the suggested protocols in this chapter, such as infra-red saunas, dry skin brushing, and dead sea salt baths. A deep cleanse involves specific cleansing protocols to cleanse the colon and liver. You will do this occasionally when your system starts to regress. If you checked off several symptoms of toxicity listed above and are new to the holistic lifestyle, a deep cleanse is an imperative.

As you will soon learn, if you haven't already, cleansing can be challenging but ... oh so rewarding. Be prepared though. When you begin a cleansing lifestyle, the liver and kidneys release massive amounts of toxins, through elimination, sweat, and lymphatic drainage, and you may initially feel worse. Nausea, vomiting, dizziness, headaches, mucous congestion, weakness, constipation or diarrhea, flu like symptoms, coated tongue, bad breath, skin eruptions, fatigue, insomnia, irritability, and nervousness are common for several days as the body releases toxins. However, few people experience all these symptoms simultaneously. One day you may feel energetic and upbeat, and the next depleted, dizzy and weak. Such discomfort is part of the healing "crisis" and will pass.

The unhealthier your lifestyle, the longer it will take your body to cleanse and you may experience ups and downs for years with decreasing intensity. Generally, though, the first two to five days of a deep cleanse are the roughest. Try to begin your cleansing program when you have a few days at home with limited responsibility.

Give yourself time to adjust to a cleansing lifestyle. A rule of thumb – it takes twenty-one days to break a habit. So as you institute something new like replacing that afternoon cup of coffee with herbal tea, reassure yourself that it might take three weeks or so before your brain switches to "Hmmm. Peppermint tea time!"

Basic Internal Cleansing Program

Detoxifying entails releasing toxins from all the body's detoxification organs.

➤ **Gastrointestinal:** colon, GI tract, liver, gallbladder
➤ **Urinary:** kidneys, bladder, and urethra
➤ **Respiratory:** lungs, bronchial tubes, throat, sinuses, and nose
➤ **Lymphatic:** lymph channels and lymph nodes
➤ **Skin:** sweat and sebaceous glands and tears

Clean the Colon

A cleansing program begins by cleaning out the colon, or large intestine, as a clean and healthy colon is sine qua non for proper digestion.

When your colon works as it was designed, you eat, absorb, and eliminate two to three times daily without strain or effort. In this way, most toxins get expelled via the feces and the rest get transported to the liver where they get transformed to an intermediate, more water soluble substance. Antioxidant nutrients convert harmful free radicals to harmless water and the liver releases the water soluble substance to the kidney which gets excreted as urine. Your system works as it should.

Does yours?

If you've been on the Standard American Diet, it is unlikely. Years of eating highly processed, low enzyme foods weaken and overwork the colon and waste builds up along the colon walls, along with unfriendly bacteria that feed off this waste, like E. coli bacteria and parasite larvae. Toxins and other poisons leak through an unhealthy intestine into the liver where they get incompletely detoxified and the toxins re-circulate in the blood. Ultimately, they get stored in fat, the brain, and the nervous system. Once the bowel is toxic, the whole body follows as toxins leak out and overburden the other detoxifying agents -- the liver, lymph, kidneys, and skin – and the body deteriorates, as does the nervous system and the mind loses clarity.

The message is clear. If you want your body and brain to function as they should, cleanse your colon. It takes some work but the payoff is immense. Basically, you will need to eat a high fiber diet and flush out debris with herbs, enemas and implants, and colonics. Fasting will speed up the process.

Don't Sit – Squat!

While eliminating, sit on the toilet with your feet placed on a stool (see Life-Step by Renew) so you are squatting, as we were designed to do while eliminating. This will ease elimination and prevent or reduce hemorrhoids

---

Eat Plenty Fiber

To quickly move waste out of your body, eat the following:

➢ **Smoothies** made with a 3HP blender (Blend-Tec or Vita-Mix) for the most fiber rich foods you can eat, broken down for easy digestion.
➢ **Beans,** lentils, whole grains, and root vegetables which, like a sponge, absorb water as it goes through the stomach and the small intestine to increase the bulk in waste products.
➢ **Oat** bran fiber and flax seeds to soak up loosened toxins.
➢ **Psyllium** husk and bentonite clay to scour and remove old debris. A caveat. Use these only if you've been on a cleansing diet for a long time and are relatively clean. If your colon contains too much waste, they could further back the colon up.

At the same time, avoid processed grains as much of what is vital for eliminating waste materials from the body has been removed. It's not hard to do. When you desist in eating products made with white flour, for instance, from which the healthy husks were removed for taste, and you eat a slice of white bread, it tastes like glue and feels heavy as it goes down the pipes.

Consider Herbs

Containing powerful cleansing action, herbs are a mainstay for any cleansing program. Here's a sample:

➢ **Red clover** extract to purify the blood.

➢ **Dandelion and artichoke** extract to stimulate healthy bile production. Dandelion root also helps to digest fat.

➢ **Slippery elm bark** and marshmallow root to release toxins in the intestines.

➢ **Peppermint** to help to reduce gas and bloating (think of your restaurant mint).

➢ **Oregano**, thyme, peppermint, and goldenseal root to inhibit further growth of Candida, bacteria, viruses, and fungi.

➢ **Aloe vera**, licorice root, pau d'arco and comfrey root to help clean the colon.

Exercise caution when taking herbs as they can cause you to detoxify too quickly. Drinking herbal tea is generally considered safe but taking other forms of herbs should be done for a limited time. In general, it's best to have a nutritionist or naturopathic doctor prescribe an herbal regimen for you or buy (from your neighborhood health food store or online) an herbal cleansing kit designed to clean, detoxify, and rebuild the colon. In general, the experts recommend that you detoxify the colon slowly, over 2-3 months: the first month is the build-up; the second the full dosage; and the last month a gradual tapering. Oxypowder, Dr. Natura's Colinix, and Rise and Shine are three superior cleansing programs that do this.

Do Enemas/Colonics

Say "enema" and most people cringe. True, they can be initially uncomfortable, but this is because your colon is dirty. When you clean it out, they become relatively easy and you will welcome the lightness and cleaned out feeling.

Follow the enema with an implant, such as wheatgrass or coffee, as this releases toxins from the liver and purifies the colon. Implants involve inserting the liquid into your rectum and holding it for fifteen to twenty minutes or as long as you can. This may sound daunting but they are, with practice, intensely relaxing and the experience meditative.

If all this sounds too repugnant and uncomfortable to fathom, look at it this way. The degree of discomfort you feel doing an enema or implant reflects the degree to which your colon is toxic-- the more uncomfortable, the more you need them.

A more invasive and thorough procedure is colonic irrigation, or colonics. Colonics moves water slowly through the entire length of the colon, softening and detaching accumulated waste matter lining the walls of the intestine. Many find it helpful in clearing out years of accumulated putrefaction. Some holistic practitioners feel colonics are essential to remove the deeply impacted matter that results from a toxic diet; others feel a deep cleansing detoxifying formula makes it unnecessary. If you do choose colonics, use the Woods Gravity Method with a trained therapist as the pressurized machines can back you up further.

How much and how often you should do an enema, implant or get a colonic depends on the condition of your colon and the nature of your cleansing program. When fasting, however, which I talk about next, doing enemas and implants or colonics are essential to expel all the toxins released from the tissues and organs. If not, they may re-circulate in the body.

Fast

Though not a typical practice in Western society, fasting has been practiced and used in most cultures since antiquity to detoxify both body and mind. So calming and rejuvenating is the experience that seasoned fasters look forward to their liquid days, self included. Greats like Edison, Einstein, Gandhi, Roosevelt and others fasted throughout their lives.

Fasting involves taking only liquid—either water or juices—for an extended period of time. In this way, your digestive system can rest and the substantial energy needed for digestion gets used for regeneration of tissues and organs. The result is deep detoxification as your body begins to eliminate disease causing elements like fat cells, arterial cholesterol plaques, mucus, tumors, and stored up worries and emotions.

Fasting benefits:

➢ **Enhanced Mental Health:** Fasting purifies cells all over the body, including those in the brain, and increases blood flow. This results in a more sharpened and focused mind and greater emotional stability.

➢ **Increased Sense of Control:** Fasting is a challenge. But after you've succeeded, you will feel greater self-control over your eating habits and your life.

➢ **Purification:** During a fast, accumulated toxins and dead cells get eliminated from the body and you feel greater energy, vitality and rejuvenation.

➢ **Increased Alkalinity:** If you do a green juice fast, you will alkalize the body and greatly enhance immune system function.

➢ **Addiction Control:** In five to seven days on a fast, you will lose your addiction to food, cigarettes, alcohol and drugs.

➢ **Reduced Allergies:** Fasting will help alleviate or even rid you of allergies as it reduces or eliminates the histamine effect.

➢ **Anti-Aging:** According to Gabriel Cousens in *Conscious Eating* (p. 234), fasting is the ultimate anti-ager. "Aging occurs when we have more cells die than are being built. 'Youthing' happens when more new cells are produced than are dying. After fasting, the experience of 'youthing' abounds. Senses get sharper, food tastes better, there is more energy, meditation is easier, and the communion with the Divine is enhanced."

➢ **Weight Loss:** On a fast, you lose weight. If you follow the fast with eating the healthy diet proposed in the last chapter, you won't gain the weight back. The more you fast, the more you will lose your desire to over-eat or eat fatty, sugary, processed foods and the easier it will be to maintain your weight.

Fasting & Schizophrenia

For the last 50 years, Russia has found therapeutic fasting the most effective treatment for schizophrenia. Since 1972, Dr. Yuri Nikolayev, director of the fasting unit of the Moscow Psychiatric Institute, reported successfully treating over 7000 patients who suffered from various mental disorders, including schizophrenia, with fasting. After 30 years of experience fasting with over 10,000 patients, Nikolayev says, "seventy percent of those [schizophrenia patients] treated by fasting improved so remarkably that they were able to resume an active life" (www.fasting.com).

Though water fasts have been traditionally used for years to rid people of illness, most holistic practitioners today recommend a raw green juice, or watermelon fast. A juice fast is safer, less depleting and more energizing and, in addition to alkalizing the body, the green juice flushes out toxins while supplying enzymes, vitamins, and minerals.

If you are new to fasting, start slowly by doing a one-to-three day fast which most can handle. Once this is less challenging, you can begin seven-to-ten days or more as the longer the fast, the greater the benefits. For best results, do long fasts under supervision as there's more involved than just juicing and doing enemas, including transitioning out of a long fast. Some holistic health spas offer supervised fasts, like Gabriel Cousens' seven-day green juice fast at Tree of Life in Sedona, Arizona.

When and how often should you fast? Typically, experienced fasters do long fasts twice a year in the spring or fall or when they begin to feel not up to par. Some people stay on track by routinely fasting one day a week to rest their digestive systems. If you wish to get into this life affirming habit, choose the day and keep it consistent week to week. Drink only greens drinks, juiced watermelon, herbal tea, and distilled or ionized water. The morning after your fast, do an enema and wheatgrass or coffee implant. To get the most benefit from fasting, check out www.juicefeasting.com.

Pregnant and lactating women, people who are obese, have neurological degenerative diseases or cancer, or are hypoglycemia should not fast or do so only under medical supervision.

Detoxify Heavy Metals

To be healthy and think clearly, you must get the heavy metals that lurk in all of our systems, particularly mercury, out of your body and brain and I will explain how to do this in detail in the next chapter. Don't attempt this though until you have completed your two-to three-month colon cleanse as, when the heavy metals release, they must have an easy passage out the body or they may re-circulate. Also be certain that your colon cleansing protocol significantly reduced parasites and especially Candida as a heavy release of heavy metals from the body may increase an out-of-control parasite load.

Cleanse the Liver

Once your colon is clean, permitting a clean path out of the body of toxic material, it's time to cleanse your liver, the organ responsible for sorting out the bad from the good and sending the toxins to the appropriate organ to exit the body. It's important to establish healthy bowel movements first because when you cleanse the liver, bile and toxins squeeze out of your liver and gallbladder and out through your intestinal tract and if the intestinal tract is clogged, many of the toxins in your liver will back up into your bloodstream and you will feel ill. Cleansing the liver is especially important in modern life as stress, food chemicals, pesticides, environmental toxins, alcohol, caffeine, nicotine, and prescription, over-the-counter, and recreational drugs tax the liver to the max.

LIVER POISONING SUBSTANCES	
◆ Antibiotics & growth hormones used in agriculture ◆ Food additives & preservatives ◆ Heavy metals, pesticides ◆ Electromagnetic fields ◆ Alcohol ◆ Tobacco ◆ Coffee ◆ Hydrogenated fats & fried foods	◆ Fluoride ◆ Pesticides ◆ Excess fat, protein & simple carbohydrates ◆ Overeating ◆ Lack of exercise ◆ Rancid oils, fried or charred foods ◆ Over-the-counter medications such as Tylenol & Advil

Cleansing the liver starts with insuring that your body has the nutrients the liver needs to detoxify and enhance your immune system. Find out from a nutritionally based health care provider your individual needs for different vitamins and minerals as deficiency in nutrients like zinc, calcium, and selenium will prevent the liver from ridding toxins from your body. When this happens, you will become more vulnerable to the environment. Also, eat only organic produce or you will continue to tax the liver.

Cleansing Food & Herbs:		
Fruits:	**Foods containing glutathione:**	**High antioxidant food:**
♦ Grapes	♦ Avocado	♦ Avocado
♦ Pineapples	♦ Asparagus	♦ Beets
♦ Cherries (dark)	♦ Watermelon	♦ Cranberries
♦ Mangoes	♦ Squash	♦ Blueberries
♦ Bananas	♦ Potato	♦ Raspberries
♦ Pears	♦ Spinach	♦ Strawberries
♦ Apples	♦ Parsley	♦ Broccoli
♦ Lemon peel (try zesting)	**Foods containing chlorophyll:**	♦ Cabbage
Vegetables:		♦ Brussel sprouts
♦ Broccoli	♦ Chlorella	♦ Carrots
♦ Collards	♦ Wheat grass juice	♦ Collard greens
♦ Kale		♦ Garlic
♦ Cauliflower	♦ Barley juice	♦ Green tea
♦ Artichokes	♦ Spirulina	♦ Nuts
♦ Asparagus	**Antioxidants like:**	♦ Onions
♦ Celery	♦ Vitamin A	♦ Red peppers
♦ Radish	♦ Vitamin C	♦ Prunes
♦ Beets	♦ Vitamin E	♦ Raisins
♦ Dandelion greens	♦ Beta-carotene	♦ Kiwis
Herbs:	♦ Selenium	♦ Oranges
♦ Rosemary	♦ Glutathione	♦ Seeds
♦ Turmeric	♦ Lycopene	♦ Spinach
	♦ Lipoic acid	♦ Sweet potatoes
	♦ N-acetyl cysteine	♦ Tomatoes
		♦ Watercress
		♦ Wheatgerm

In addition to these foods,

> **Take:**
>   o **Milk thistle** (80% silymarin and formulated in patented process with phosphatidylcholine).
>   o **Red** clover extract

- o **L-Arginine** and L-lysine.
- ➤ **Try Castor Oil:** A castor oil pack helps your liver, lymphatic circulation, and the immune system. Apply castor oil to the liver area (your right side, under your ribs) and cover with a flannel cloth. Rap a piece of plastic over the cloth, and place a hot water bottle over it. Leave it on for an hour.
- ➤ **Drink Flaxseeds:** Put one tablespoon of flaxseeds, preferably golden and organic, into a glass of filtered water and let it sit overnight in the refrigerator. Drink in the morning.

Move Your Fluids

Now that you have some idea on what to do to detoxify your colon and your liver, let's look at how to cleanse your other detoxifying organs:

- **Kidneys,** the "water management" organs that maintain blood alkalinity by filtering out acid wastes;
- **Skin,** the "temperature/humidity controller" of the body;
- **Lungs,** the blood's "air purifiers;"
- **Lymph glands,** the "garbage arteries" of the body that carry the waste from the cells to the final elimination organs.

Hydrate

If you increase urine flow, you increase detoxification. Logically, you do this by drinking a sufficient amount of water. But most people don't and, unknowingly, many are dehydrated. Unfortunately, by the time you *feel* thirsty, you are already dehydrated. At the same time, many people traditionally drink during meals, a bad habit because, as previously noted, doing so dilutes your digestive juices and reduces your ability to properly break down food.

To get hydrated, throughout the day,

Drink:
- ➤ **Filtered** water to equal half your body weight (128 pounds equals 8 glasses of water, or 64 ounces).

➤ **Herbal** teas.
➤ **Juiced** natural diuretics like celery, cucumbers, and watermelon in season (juice with rind).

Eat:
➤ **Raw** veggies as they have a high water content, and especially celery and cucumbers
➤ **Juicy** fruits like grapes and watermelon, a great hydrator.

Sweat It, Slough It

The skin is the largest organ of the body and must be detoxified in a cleansing protocol.

The first way to detoxify the skin is to sweat out toxins. You can do this in several ways:

➤ **Exercise:** Move until you sweat, especially in warm weather.
➤ **Infrared sauna or steam**: Sit and chill out for 15-30 minutes 2-3 times a week. To increase cleansing and detoxifying, throw eucalyptus, tea tree or pine essential oil onto the heat source of a sauna or the steam source in a steam bath, or diffuse the oil.
➤ **Hot bath**: Lie back and relax in a bathtub. Filter the water using salts such as Epsom or Dead Sea salts and baking soda or green clay as these will pull toxins out of the body, and especially heavy metals. Follow the bath with a quick cold shower as this will boost your immune system.

Second, exfoliate the skin. Use a vegetable fiber brush, using circular and long strokes towards your navel. Brush for three to five minutes before taking your daily shower. This will slough off dead skin cells, stimulate acupressure points, activate lymphatic drainage, and keep your skin soft and healthy. Getting a massage or bodywork are also great ways to stimulate your skin, release toxins and to relax you.

Breathe It Out

Stressed out, rushed, our world speeded up, many of us have lost the art of deep breathing. This is a problem. If the breath isn't deep, it doesn't reach completely into the diaphragm and the toxins in the bloodstream don't get expelled in the outgoing breath. Some go to the brain and you don't think clearly. This is why deep breathing is paramount to good mental health and a necessary part of detoxification.

To deepen breathing, see the breathing exercises outlined in chapter seven. Also, try Kundalini yoga which focuses on the breath, and consider using the chi machine (the original Sun Ancon) which both oxygenates the body and enhances lung functioning.

Boost Lymphatic Drainage

Most of us become aware of our lymph nodes because they are swollen. In fact, the lymphatic system, consisting of a network of vessels and ducts that move fluid throughout the body, is a crucial detoxifying system in our body as it is responsible for bringing nutrients to as well as wastes away from cells. As the lymphatic system does not have its own pumping mechanism, external means that encourage lymphatic drainage help the body produce a free-flowing lymphatic system.

Here are some ways to encourage lymphatic drainage.
- **Exercise** (especially jumping on the rebounder)
- **Lymphatic** massage
- **Clay bath**
- **Chi** machine
- **Herbs**--red clover, astragalus, echinacea, goldenseal, wild indigo root and burdock
- **Skin** brushing – see above

Get out in the Sun

The sun has gotten a bad rap. In addition to the health benefits of Vitamin D3 that the sun provides, it is the biggest killer of toxins, the most powerful immune system builder and, as sunbathers know, a potent anti-depressant.

But is it safe to *be* out in the sun's rays? The experts believe it is if we use caution and common sense to avoid getting burned. To get sufficient vitamin D, we should expose our skin for about 20 to 30 minutes a day, preferably before 10 a.m. and after 4 p.m. Don't wear sun block as it will not only block out the bad UV rays but the good, healing rays as well. If you are very fair, cover your skin with clothing and wear a wide-brimmed hat.

On a skin-deep level, the more we are able to absorb solar electrons the less sunburn and, theoretically, the less our risk for skin cancer. Perhaps the two highest solar electron-rich foods and foods able to absorb solar electrons are *spirulina* and *flaxseed* in various forms, including flaxseed oil. If you cannot get sufficient sunlight, take Vitamin D3 (see **www.mercola.com** for a vitamin D3 spray).

Move

In the sedentary society in which we live, we approach exercise as a choice. It's not. We were designed to move. Not doing so goes against human nature and causes our 700 muscles atrophy. When this happens, moving takes effort, we become arthritic and live in pain, we don't digest our food as well, our metabolism slows and we gain weight, lymphatic drainage suffers and our bodies don't detoxify well. Further, we are more prone to anxiety and depression.

Exercise Benefits	

◆ Alleviates anxiety & depression
◆ Boosts energy
◆ Increases:
  ○ Blood flow
  ○ Energy reserves
  ○ Oxygen
  ○ Well being
◆ Helps body detoxify
◆ Forces minerals into bones
	◆ Enhances skin tone
	◆ Oxygenates brain, enhancing clear thinking
	◆ Improves digestive function by 75%
	◆ Stimulates lymphatic flow
	◆ Supports immune function
	◆ Raises metabolism
	◆ Improves sleep
	◆ Reduces stress

In chapter three, I discuss the many ill effects of taking anti-depressant medication and I list many natural herbs and amino acids you can take instead. Exercise is also part of nature's pharmacy. Exercise boosts serotonin level, the neurotransmitter responsible for mood control and the fear factor: worry, anxiety, phobias, and panic all reflect low serotonin levels. During exercise, tryptophan, the amino acid your brain uses to make serotonin, more easily penetrates the blood-brain barrier and quickly converts into 5-HTP and then serotonin, increasing serotonin levels. Serotonin boosts as well by the increased oxygen intake from exercising. These processes help explain why exercise is, as several studies attest, as strong an anti-depressant as Prozac and others if not stronger.

There is a caveat. Exercise elevates blood lactic acid level and, in the panic attack sufferer, will evoke a severe panic attack as they are sensitive to lactate. According to Michael Murray, ND and author of *Encyclopedia of Natural Medicine*, one can reduce lactate levels with the following steps:

- Avoid alcohol, caffeine and sugar
- Eat foods high in B-vitamins niacin, pyridoxine, and thiamin
- Get sufficient calcium and magnesium
- Avoid food allergens

Exercise Uses
◆ **Flexibility:** yoga or Pilates
◆ **Strength:** weight lifting or anything that heavily uses your muscles like mountain climbing or biking, surfing, skiing and rock climbing
◆ **Endurance:** swimming, bicycling, running, or walking (constantly overcoming gravity strengthens muscle & skeletal system)
◆ **Lymphatic drainage:** Rebounding
◆ **Oxygenation:** Qigong; tai chi

So why do so many people avoid exercise? There are many reasons, from lack of time, to pain from exercising as when you have fibromyaligia (see chapter five), dizziness if you have balance issues (see chapter ten), a stress reaction from lactic acid in the panic prone (see introduction), weak muscles from structural misalignment (see chapter eight), and lack of strength because your body is depleted (see chapter twelve).

Another frequently overlooked reason is lack of coordination that made you often fail in sports and therefore evokes negative emotions. Low muscle tone and lack of firm musculature makes you clumsy and, as moving feels effortful, you seek ways to *not* move your body (see chapter nine). Hand in hand with low muscle tone and dislike of exercise is a low metabolism and it's hard to lose weight, and, overweight and unmotivated to get your body going, especially in the morning, you feel easily depressed. Unfortunately, this pattern self-perpetuates if you don't exercise because you need muscles to raise your metabolism and to give you the body awareness to make exercising pleasurable. In other words, the only solution is ... dreaded exercise.

How do you make moving pleasurable so it doesn't feel a chore? The answer is to find movement that gives you satisfaction and there *is* something for most everyone, from lifting weights, to running, to swimming. If nothing else, most everyone can take a stroll out in nature to unwind, especially after meals. Take deep breaths as you amble along and you will increase oxygenation and therefore detoxification, and enhance relaxation. To increase input into the proprioceptors and therefore body awareness, walk on an uneven surface. For full exercise benefit, always work up a sweat.

If exercise continues to feel effortful, persevere because *you must*. Keep telling yourself that, by following the holistic lifestyle outlined in this book, you will transcend pain, exhaustion, depression, anxiety, poor motivation, discouragement and, for some, a frustrating tendency to gain weight easily.

Supplement

As toxins release, you lose nutrition and may become deficient. Proper supplementation, and especially during a cleansing protocol will help avert this. Don't take individual synthetic vitamins, whose value is questionable but rather whole food nutritional supplements, live blue-green algae (E3Live or BSP (Biosuperfood), phyloplankton (Frequensea), along with other algae like spirulina and chlorella (see the next chapter). Containing the full range of vitamins and minerals your body requires in a quick and easy to assimilate form, these amazing sea treasures are an elixir for optimal health. For additional minerals, take a bath with Epsom salts and baking soda, Dead Sea salts or add Adya Clarity to your water. You may also wish to add more magnesium to your body with a popular product called *Calm*.

Basic Detoxifying Tips:

- ➤ **Eat** nutritious, raw, organic vegetables and fruits along with detoxifying minerals and herbs.
- ➤ **Avoid** meat, sugar, dairy, and wheat.
- ➤ **Do** occasional colon and liver cleansing and, if you wish fasts and enemas/colonics.
- ➤ **Drink** enough pure water to keep your body hydrated.
- ➤ **Remove** silver amalgams from your mouth.
- ➤ **Sweat** out poisons through exercise, saunas, steambaths and so forth.
- ➤ **Oxygenate** your body with exercise, the chi machine and deep breathing.
- ➤ **Encourage** lymphatic drainage with exercise, especially the rebounder, massage and the chi machine.
- ➤ **Rid** your body of problems that inhibit digestion and cause malnutrition like *Candida* overgrowth and food sensitivities.
- ➤ **Take** enzymes with your meals to enhance digestion, and probiotics to insure healthy flora.
- ➤ **Supplement** with whole foods like algae and phyloplankton.
- ➤ **Get** out in the sun.

To enjoy a healthy, vibrant life, we need to not only detoxify the bad stuff out but to prevent toxins from entering our bodies. The next two chapters will cover these topics.

Quick Review

- ➤ **Toxicity** from drugs, junk food diets, smoking, drinking, yeasts and parasites, environmental poisons, and electromagnetic radiation are accumulating dangerously in our systems. Eventually, our entire body becomes toxic as the liver, lymph, kidneys, skin, and other organs involved in detoxification become overwhelmed. Inevitably these toxins hit the brain and psychiatric symptoms, like anxiety, emerge.

- ➤ **Detoxifying** your body will help alleviate the toxicity that creates or contributes to irritability, stress, nervousness, anxiety or panic, and anxiety mimickers, such as hypoglycemia, thyroiditis and chronic fatigue.

- ➤ **Detoxifying** entails different levels. Some things should become part of your lifestyle, like eating foods with the most nutritional value, and avoiding toxic exposure in your food, air, water and environment. As you get deeper into cleansing, you will want a more rigorous protocol to purify the body, such as fasting, enemas, and colonics.

- ➤ **The** first two to three days of detoxifying constitute a healing crisis and most people feel worse. Nausea, vomiting, dizziness, headaches, mucous congestion, weakness, constipation or diarrhea, flu like symptoms, coated tongue, bad breath, skin eruptions, fatigue, insomnia, irritability, and nervousness are common. These symptoms will pass.

- ➤ **Cleaning** out your colon is a major part of any detoxifying program and requires eating a high fiber diet, and flushing it out with herbs, enemas and enema implants. Fasting is helpful.

- ➤ **As** the body's main detoxification factory, it's important to cleanse the liver and to clean out the kidneys, skin, lungs and lymph system. We can do this by drinking plenty of water to stay hydrated, encouraging lymphatic drainage through exercise and herbs, sweating out toxins as well as brushing our skin, and breathing deeply.

Resources

Suggested Books

Colon Health
- *Colon Health* by Norman Walker (Norwalk Press, 1979).
- *Tissue Cleaning Through Bowel Management* by Bernard Jensen (Avery, 1998).

Fasting
- *Fasting and Eating for Health : A Medical Doctor's Program for Conquering Disease* by Joel Fuhrman, Neal D. Barnard (St. Martin's Griffin, 1998).

Herbs
- *Herbal Prescriptions for Health and Healing* by DJ Brown (Prima, 2000).

Websites:

jonbarron.org/baseline-health-program

14

*

Toxic Environment, Toxic Brain

Sprinkled throughout the writings of Edgar Allen Poe are references to anxiety, panic, and hypersensitivity. Note these from *The Fall of the House of Usher* (1839):

➢ *"Constant nervous agitation"*
➢ *"Suffered much from a morbid acuteness of the senses"*
➢ *"Insipid food was alone endurable"*
➢ *"Could wear only garments of certain texture"*
➢ *"Odors of all flowers were oppressive"*
➢ *"Eyes were tortured by even a faint light"*
➢ *"Had hysteria in his whole demeanor"*
➢ *"Struggled to reason off the nervousness which had dominion over me"*
➢ *"Overpowered by an intense sentiment of horror, unaccountable yet unendurable"*

Poe appears to have suffered MUSES SYNDROME, a specific kind of toxic poisoning caused by carbon dioxide (CO) poisoning and characterized by multiple chemical sensitivity, acute hypersensitivity to stimuli (sensory defensiveness), anxiety, and panic. Poe was likely poisoned by exposure from gas lighting in 1829, while rooming for a few months with his cousin Edward Mosher in Beltzhoover's Hotel in downtown Baltimore.

In Poe's day, gas inhalation was a common potential hazard. Today the list of hazardous toxins to which we are exposed has increased exponentially: Over 100,000 different chemicals pervade the air and make their way into our bodies, through air, water, and food. Inhaling modern life has become dangerous to our physical, mental and emotional health.

In this chapter, you will learn how to block further invasion of chemical poisons through:

> ➢ *Natural hygiene*   ➢ *Clean air*
> ➢ *Natural cleansers*   ➢ *Clean water*
> ➢ *Natural furnishings*   ➢ *Organic food*
> ➢ *Natural wardrobes*   ➢ *Natural cookware*

Chemical Sensitivity

Living in modern civilization is a living in a chemical cesspool: We spray our foods, fertilize our lawns, paint our walls, carpet our floors, dry-clean our clothes, exterminate our homes, dye our hair, and perfume our bodies. All this fills us with massive amounts of toxic chemicals that get stored in fat and nerve tissue. Added to this are heavy metals and dangerous gases. We breathe in small amounts of lead in the air, absorb mercury from amalgam fillings and contaminated fish, eat aluminum from pans, foil, certain medications, baking powder, table salt, and vanilla powder, inhale cadmium from auto tires spinning on the road and from cigarette smoke, and volatile hydrocarbons from gasoline.

The conventional wisdom is that the levels of chemicals present in water, food, air, dust and soil are too low to pose a health hazard. But are they? A little lead from water, aluminum from antacids, mercury from dental fillings, pesticides from food, formaldehyde from furniture and so on adds up. And while most people's systems appear to detoxify small amounts of chemicals well enough so this chemical cocktail doesn't interfere with ordinary functioning, the constitutionally sensitive or immune-system-compromised get easily overloaded when even small levels of toxic elements enter the bloodstream. Such toxicity upsets brain chemistry and triggers panic or anxiety and other psychiatric conditions.

How wide is the problem of chemical sensitivity? Estimates vary. As many as 37.5 million people report allergic reactions to a multitude of chemicals, along with a myriad of psychological symptoms. This figure may be low. A 1991 survey by the U.S. Environmental Protection Agency found that approximately one third of inhabitants of sealed buildings report chemical sensitivity to one or more common chemicals. That's around 80 million people!

Of those, few will make the connection between feeling anxious or having a panic attack and chemical sensitivity. For instance, many people get edgy while driving home from work which they attribute to job stress and rush hour traffic. In fact, the carbon monoxide fumes attacking you might actually be precipitating your anxiety.

Symptoms

How do you know if your anxiety relates to chemical sensitivity? Your nose knows. If you are chemically sensitive, the odor of some or all of the following substances will be noxious.

♦ Gasoline or diesel fumes	♦ Soaps, detergents
♦ Perfume	♦ Tobacco smoke
♦ New car smells	♦ Chlorine & chlorinated
♦ Dry cleaning, hair spray or other strong odors	water
	♦ Musty odors
♦ New carpeting	♦ Pesticides

As odor goes directly from the nose to the limbic system in the brain, our emotional center, an adverse reaction to a scent immediately triggers a red flag in the brain that shouts "Danger!" Immediately anxious, you flee as you cannot shut out or ignore a noxious odor. Nature designed us this way lest we eat that piece of rotten meat.

Most people with chemical sensitivity have a mild reaction to common toxins and get a headache after smelling perfume, or they sneeze when someone's clothing has been newly washed with detergent. But sometimes people become exposed to dangerous heavy metals or organophosphates that wreak havoc on all the body's systems, including the nervous system and they feel not only physically ill but extremely anxious, panicked, depressed and even psychotic. If you are reading this book, you could be one of those people.

SYMPTOMS OF CHEMICAL SENSITIVITY		
PHYSICAL	**PHYSICAL CONT.**	**PSYCHOLOGICAL**
Autonomic	Head	Feelings
♦ Fast heartbeat	♦ Headaches	♦ Irritability
♦ Low body temperature	♦ Dizziness	♦ Anxiety
	Muscles & Joints	♦ Panic
♦ Sweating	♦ Muscle twitching	♦ Depression
GI System	♦ Poor muscle stamina	Thinking
♦ Nausea		♦ Confusion
♦ Vomiting	♦ Muscle pain	♦ Forgetfulness
♦ Diarrhea or constipation	Sleep/Wake	♦ Poor concentration
	♦ Fatigue	
Skin	Other	Behavior
♦ Red ears or cheeks	♦ Drug intolerance	♦ Hyperactivity
♦ Dark circles under eyes	♦ Numb patches	♦ Stranger anxiety
	♦ Clumsiness	

Poisonous Culprits

Chemicals, chemicals everywhere! Virtually all man-made products contain chemicals that are potentially toxic and unless you live on a pristine island, they are hard to avoid.

The most dangerous to the nervous system fall into two categories: heavy metals and organophosphates.

Heavy Metals

Heavy metals like lead, mercury, arsenic and bismuth can be extremely toxic to the body. Our brain especially is vulnerable to these toxins. High levels of mercury, cadmium, lead, copper, and manganese, for instance, go hand in hand with learning disabilities.

Lead

Today, the average person has 500 times more lead in their bodies than before the industrial revolution. This is of concern. Taken up by red blood cells and gradually transferred to the bones, teeth, and other tissues, lead is stored in and released from bone for up to ten years. Toxic levels damage brain and nervous tissues.

SYMPTOMS OF LEAD POISONING	
PHYSICAL	**PSYCHOLOGICAL**
◆ Nervousness	◆ Headache
◆ Irritability	◆ Abdominal cramps
◆ Depression	◆ Fatigue
◆ Mania	◆ Anemia
◆ Delirium	◆ Pins-and-needles
◆ Hallucinations	sensations in hands & feet
◆ Delusions	◆ Paralysis

How does lead get into your system? If you drink tap water, lead and other heavy metals leach into your body from pipes and water mains. Lead can also seep into food kept too long in lead-containing pots or leak out through the glaze of some imported pottery that, if used to serve food, can result in toxic levels if ingested. If your home was built before 1978, there's probably lead paint on the walls. In severe cases in children, brain damage may occur and leave the child blind, epileptic, mentally retarded or with cerebral palsy.

Mercury

Do you recall ever dropping a thermometer and trying to pick up the mercury with your fingers? If so, you'll probably cringe when you learn how dangerous that actually was.

Mercury is the second most toxic heavy metal in the world and is everywhere and present in all our systems. We inhale mercury vapors from pesticides, fungicides, petroleum products and fluorescent lights, and absorb it from mercury-based skin creams, laxatives, douches, and from vaccines preserved with Thimerosal. Do think twice before you get that flu shot! We drink mercury contaminated water and eat mercury-tainted food, especially tuna (remember the ban against canned tuna fish from Japan several years ago), as it is touted as a source of high quality protein and heart-healthy omega-3 fatty acids.

How concerned should we be about mercury exposure? Very. Mercury affects every cell in the body--the medical literature lists over 200 symptoms of mercury poisoning–and causes or contributes to a multitude of illnesses, from cardiovascular to neurological including Alzheimers. And, according to the World Health Organization (WHO), there is no known safe level of mercury that the human body can tolerate.

The Environmental Protection Agency (EPA) lists the following symptoms of mercury poisoning.

◆ Impaired peripheral vision ◆ Disturbances in sensation ("pins and needles" feelings, numbness) usually in hands, feet, sometimes around mouth ◆ Memory loss ◆ Mood swings	◆ Mental disturbance ◆ Uncoordinated movement, such as writing ◆ Impaired speech, hearing, walking ◆ Muscle weakness ◆ Skin rashes

As the brain is one of the first organs affected, initial signs of mercury poisoning are psychiatric, including:

◆ Forgetfulness ◆ Heightened anxiety ◆ Depression ◆ Mood swings ◆ Severe irritability ◆ Fits of Anger	◆ Poor concentration ◆ Personality changes ◆ Fatigue ◆ Xenophobia (fear of strangers)

Mad as a Hatter

Felt hat makers inhaled the hot mercuric nitrate that they used in making the felt, causing mercury poisoning -- hence the origin of the phrase "mad as a hatter."

Many of the medical conditions related to mercury poisoning are common anxiety mimickers. These include autoimmune diseases, like thyroiditis and fibromyalgia, as leaked mercury confuses the immune system into attacking the body's own tissues, and food sensitivities, as the immune system sets up antibodies against certain foods. Many with mercury poisoning also have yeast overgrowth.

Arsenic

Toxic levels of arsenic, a tasteless, odorless metal found naturally in the environment and used in several industries, can result in anxiety, depression, psychosis, and personality changes. To deter pests, arsenic is used in lumber to make outdoor decks, play equipment, and picnic tables and can leach into the soil and groundwater and get on your hands. It's also used in some water supplies.

Bismuth

A major ingredient in skin-lightening creams, and popular stomach medications made in Europe and Australia, bismuth toxicity begins with anxiety symptoms, apathy, depression and delusions. If the condition progresses, it leads to terrifying hallucinations, altered consciousness, and babbling.

Organophosphates

Organophosphates are extremely toxic chemicals that can adversely affect every system in the body, including: the central nervous system to produce psychiatric symptoms; the endocrine system to offset hormonal balance and result in conditions like hyperthyroidism or PMS, which are common anxiety mimickers; and the immune system to produce disease like chronic fatigue and other common anxiety mimickers.

Volatile Substances

Volatile hydrocarbons, as found in glue, paint, gasoline, and nitrous oxide, can cause anxiety, panic, depression, personality changes, and other psychiatric symptoms and in high doses disorientation, confusion and coma.   At special risk are those exposed daily to inhalation of volatile fumes -- painters, refinery workers, and members of airport crews who refuel aircraft, for instance -- as well as people who sniff glue, gasoline, nitrous oxide, and other agents to get high.

Of special note is formaldehyde, a common allergen used extensively in home furnishings, and especially in carpeting. Formaldehyde can produce lethargy, memory lapses, irritability, disorientation, sleep disturbance, and depression, along with chronic headaches, dizziness, menstrual problems, breathing difficulties, chest pains and heart problems.

Products Containing Formaldehyde	
♦ Contemporary furniture, solid wood as well as upholstered ♦ Synthetic carpets ♦ Carpet glue ♦ Drapes ♦ Oil-based paints & resins ♦ Permanent press fabrics	♦ Plastics ♦ Ceiling tiles ♦ Combustion from tobacco smoke, gas stoves, woodstoves, and kerosene space heaters ♦ Clothing & bed linen ♦ Cosmetics & deodorants

Insecticides

Used routinely in crop production, bug-killing chemicals contain organophosphates that inhibit production of an essential brain enzyme and can produce anxiety, irritability, depression, restlessness, drowsiness, and decreased memory and attention span.

CO Poisoning & MUSES Syndrome

Carbon monoxide (CO) is the most common cause of toxic poisonings and deaths in America. As in Edgar Allen Poe's case, it causes Multi-Sensory Sensitivity or **MUSES Syndrome**, marked by a deficiency in the body's ability to absorb oxygen from the blood and characterized by multiple chemical sensitivity and hypersensitivity or sensory defensiveness to light, sound, touch, hot or cold weather (see chapter nine) and (in extreme cases) electromagnetic fields (see chapter 13). It results as well in cognitive deficits such as problems learning, confusion, and memory loss.

MUSES syndrome is easily tested for and treated with 100% oxygen (humidified) via a tight fitting non-rebreather mask. Symptoms usually improve within weeks of daily oxygen therapy (2hours per day), although it usually takes 3 to 4 months of daily therapy until people can stop taking oxygen without their CO symptoms returning. For more information, see mcsrr.org.

After one huge chemical dose or prolonged or recurrent chemical exposure to heavy metals or organophosphates, some people will become not only sensitized or abnormally reactive to the volatile chemical but to many man-made chemicals. To avoid feeling ill, anxious or depressed, they must alter their lives to avoid contact with the multitude of toxins that pervade every inch of modern life. They have multiple chemical sensitivities or MCS.

Multiple Chemical Sensitivity & Gulf War Syndrome

Imagine living side-stepping modern life. Needing to avoid scent used in perfume, aftershave, deodorants, hair sprays, and body lotions, you avoid elevators, buses and other places entailing close contact with people. Needing to avoid formaldehyde, you buy carpeting and furniture without the offending substance, and may need to quickly flee offices or homes laden with the chemical. Needing to avoid solvents, you must strip your paint, cleaning fluids and fabrics of any residue. Such is the fate of the multiply chemically sensitive, an acquired condition affecting the nervous system, and particularly the brain.

How It Happens

Following chemical exposure to a toxic chemical or metal, your defenses against the world slowly depress and in a "spreading phenomenon" you develop multiple chemical sensitivities (sometime referred to as allergies) to chemicals in the environment that most take for granted. Incurring subtle toxic brain damage, you experience physical, mental, and emotional symptoms in response to very low chemical exposure that persists long after initial exposure.

At large risk are those whose occupation entails overexposure to chemicals, like exterminators who may get organic phosphates poisoning or printers who are exposed to toxic photochemicals.

Many who suffer MCS have worked in high-rise "sick" buildings, where many employees in the same building develop symptoms with no apparent cause. The idea of a sick building began in 1976 when a mysterious lung ailment killed twenty-nine people who attended an American Legion convention at the Bellevue-Stratford Hotel in Philadelphia. But it didn't quite hit home until it hit the headquarters of the *Environmental Protection Agency (EPA)*, housed at Waterside Mall in Washington, D.C.. Shortly after remodeling and installing new carpeting in Waterside Mall in 1987, hundreds of employees of EPA began experiencing headaches, fatigue, dizziness, nausea, and respiratory problems. Around seventy-five people were forced to work at home. A survey in 1991 by the EPA found that approximately one third inhabitants of sealed buildings reported sensitivity to one or more chemicals.

Living in a Sterile Cocoon

To avoid omnipresent chemicals in manmade products, some MCS sufferers live isolated within sterile cocoons and, rarely leaving their house, appear agoraphobic. When going out, they wear a mask and, assumed to be fearful of germs, appear obsessive-compulsive. Marcel Proust, Florence Nightingale and William James all complained of vague, unsubstantiated illness that fit the profile of MCS. Proust lived the last twelve years of his life encased in a cork-lined room to protect him from the outside environment and shooed away friends with a hint of fragrance.

MCS Denied

A classic case of throwing out the sick baby with the dirty bath water, MCS is denied by the American Medical Association as a clinical entity. Similarly, Gulf War Syndrome, affecting over 80,000 vets (around 30%) exposed to toxic fumes, pesticides, local microbes, and chemical warfare while fighting in Iraq, and with symptoms virtually identical to MCS, including fatigue, memory loss, poor sleep, mood changes, digestive troubles and rashes, continues to be denied by the Federal Government. As recently as September, 2006 a panel of the National Academy of

Science's Institute of Medicine concluded that Gulf War syndrome *does not exist*. Since both MCS and Gulf War Syndrome cover an array of physical symptoms that do not contain a definitive physiological marker, like a proliferation of white blood cells, and since the dosage for damage is so low, and since people react "neurotically" for years, both syndromes are considered to be "in one's head." MCS is attributed to stress, while Gulf War Syndrome is thought to be post-traumatic stress disorder. Many psychiatrists and psychologists concur, describing many MCS sufferers as fitting the personality profile of someone with a major mental disorder. To them, the answer lies in deprogramming "false beliefs" with cognitive-behavioral therapy.

Such denial of a real illness has further traumatized the thousands of Gulf War survivors with the syndrome. Prominent among them is veteran Brian T. Martin, a major spokesperson for Gulf War syndrome activists. At a 1996 Congressional hearing, Martin described his symptoms as starting in 1991 with "…. blurred vision, shaking and trembling like I was on a caffeine high." His muscles felt weak and his chest pounded.

All in all, Martin has experienced:

◆ Excruciating headaches ◆ Low back pain ◆ Diarrhea ◆ Burning & swelling of feet ◆ Blood in the stool ◆ Burning, swelling, & pain of joints of knees & hands ◆ Mood swings	◆ Insomnia ◆ Getting lost driving ◆ Lumps in thigh, stomach, and rib cage ◆ Tinnitus (ringing in ears) ◆ Debilitating fatigue ◆ Vomiting from perfumes, vapors, other chemicals

Psychiatrist Stephen Barrett and physician Ronald Gots believe Martin's story is implausible and nothing more than anxiety. In their book *Chemical Sensitivity: The Truth about Environmental Illness*, they write:

Blurred vision, shaking, trembling, and pounding of the heart are typical of anxiety attacks ... in which a sudden release of adrenaline ... into the bloodstream causes responses throughout the body. Although Martin probably has some physical problems as well, his countless symptoms do not constitute a syndrome, and most of them could not possibly result from exposure to environmental toxin.

Elaine Showalter, who teaches humanities at Princeton University, has gone further. In her book, *Hystories: Hysterical Epidemics and the Modern Media*, she classifies Gulf War syndrome with other "hysterical epidemics" including alien abductions, satanic ritual abuse, recovered memory, and multiple personality syndrome and cites Brian T. Martin as an example.

Psychological or Neurological?

Why have so many in the medical and psychiatric community pushed the problem of MCS and Gulf War Syndrome under the formaldehyde laden carpet? To begin, there are too many symptoms and these vaguely resemble other conditions. For instance, MCS often overlaps with fibromyalgia and chronic fatigue syndrome, the latter believed caused by a virus, such as Epstein-Barr. And routine blood tests don't show a clinical marker for MCS. Nor do all exposed to the same chemicals become reactive.

Some specific tests do, however, show significant changes in people suffering multiple chemical sensitivities consistent with neurotoxic brain damage, such as the Auditory Evoked Response Potential and SPECT. As for the argument that not all exposed become sick, people react differently to chemical exposure depending on inborn constitution, and history of illness or trauma. Those born with a more fragile nervous and immune system -- the colicky babies who as toddlers clung to their mother's apron string -- are more likely to suffer allergies of any type than their hardier counter types. For instance, when a shy person enters a dusty, unfamiliar room, he's likelier than others to have an allergic reaction.

Such vulnerability may start with poor absorption in the colon. If you were born with a strong enzyme system, a cast iron stomach and the liver of an ox, you can abuse your body by eating junk food, smoking, and abusing drugs and your body will digest the necessary nutrients and your liver will pull the bad stuff out for elimination. You don't appear edgy or sick after the exterminator sprays your house with pesticides. Other people have less enzymes and what you have don't work well and your liver may be inefficient. After your house is sprayed, you start to destabilize and feel anxious, weak, shaky and depressed, sleep poorly and feel sick. You are environmentally susceptible. It's not that other hardier types aren't being affected by the poisons in the environment. Rather, the more vulnerable are the first to smell the perfume from across the room, or natural gas. They are the canary in the coal mine.

Nor is the argument of any illness being "all in your head" valid. There is no split between mind and body. Every physical illness has an emotional component and every felt emotion triggers a physical response.

Autism, Mercury and MCS

Could vulnerability to chemical sensitivity lie in a body poorly able to detoxify chemical poisons? Evidence from the long raging controversy between mercury containing vaccines and autism, a developmental disorder that affects a person's ability to communicate, form relationships and relate to the world, suggests yes.

Autism is rising at an alarming rate. In 1980, autism struck one child out of every 10,000 births in the US. In 2009, autism struck one child out of every 100 births! For years, a controversy has raged over whether the rise may relate in part to vaccinations containing thimerosal, a mercury containing preservative, as some normal infants begin showing autistic characteristics following vaccination. The medical community denies an association. But research that tested hair samples from the first haircuts of children with autism and children without autism argue otherwise. Both studies found children without autism had about twice the level of mercury in their hair as children with autism, an indication that children with autism may be retaining mercury in their bodies.

Dr. Steven Edelson studied and tested the blood and urine of 56 young autistic children. All showed toxic heavy metals in their blood and urine. Fifty-three out of fifty-six showed the presence of one or more toxic chemicals in excess of the adult maximum reference range. Ninety-seven percent demonstrated liver detoxification malfunction. Mercury and lead were the most commonly found heavy metals. In addition, he found:

> ➤ **Aniline** *dyes* from women who dyed their hair during pregnancy with the transfer of these toxic chemicals through the skin;
> ➤ **Styrene** from pregnant women drinking hot liquids from styrofoam cups;
> ➤ **Trichloroethylene** from pregnant women wearing dry cleaned clothes;
> ➤ **Diazinon** from pregnant women coming in contact with fire ant poison;
> ➤ **Other** organic toxins like **benzene** and **xylene,** solvents used in perfumes and body lotions.

Even though thimerosal has not been officially linked to autism, it was removed from some but not all vaccines given to infants in 2001, upon recommendation of a committee of the National Academies of Science. And while this is a first step, the problem is not just vaccines. Children are exposed to mercury in the womb through their mother's blood. In fact, recent studies found blood from the umbilical cords of newborns to have mercury levels 70 percent higher than the mercury levels in their mother's blood! The Environmental Protection Agency recently doubled its estimate of the number of children annually exposed to unsafe levels of mercury in the womb from 320,000 to 630,000. Later exposure in infancy and early childhood through vaccines may simply add to the mercury burden in autistic children or may be enough to trigger the disorder.

Why do most infants tolerate mercury exposure while others appear to get autism? A recent study conducted by Dr. Jill James offers an explanation. It appears that children with regressive autism have a defect in the pathways used by the body to detoxify and excrete heavy metals such as mercury. Existing within the body, the amino acid glutathione (GSH) is the most powerful antioxidant free radical scavenger to help eliminate heavy metals. GSH binds with toxins like mercury to prevent them from damaging structural proteins and inactivating enzymes, enabling the toxins to get excreted via the kidneys and bile. Autistic children may have an impairment of the natural glutathione based detoxification mechanism in their bodies and the metals don't get excreted.

This not only helps explain why some children are more sensitive to environmental toxins, including vaccines and the mercury they contain, it also sheds light on MCS and Gulf War syndrome. Sufferers of these conditions too may have a body that poorly detoxifies and they get easily overloaded with toxins, stretching the available supply of GSH to the limit. This can reduce immune function and increase vulnerability to infection and explain why some people seem to be more sensitive to environmental factors than others.

Diagnosis

If you are chemically sensitive, it's crucial that it be diagnosed -- both to alleviate anxiety and because it poses a major health risk and can lead to MCS.

To start, you need a complete physical and neurological exam from your personal physician, an environmental physician, or a holistic doctor. The latter two will provide more extensive testing that, in addition to a physical exam, and neurological work-up, will include specific blood tests. In addition, they will likely give you a hair-mineral analysis (by taking a small sample of hair) to test for levels of toxic chemicals and metals in the body's tissues, as well as tests for yeast and nutritional level. They may also do a repeated 24-hour urine analysis with an intravenous chelation procedure, a test for creatinine clearance to detect toxicity like heavy metals stored in the kidneys or brain. Based on the results, the physician will outline natural ways to eliminate toxicity from your system.

You should also check out whether you are an under-or overmethylator through a histamine test from your physician (under-methylator, high histamine; overmethylator, low histamine). According to Dr. William Walsh of the Pfeiffer Treatment Center, perfume and other chemical sensitivities appear associated with overmethylation low blood histamine, and elevated norepinephrine that is associated with anxiety and panic. In evaluating around 19,000 persons, including about 1500 with anxiety disorder or panic disorder, Dr. Walsh found that hundreds reported sensitivity to perfumes. Nearly 90 percent of the perfume-sensitive group were overmethylators, and reported multiple chemical and food sensitivities, usually in the absence of seasonal inhalant allergies.

Overmethylators generally respond well to folic acid, and B_3 and B_{12} therapy.

Getting Toxins Out

If you suffer chemical sensitivity, you can do much to improve your condition. In addition to eating correctly, supplementing and detoxifying your body as discussed in the last two chapters, you can remove toxins from your body through chelating, sweating, removing mercury amalgams and other means that we will discuss.

Remove Chemicals

Getting the chemicals out of your system will happen naturally by following the diet in chapter twelve and the detoxifying protocols in chapter thirteen. If you are chemically sensitive, this is paramount as you are likely deficient in nutrients necessary to clear toxins from your system, like zinc, calcium, and selenium and this burdens the liver, the body's main detoxifying organ. As the liver cannot do its job, you become more vulnerable to the environment. Ideally you should find out from a nutritionally based health care provider your individual needs for different vitamins and minerals.

Here are some general guidelines for removing toxic chemicals.

> ➤ **Eat** organic food, and avoid meat, sugar, dairy, and wheat products (see chapter 12).
> ➤ **Get** sufficient quantities of B vitamins, iron, antioxidants like vitamin C, and specific trace minerals, like calcium, magnesium, zinc and selenium.
> ➤ **Take** enzymes with your meals to better digest your food as chemical sensitivity interferes with enzyme production and efficiency.
> ➤ **Skip** the coffee which has traces of pesticides and toxic chemicals used in the growing and extraction processes.
> ➤ **Check** for food related problems like *Candida* overgrowth or food sensitivities which will prevent you from absorbing nutrients properly and cause malnutrition, even if you are eating the right foods (see chapter one).

> **Detoxify** your entire system to help clear toxins from your body (see chapter 13).
> **Avoid** over-the-counter laxatives which contain mercury and, when overused, can create mercury poisoning and mimic heightened anxiety and phobic behavior.

Remove Mercury

To effectively alleviate anxiety and other mental health issues, you must get the mercury and other heavy metals out of your body and brain. Start by assessing your levels of mercury and other heavy metals with a diagnostic test, like a hair analysis, from a holistic physician.

Mercury Poisoning and Zinc

Low levels of zinc indicate possible mercury poisoning as mercury cancels out the zinc in the body, and inactivates the enzymes necessary for digestion.

Get the Silver Out of Your Mouth

Do you have silver amalgam fillings? If so, they may well be contributing to your anxiety. According to the World Health Organization, mercury fillings in your mouth are a prime source of mercury exposure. "Silver" fillings are actually misleading. In truth they are only 35% "silver" and **50% mercury**, 9% tin, 6% copper and have with trace amounts of zinc and mercury that stays in your mouth for many years. Every time you eat, you unknowingly ingest mercury vapor from amalgam tooth fillings from acids in your saliva, the digestive juices in your mouth, and corrosion, and chewing and grinding motions. The vapors go up through your nose and to your brain in areas that don't have a blood-brain barrier, like the hypothalamus, the master controller of the nervous system. Once the amalgam fillings are removed, people commonly report that fatigue, moodiness, panic attacks, irritability, poor memory, confusion, and many other symptoms abate or disappear.

SIGNS & SYMPTOMS OF MERCURY VAPOR EXPOSURE FROM AMALGAM DENTAL FILLINGS

Psychological

- Irritability
- Nervousness
- Fits of Anger
- Memory Loss
- Lack of Attention
- Anxiety
- Depression
- Low Self-Confidence
- Drowsiness
- Shyness/timidity
- Decline of Intellect
- Insomnia
- Poor Self-Control
- Mild Fatigue

Endocrine

- Subnormal Temperature
- Cold Clammy Hands & Feet
- Excessive Perspiration
- Muscle Weakness
- Fatigue
- Hypoxia
- Edema
- Loss of Appetite
- Loss of Weight
- Joint Pain

Neurologic

- Chronic or frequent
- Headaches
- Dizziness
- Ringing or Noises in Ears
- Sensitivity to Sound
- Fine Tremors (Hands, Feet, Eye Lids, Tongue)

Systemic

- Cardiovascular
- Irregular Heart Beat
- Changes in Blood Pressure
- Feeble or Irregular Pulse
- Pain or Pressure in Chest

Immunological

- Allergies
- Asthma
- Rhinitis
- Sinusitis
- Swollen Lymph Nodes in Neck

Oral Cavity Disorders

- Bleeding Gums
- White Patches-Mouth
- Stomatitis
- Bone Loss Around Teeth
- Loosening of Teeth
- Ulcers of Gums-Palate-Tongue
- Excessive Saliva
- Burning of Mouth
- Foul Breath
- Gum Pigmentation
- Metallic Taste

Gastrointestinal

- Abdominal Cramps
- Colitis
- Crohn's disease
- Gastrointestinal Problems
- Diarrhea

Respiratory

- Persistant Cough
- Emphysema
- Shallow or Irregular Breathing

To remove silver amalgam tooth fillings, find a specifically trained holistic mercury-free dentist as your body is exposed to some mercury during the procedure. These dentists employ some or all of the following protocols. The more used the less mercury will enter your system.

➢ **Protective** dam around the tooth worked on

➢ **Special** magnets on the water source sprayed in your mouth

➢ **A mask** to supply fresh oxygen so you don't breathe the fumes

➢ **A special** air system that pulls the mercury fumes out of the air during this procedure

➢ **A mercury** detoxification protocol to be done before, during removal and after. The leading protocol is the 9 step Klinghardt Neurotoxin Elimination Protocol (klinghardt.org).

Supplement

Glutathione Power

Essential to excrete heavy metals and other toxins from your body is glutathione, the body's master antioxidant. A specific blood test can reveal if you are low and need to supplement. If so, don't waste your money on glutathione supplements -- a protein, glutathione is digested in the stomach before reaching the blood stream or tissues of the body. Instead increase glutathione:

With food rich in the antioxidant:

Natural Foods & Herbs to Boost Glutathione Levels	
◆ Wheatgrass ◆ Asparagus ◆ Broccoli ◆ Avocado ◆ Spinach ◆ Raw eggs ◆ Garlic ◆ Cilantro	• Undenatured whey protein (a non-heated product that preserves bioactive amino acids like cysteine) • Curcumin (Turmeric) • Balloon Flower Root ◆ Chlorella

With natural precursors and glutathione supports:

➢ **N-Acetyl-Cysteine (NAC)**–a natural precursor of glutathione clinically proven to boost intracellular production of glutathione

> **Milk Thistle, Silymarin**–a powerful antioxidant that supports the liver by preventing the depletion of glutathione
> **Alpha Lipoic Acid**–a powerful antioxidant and free radical scavenger, ALA increases the levels of intra-cellular glutathione, and boosts brain functioning.

With the glutathione patch made by Lifewave, clinically proven to increase glutathione levels 300% within 24 hours (see resources).

Zeolite Wonder

A naturally occurring mineral formed from the fusion of lava and ocean water, zeolite is an amazing new natural chelater of heavy metals. It does so by a unique, negatively charged, crystalline structure that captures heavy metals, particularly lead, mercury, cadmium, and arsenic, and also pesticides, herbicides, PCBs, and other toxins from the body into a molecular cage that the body excretes.

How well does it do its job?   To find out, natural holistic physician Gabriel Cousens, MD, director of the Tree of Life Rejuvenation Center in Sedona, Arizona conducted a pilot study. The subjects were 55 people who tested positive for a whole set of toxins consisting of 14 to 26 of the common heavy metals, pesticides, and herbicides. They all received 15 drops of Natural Cellular Defense (liquid zeolite) 4x/day combined with a one-week green juice fast. The results are impressive.

> **Eighty eight percent** of the toxins were removed from the liver, breast, and brain, leaving only 12% of the toxins in their systems overall.
> **Four** subjects who continued the green juice fasting with NCD for two weeks experienced a 100% removal rate.
> **Seventeen** of the 18 people who tested positive for depleted uranium (DU), a very serious worldwide radioactive contamination resulting from the use of DU armaments, especially used in Iraq, were DU-free.
> **All** but two of 32 people tested for Teflon and Perfluorooctanoic acid (PFOA), the carcinogenic element of Teflon, became Teflon-free.

Chelate Nutritionally

The following nutrients naturally chelate heavy metals out of your body:

➢ **Garlic** and onions, vitamin C, cilantro or parsley, the chlorophyll in all green vegetables, pectin (found in apples) and alginic acid (found in seaweed).

➢ **Chlorella** tablets contain high levels of sulphur that bind with mercury and aid in pulling it out of the body. A half hour after taking chlorella, eat some cilantro to release the mercury. For more information see the 9 step Klinghardt Neurotoxin Elimination Protocol (klinghardt.org). To buy liquid cilantro, see kitchendoctor.com.

➢ **N-acetyl-cysteine**, and alpha-lipoic acid boost glutathione.

➢ **Vitamins** C, E, B_2 and B_3, iron, beta-carotene and selenium (taken with vitamin E) and specific trace minerals, like calcium, magnesium, zinc and selenium. Calcium, iron, and zinc helps reduce lead absorption. Zinc and calcium act as antagonists to lead and reduce their accumulation in the body. Selenium binds with mercury, cadmium, and arsenic to help destroy dangerous chemicals in the body.

➢ **Lecithin** helps protect the brain from mercury poisoning. Throw lecithin granules into your cereal, and buckwheat sprouts, loaded with lecithin, into your salad.

➢ **Humifulvate**, an extract from Hungarian peat that reduces lead and cadmium levels by binding harmful metals in the intestinal tract, without depleting the body of healthy minerals, such as calcium or magnesium.

➢ **Malic** acid, found in many citrus fruits and apples which decreases aluminum toxicity in the brain.

You can also get chelation therapy from your physician who will apply a protein substance intravenously to help bind heavy metals and drag them out of the body. This is recommended as a last step as there are some risks involved.

Detoxify the Skin

Sweat It Out

A relaxing and enjoyable way to alleviate heavy metals and other toxins from your body is to sweat them out with infrared rays, which penetrate 6-8 inches into the body. Doing so will

➢ **Improve** lymph flow, reducing swelling and inflammation;
➢ **Increase** blood flow;
➢ **Knock** toxins loose from fat cells into the body, and the toxins release through sweating;
➢ **Increase** enzyme activity.

You can do this in a few ways:

➢ **Infrared** sauna (see page 286)
➢ **Infrared** mat or mattress such as the *BioMat*. The *BioMat* combines far infrared light with negative ions, which increase the flow of oxygen to the brain, and amethyst quarts which boosts hormone production. Delivering the highest vibrational resonance deep into all tissues of the human body, the BioMat opens the channels for cellular communication and this leads to DNA repair and total body wellness. The experience is both healing and calming. See resources for more information.

Bathe It Out

An ionic detoxifying footbath efficiently draws heavy metals and other toxins out through the large pores in your feet. Treatments range from 30 minutes to an hour. Make sure you use a high quality system as the results come from the low wattage power that stimulates the cells to release toxins. Drink plenty of filtered water before and after your treatments to aid in the detoxification.

Blocking Toxic Entrance

Now that you know how to rid your body of chemical and heavy metal inside you, you must prevent further intrusion of environmental poison into your body as much as possible. To do so, use natural products on your skin and natural products in your environment.

Watch What Touches Your Skin

Watch anything that touches your skin. Synthetic fabrics, bedding and personal care all contain chemicals that your body will absorb. Replace them with safe, healthy natural ones.

Clothing

➢ **Wear:**
  o 100 percent natural fibers, like linen, cotton, wool, silk, bamboo and hemp, as these fabrics allow your skin to breathe.
  o Organic when possible. Even natural fibers may be produced using chemicals and pesticides, and synthetic dyes for color.
  o Soft tone colors of untreated fabrics or the subtle beauty of natural dyes.
  o Washable clothing materials and wash a garment several times before wearing it.

➢ **Avoid**
  o Polyester clothing and bedding as they coated with formaldehyde to resist wrinkling, and emit positive (bad) ions.
  o Dry cleaning your clothes as the process is one is done with toxic chemicals, primarily perchloroethylene, or tetrachloroethylene. The noxious odors stay on clothes after cleaning and especially if clothes are kept in a plastic bag, which doesn't permit these chemicals to off-gas well. Instead, gently hand-wash and hang-dry.

Bedding

➢ **Sleep** on
  o organic cotton, cotton linen sheets or those made from the eucalyptus. If not, you will be inhaling toxic fumes while you sleep.
  o an organic cotton mattress or futon as it will breathe and pull water from your body, helping repel dust mites, and

keeping your body at a more temperature constant. Shoot for a slatted bed frame that floats on beams as it will allow the mattress to breathe and provide better back support.

o   a buckwheat pillow or other natural materials in lieu of feather or foam.

Personal Care Products

When it comes to cleansing your body, the rule of thumb is: if you wouldn't eat it, don't put it on your skin. What goes onto your skin goes into your body. This is why the patch has become an important delivery system--the medicine goes right into the bloodstream. In Victorian times, some women used arsenic solution to whiten their faces and became sick and even died. The message is clear: Replace synthetic hygiene products with natural ones. They are easily found at health food stores and no more expensive.

Cleansing

➤ **Wash** with vegetable oil soaps made with natural plant extracts and mixed with essential oils which leave your skin aromatic and smooth.

➤ **Use** natural shampoo and conditioners to clean, soften, and strengthen your hair.

➤ **Use** white, unscented facial tissues, toilet paper, and paper towels, which are less irritating on the skin and readily available in supermarkets.

Beautifying

➤ **Use** natural hair spray, deodorant, nail polish, and nail polish remover as commercial products emit toxic fumes.

➤ **Use** natural, environmentally friendly non-toxic, fragrance free or scented cosmetics with natural essential oils as commercial cosmetics contain harmful chemicals.

➤ **Use** a henna to enhance color and texture. Non-toxic hair coloring and dyes are also available.

Home Clean-Up

A crucial step for coping with chemical sensitivity is to vary your lifestyle to reduce or eliminate exposure to irritants, even if it means, for some with MCS, living in a sterile bubble.

Start by touring your house to identify toxic chemicals. Replace them with non-toxic, nonpolluting, sustainable, and renewable natural ones. Everyday, "green" products become more readily available and affordable at health food stores, the internet and even commercial enterprises, like supermarkets which are beginning to carry at least some natural products.

Think Green

From the paint on our walls to the carpets on our floors and the leather on our couches, our homes are replete with toxic materials. When you can, make your home generic by substituting these materials with those that are natural and non-toxic.

Wood and Wood Products

Though the smell of new wood furniture is often pleasant, it's often not safe. Softwoods like pine, spruce, cedar, redwood, and other conifers contain volatile resins that outgas for years (outgassing is the gradual release of gases from a substance). Wood paneling, cedar closets, fireplace wood, and Christmas trees can all produce toxic vapors that cause reactions in sensitive people. Use older, recycled wood or other species.

Products containing formaldehyde emit dangerous vapors. These include medium density fiberboard or particleboard products, such as subflooring, floor decking, paneling, solid-core doors, shelving, and cabinetry, including almost all kitchen cabinets. What can you do?

➤ **Replace** them with solid wood, formaldehyde free medium-density fiberboard (MDF) boards and metal or hardwood cabinets.
➤ **Buy** old wooden furniture that has already outgassed, or buy solid wood, rattan, bamboo or wicker furniture.

➢ **Replace** particleboard or hardwood plywood wall paneling with decorative hardboard, drywall, or plaster.

Paints, Varnishes, Stainers, Removers

The whiff of newly painted walls, the biting scent of turpentine, or the tang of polyurethane paint sealer smell bad for a reason: they are poisons. Replace them with natural substitutes.

➢ **Paint** with colored natural pigments made from plants, minerals, and resin oils or with milk paint.
➢ **Use** commercial paint with low or no VOC (volatile organic compounds), widely available in commercial paint stores.
➢ **Seal** new and restored wood with a nontoxic finish of linseed oil, beeswax, or a natural resin.
➢ **Seal** some of the formaldehyde in kitchen cabinets, particleboard shelving, hardwood plywood paneling, cabinet joints and edges, countertop undersurfaces, and unfinished furniture with a water-based sealer or nitrocellulose-based varnish.
➢ **Use** shellac, a pure resin varnish, as a sealant to paint over chemically treated building materials such as composite or plasterboard as it will seal the fumes. For faux painting, a coat of shellac will stop the surface from absorbing the glaze or color wash, giving you time to form your pattern.
➢ **Clean** paint with pure turpentine with white spirit turpentine, distilled from resinous oil derived from balsa wood or citrus peels.

If you must use synthetic oil-based paints and varnishes, use them sparingly and only in dry warm weather. Open the doors and windows to allow the fumes to escape.

Floor coverings

Get rid of that carpet. Nylon and polyester carpets give off vapors, especially formaldehyde, and insecticides that we breathe in, and are a breeding ground for microorganisms that contribute to allergies and chemical sensitivity. The adhesive used in underlay can also give off vapors. Vinyl and plastic floor coverings also emit vinyl chloride vapors and are environmentally harmful.

Here are some alternative flooring ideas.

➢ **Old** or recycled wood, sealed with a natural varnish or sealant
➢ **Bamboo,** an environmentally sound fast growing grass
➢ **Linoleum,** a natural product, or stone or ceramic tiles
➢ **Naturally** sealed cork, especially where warmth is needed
➢ **Area** carpets made from a natural material like wool, Hessian, seagrass or coir with a natural underlay of cotton, hessian, or linen
➢ **Wool** carpets dyed with Ecolor, a non-toxic, biodegradable dye

Fabrics

Many fabrics contain formaldehyde. And though its presence in each product is small, the cumulative effect of having many items together in an enclosed space could be giving off unsafe fumes.

➢ **Purchase** organic cotton, linen, silk, bamboo or hemp fabrics for your home furnishings. These natural fabrics allow light, air and aroma to pass freely though them and don't contribute to indoor pollution. Rayon, a synthetic fiber made from plant material, is also safe.
➢ **In place** of polyester batting, stuff furniture and cushions with natural horsehair stuffing (if you're not allergic), or cotton bump batting.

Reduce Plastic Use

Whenever possible, replace plastic with a natural material like wood or cork. Plastic contains chemicals that act as endocrine disrupters. Resembling hormones in their chemical structure, endocrine disrupters trick the body into treating them as hormones. This disrupts normal hormonal processes and can cause genetic damage, especially in developing fetuses and children. Animal studies have revealed interference in sexual development as well as hormone-related cancers, leading researchers to speculate that endocrine disrupters may be responsible for early menses in young girls. Especially alarming is the recent finding that water stored in a plastic bottle pulls the plastic into the liquid. One solution is to make your own safe drinking water at home by using a water filter and a water ionizer.

Clean Naturally

If you are like many, you probably use commercial household cleaners unaware of their toxicity and irritability, even danger. Here are a few of the most dangerous and what's in them:

- ➤ **Air Fresheners:** formaldehyde and phenol, which can cause hives, convulsions, circulatory collapse, coma, and even death.
- ➤ **Carpet and Upholstery Shampoos:** perchlorethylene, a known carcinogen that damages the liver, kidneys, and nervous system; ammonium hydroxide, a corrosive that irritates eyes, skin, and respiratory passages.
- ➤ **Dishwasher Detergents:** highly concentrated chlorine, the #1 cause of child poisonings.
- ➤ **Drain Cleaners:** lye which can burn skin and eyes, and the esophagus and stomach if ingested; hydrochloric acid, a corrosive eye and skin irritant that damages kidneys, liver, and digestive tract; tricholoroethane, eye and skin irritant and nervous system depressant.

Substitute these toxic products with safe, natural, non-toxic, fragrance free, environmentally-friendly household cleaners or else you just replace dirt with chemicals. You can find a wide array of these products at health food stores and some supermarkets. Or use time-tested natural cleaning products, like vinegar, baking soda, salt, borax, lemon juice, and reusable steel wool.

Here are some useful natural cleaning tips.
- ➤ **In place of air fresheners, control** odors by cleaning or ventilation, or diffusing essential oils.
- ➤ **Replace** scented laundry products with natural ones and, for scent, add a few drops of essential oil, like lemon and eucalyptus, to the rinsing water during a wash.
- ➤ **Replace** aerosol sprays, which emit chlorinated fluorocarbons and break down the ozone layer around the earth, with a liquid or

dry form of a product and buy products with natural pump action sprays.

➤ **When** drying clothes, leave a window open and when using a dishwasher, wait several hours after the dishwashing cycle has completed to remove the dishes as both clothes dryers and dishwashers emit chlorinated fluorocarbons.

➤ **Never** use lye-based oven cleansers, drain openers and commercial toilet-bowl cleaners.

Cook & Store Wisely

In place of aluminum cookware which can leach aluminum into your system, cook in iron, stainless steel, glass, or porcelain cookware. Store foods in glass containers or cellophane wrap rather than plastic containers.

Use Pest Control Cautiously

Among the most dangerous products that people have inside their homes, both from use and from storage are pesticides include roach spray, bug repellent or a lawn care product. Before purchasing these dangerous products, consider the potentially enormous health consequences to you and your family. What is the best course of action to rid your homes of pesky creatures? Get educated on prevention practices and non-chemical methods; use the least toxic chemicals lastly.

Pay Attention to Air Quality

Modern life is lived largely indoors: even in the best of climates, the average person spends 80% of their time inside, and more than half in their homes. This does not bode well for our health. Air pollutants, some of which are undetectable by odor or color, are two to five times more concentrated inside than in outdoor air, estimates the Environmental Protection Agency, and occasionally even one hundred times more concentrated indoors. Don't despair. Rather, employ the following tactics to reduce this pollution.

Clean Indoor Air with:

Negative Ion and Ozone Generators

"Ozone and negative ions" are unfamiliar terms to the average consumer. It's a good idea to learn about them. Found where the air is most pure and healthy, they are nature's most powerful air-cleansing agents *and* tranquilizers. Think how calm you feel following a thunderstorm, or walking along the ocean shore with its crashing waves, or by a cascading waterfall, dense with negative ions, as moving water ionizes air. Conversely, "positively charged ions" in the air, found in our industrial cities and in enclosed spaces, like our homes and cars, drain us.

Fortunately, you can add ozone and negative ions to your air with ozone and negative ion air cleaners that will alleviate allergens and toxins from the air. Negative charged ions attach to positively charged contaminates and allergens, pull them out of the air and drop them to the ground in clumps where they can't be inhaled. A negative ion air cleaner can effectively remove particles as small as 0.01 microns out of the air. For relatively little cost, you can also introduce negative ions to the air, *and* embellish your living space by lighting up with Himalayan Crystal rock lights. Emitting a calming amber glow, these rock lights produce a low heat that frees the crystal's natural negative ions.

Green Plants

The easiest way to bring nature into your home, relax your body, invigorate your soul, and purify the air is to fill your rooms with live green plants. Houseplants breathe during the day, giving off fresh oxygen and purify the air. You don't need many--although if you're like me, the more the better--as one plant in every 100 square feet of floor space enhances the air you breathe. The best plants to absorb pollutants include: areca palm, Boston fern, spider plant, azalea, dieffenbacia, philodendron, Golden pothos, Crysanthemum, Bamboo plant, corn plant, and draecena.

Aromatherapy

Do you love scents? If so, try detoxifying your air, and at the same time deodorizing it with pure essential oils from plants. When diffused, essential oils release oxygenating molecules with captivating scents as well as negative ions that kill microbes in the air, cleaning and purifying it. Be sure to also add a few drops of lemon or peppermint essential oil to dishwater, the washing machine, or the dishwasher.

As an added benefit, the scents you inhale also balance emotions. When we inhale essential oils, they go straight from the nose to the limbic system, the emotional center in the brain and alter mood. This is why certain scents evoke emotional memories and transport you to an earlier time and place.

Ventilate Well

Your air-conditioning, ventilation systems, humidifiers and heating ducts contain airborne microorganisms, like fungi, bacteria, and molds. You can help contain some of the toxins by ventilating to the outside, maintaining comfortable indoor humidity, and by using porous, breathable natural materials in your home like brick, stone, timber and plaster. Clean out the central air ducts of your air conditioner at least seasonally to limit allergic reactions to molds and other airborne microorganisms.

Stay Out of Your Garage

If you park inside a garage, fumes from car exhausts, which contain potentially lethal amounts of CO, lead, and other pollutants can permeate the whole house. If your garage is not separate from the house, keep doors and windows shut while warming up your car and keep your garage door open long enough to let out any exhaust fumes. Even better, park your car on the outside driveway and use your garage for storage.

Pay Attention to Your Water

Drinking water has become hazardous to our health. For this, we can thank in large part the unleaded gas on which we depend to drive our cars, as it contains heavy metals and other toxic products that get into the air. When it rains, these toxins seep through the ground and contaminate our drinking water. Most city water departments only take out bacteria using chlorine, another chemical, and filter out particles, leaving in the water pesticides, heavy metals, and sometimes formaldehyde. Ninety percent of chemically sensitive people react to contaminants in water. If you are one, you should drink distilled water or that processed with reverse osmosis, and ideally in a glass bottle, not plastic.

To protect against these toxins, drink distilled water or that processed with reverse osmosis. Check out a product called Adya Clarity black mica (see www.therawfoodworld.com). A teaspoon mixed in a gallon of water will filter out the toxic sediments and sink them to the bottom while at once providing you with needed minerals. Use sink and shower filters to reduce your exposure to chlorine through your skin, as many sensitive people react to chlorine. This is particularly important if you suffer *Candida* overgrowth, as chlorine induces yeast growth.

Light Up Nature's Way

Spending most our time indoors, we have become accustomed to artificial means of light, unaware often of their dangers. Incandescent bulbs become hot when turned on and this heat can cause plastics and paints in or around the fittings and shades to vaporize and pollute the air. Older fluorescent lights in your home, usually in a kitchen or bathroom, may be fitted with a starting device known as rapid-start ballasts. These devices contain highly toxic polychlorinated biphenyls (PCBs) that can leak and emit high concentrations of PCBs.

To avoid these ill effects, use full-spectrum light bulbs (see chapter nine) in place of common incandescent bulbs and fluorescent lights. And open your windows to natural sunlight which will destroy many noxious chemicals.

Quick Review

➤ **Over** 100,000 different chemicals pervade the air and make their way into our bodies, through air, water, and food. Though assumed to be in too small amounts to be dangerous to our health, these toxins add up. The constitutionally sensitive or immune-system-compromised get easily overloaded when even small levels of toxic elements enter the bloodstream and this triggers panic or anxiety and other psychiatric conditions.

➤ **Heavy metals,** such as lead and mercury, and organophosphates, like formaldehyde and pesticides, can lead to serious psychiatric symptoms, including anxiety, panic attack, depression, hallucinations, and psychosis.

➤ **The** problem of chemical sensitivity is widespread. And though most people affected will show minor signs of chemically sensitivity, some people, after one large dose of volatile chemicals or heavy metals become sensitive to many manmade chemicals and get physically ill, agitated and anxious from the slightest exposure. Often people with multiple chemical sensitivities are forced to live in sterile cocoons.

➤ **As** there are no specific medical markers for MCS and as many who suffer it also fit a psychiatric profile, both Multiple Chemical Sensitivity and Gulf War Syndrome, which has identical symptoms, are denied by the medical community and considered "all in the head."

➤ **Strong** evidence points to MCS and Gulf War Syndrome as being real, horrifically debilitating illnesses. Sufferers may react more severely than others to chemical exposure because their system poorly detoxifies chemicals.

➤ **Diagnosing** chemical sensitivity requires a physical exam, neurological work-up, and specific blood tests. Some holistic physicians test for heavy metals with a repeated 24-hour urine analysis and hair-mineral analysis.

➤ **Treating** chemical sensitivity requires avoiding exposure to toxic chemicals in the air and water. You must remove them from your home environment, clothing, bedding and personal care products and replace them with natural, non-toxic materials. Ionizers, green plants, and essential oils can help clean the air naturally. You must detoxify the chemicals out of your body through proper nutrition, chelation therapy, sweating it out, as well as removing mercury amalgams, if necessary.

Resources

Suggested Books

- *Toxic Metal Syndrome* by Dr. H. Richard Casdorph and Dr. Morton Walker (Avery, 1994).
- *A Clinician's Guide to Controversial Illnesses: Chronic Fatigue Syndrome, Fibromyalgia, and Multiple Chemical Sensitivities* by Renee R. Taylor, Fred Friedberg & A. Jason Leonard (Professional Resources Exchange, 2001).
- *Allergic to the Twentieth Century* by Peter Radetsky (Little, Brown, 1997).
- *A Mouth Full of Poison: the Truth about Mercury Amalgam Fillings* by Myron Wentz (Medicis, 2004).
- *The Natural House Catalog* by David Pearson (Fireside/Simon & Schuster, 1996).
- *Home Safe Home: Protecting Yourself and Your Family from Everyday Toxics and Harmful Household Products in the Home* by Debra Lynn Dadd (Jeremy P. Tarcher, 1997).
- *Home Enlightenment: Keeping House in the 21st Century* by Annie Berthold-Bond (Rodale, 2005).

Websites

Green Products
Care2.com
Gaiam.com
Alerg.com

MCS Referral & Resources
Mcsrr.org

Mercury Free Dentists
Mercuryfree.com
Iaomt.org

Biomat
bionicwoman.thebiomatcompany.com

Glutathione Patches
Lifewave.com (#699520)

15

★

Invisible Toxic Rays-EMFs

> *Demoniac frenzy, moping melancholy,*
> *And moonstruck madness.*
>   -Milton, Paradise Lost

When Jonathan feels too jumpy to sleep, he looks out the window to check for a full moon. The belief that the moon's trajectory creates *lunacy* has colored our thinking since time immemorial. And though scientific evidence of the moon's influence on our behavior is scant, lunar and solar activity does affect the earth's electromagnetic energy fields. And this reportedly affects our mood. For instance, drops in the earth's magnetic field during various solar and lunar events cause a drop in melatonin, the sleep inducing hormone, and creates insomnia.

We are profoundly skeptical of forces that we cannot see, like electromagnetism. Yet our bodies, like our microwave and TV, run on electricity: the electromagnetic forces that bathe the earth affect us profoundly and alter our mood and health in subtle ways that are hard to put a finger on. Accidents, seizure activity, migraines, circadian rhythm disturbances, alcohol abuse, and even suicide all increase in relation to sudden changes in electromagnetic levels. A week or two following geomagnetic storms, which affect the ions in the air, hospital admission rates for certain psychiatric disorders increase. One study showed that suicide rates doubled on days of falling geomagnetic activity compared to days of rising levels.

Today, the need for balancing the body's energies is greater than ever. The artificial, technology-generated electromagnetic fields that surround us from our EMF-generating devices throw off the body's natural balance and disturb state of mind. Says Dr. Andrew Weil in *Spontaneous Healing*, "Electromagnetic pollution may be the most significant form of pollution human activity has produced in this century, all the more dangerous because it is invisible and insensible."

Dangers of Electromagnetic Fields

EMFs cannot be seen or smelled, leaving many unaware of the ways in which living in a digital society has created harmful energies from electromagnetic radiation. Yet it's there all around us: televisions, computer monitors, cell phones, high tension wires, industrial radar, ordinary sixty-cycle electric current, fluorescent lights, microwave beams, electric blankets, hair dryers, and other electrical appliances all emit radiation.

Too Close for Comfort

The more you use these devices and the closer you are to them, the higher is your exposure to EMFs. TVs and computer monitors emit EMR radiation about three feet to the front and up to six feet to the sides and the rear, the range in which most of us sit or lie near them. This means that we unknowingly soak in about 1.5 millirems of radiation -- equivalent to around three x-rays a year. And unless you have lead walls, radiation penetrates through them, along with ceilings and floors, to other rooms and could conceivably affect sleeping children.

How might this affect behavior? In a study done with rats, the radiation emanating from TV sets fifteen feet from their cages created hyperactivity and aggressiveness, even though the sound was turned off and all visible light from the screen was shielded by a piece of black cardboard. When a lead shield was placed over the black cardboard, the rats behaved normally.

Beyond Safe Limits

Food mixers, hair dryers, and vacuum cleaners emit EMFs 30 to 100 times greater than the suggested safe limit, while the fuse box that connects the outside line with the inside wiring generates large amounts of EMFs on a continual basis.

Even microwaves, generally considered safe, may be emitting a dangerous level of radiation. Though all microwaves are presumed to stay inside the microwave oven, crumbs or grease stains make the seal permeable and a few of the high-speed microwaves almost always spurt out. What does this mean for our mental health?

Microwaving Dangers

Microwaving food or liquids distorts the molecular structure of the food and the human body cannot metabolize these unknown substances and what is absorbed cannot be broken down. In 1992, the Journal of Pediatrics reported that microwaving breast milk to warm it destroyed 98% of its immunoglobulin-A antibodies, needed to strengthen the infant's immune system, and 96% of enzyme activity that inhibits bacterial growth.

Overexposure

Though most radiation has been assumed too low in frequency to harm us, some experts worry that cumulative exposure may give us doses beyond safe. Hours, days, years of using a hair dryer, staring at a TV, typing at the computer, chatting on the cell phone, cooking in a microwave, and sleeping in a bed with an electric outlet behind us create on-going exposure of high levels of EMFs.

This takes its toll in a number of ways that affect the brain and nervous system. According to scientific research, such continuous everyday exposure to electromagnetic frequency zones create a constant source of stress, altering body polarity, and magnifying our body's self-protective fight or flight response. This compounds adrenal loads from all other stressors, physical and emotional, and significantly reduces our ability to effectively cope, leading to fatigue, tension, and illness. Highly disruptive to our nervous system, EMFs also numb or dull our sense perceptions and interfere with normal brain wave activity. And they disrupt neurotransmitters such as dopamine, which helps us focus, experience pleasure, and feel energized, and serotonin, which helps stabilize our moods.

Artificial EMFs interfere with our sleep in a variety of ways. To begin, they offset the body's natural rhythms during sleep. While the voltage of the electric current used in homes in the United States is 60 Hz (cycles per second), the ideal frequencies of the human brain during waking hours range from 8 Hz to 20 Hz and during sleep may drop to 2 Hz. If you have an electric clock radio on your bedside nightstand, only a few feet from your head, as many do, EMFs pounce on your brain and could throw off your sleep patterns.

Such alterations of our body's polarity, neurotransmitters and brain waves are especially detrimental for those who suffer anxiety and panic as the body is already disharmonious. Forces that further throw off the body's rhythms further destabilize you and result in a variety of mental and physical symptoms that probably will not be associated with EMFs.

SYMPTOMS OF EMF POLLUTION	
Feelings	**Behavior**
♦ Anxiety	♦ Alcoholism
♦ Restlessness	♦ Procrastination
♦ Irritability	♦ Eating disorders
	♦ Alcoholism
Thinking	♦ Procrastination
♦ Confusion	♦ Eating disorders
♦ Forgetfulness	
♦ Learning disability	**Physical**
♦ Poor concentration	♦ Headaches
	♦ Weight Gain
Sleep/Wake Regulation	♦ Chronic aches & pains
♦ Insomnia	♦ Reduce coordination
♦ Fatigue	

EMF Sensitivity

Associated with CFS, figromyalgia and autism, EMF sensitivity is a syndrome suffered by a small percentage of the population who has weak immune systems. About half of those with EMF sensitivity also report MCS.

When anywhere near EMFs, sufferers experience headache, fatigue, dizziness, head fog, tinnitus, poor memory, irregular heartbeat, sleep disturbances, eye burning and whole body skin symptoms. As those with MCS must avoid chemical exposure, these people must avoid EMF exposure and they live inside a house lit with candles, appliances, TV and computer and phone turned off. They avoid going out except in pristine nature as they are fearful of bumping into power transmission lines.

EMF hypersensitivity was initially reported with exposure to computer monitors. Sufferers now report symptoms near base stations for mobile and cordless phones, overhead power lines, electrical transformers, and mobile phone handsets.

EMF Protection

Flooded by EMF-producing devices, what can you do to reduce your exposure? Start by measuring EMF levels with a gauss meter. According to the US Environmental Protection Agency, 2.5 milligauss is safe for the surrounding background EMF field. Maintain a reasonable distance from those that are not safe. Even so, short of giving up many modern day appliances and conveniences, including your cell phone, computer, and TV, and moving away from electric power lines or transformer boxes, controlling EMF exposure is hard. You can, however, take some direct measures.

Avoid Exposure

Phones:
➤ **Don't** use a wireless Blue Tooth headset or other cellular phone accessories, Bluetooth adapters that allow you to use your laptop wirelessly, or blue tooth wireless keyboards.
➤ **Do** not use the cell phone in enclosed metal spaces such as vehicles or elevators, where more power is needed to establish connection. Also, the metal enclosure traps the radiation and reflects it back onto the occupants.
➤ **Keep** the cell phone as far from your body as possible as radiation drops dramatically for every inch from your body.
➤ **Prohibit** children from using a cell phone except in an emergency.

Microwave:
➤ **Ideally,** never use a microwave. If you choose do so, exercise precaution:
  o **Keep** it outside the house.
  o **Don't** stand near a microwave while it is operating.

- o **Use** it as briefly as possible to defrost, reheat, or rapidly cook food and never for long cooking.
- ➢ **Never** microwave food in plastic containers or plastic wrap as the microwave radiation can drive plastic molecules into the food.   Microwave using glass, Corning Wear, or ceramic containers, and waxed paper or a paper towel for a cover.

Other Appliances:

- ➢ **Avoid** cordless electronic devices such as electric toothbrushes, cordless phones (especially digital ones) and razors, all of which use magnetic induction to charge the battery. Such devices create large magnetic fields.
- ➢ **Don't** use plug-in electric blow-driers for the hair, electric razors or electric toothbrushes.
- ➢ **Don't** stand in front of the dishwasher while it is operating.

Lights:

- ➢ **Don't** use dimmers or three-way electrical switches as they emit strong EMFs.
- ➢ **Don't** stand under fluorescent lights which emit higher EMFs than incandescent light. Photobiologist John Ott placed geranium plants near the ends of the tubes and they wilted.   When he covered the x-ray emitting cathode ends with lead foil to absorb the suspected x-rays, they flourished.

During Sleep:

- ➢ **Don't** sleep with an electric blanket or heating pad as they expose you to EMFs at high levels (50-100 milligauss) all night long that disturbs sleep and disrupts melatonin production. If you wish warmth during the night, sleep with a biomat or a jade infrared mattress.
- ➢ **Place** electric clock radios at least six feet from your bed as they emit powerful radiation.   Better yet, replace your clock radio with a Zen battery operated one that gently awakens you to a soothing Tibetan bell-like chime.

Other Don'ts:

- ➢ **Don't** take unnecessary x-rays.
- ➢ **Don't** live near power-transmission lines.
- ➢ **Don't** use wireless connections as WiFi is the main contributor to household electro pollution.
- ➢ **Don't** use digital baby alarms.

Take Protective Action

Lighting:
➢ **Replace** fluorescent lights with full spectrum lights. Use an Ott full-spectrum lamp while working at your computer or watching TV.

Cell Phone:
➢ **Purchase** a cell phone with a low SAR (Specific Absorption Rate).

➢ **Use** a protective device on your cell phone.

➢ **Use** your cell phone on speakerphone and a hand free, wired set/head set which uses less radiation than does the cell phone.

➢ **Replace** cordless phones with landline phones.

➢ **Keep** calls short and minimize usage. A call as short as two minutes alters the natural electrical activity of the brain for up to an hour afterwards.

Computer Monitor:
➢ **Sit** 30 inches from your computer monitor and more than three feet away from the TV and don't face it directly. The bigger the screen, the further you should sit.

➢ **Place** a screen over your computer monitor to block glare and electric and magnetic fields.

➢ **Use** a flat screen monitor which emits far less radiation than old standard ones. This applies as well to your TV.

Electronic Devices:
➢ **Unplug** all your electronic devices after using.

Sleeping Safety:
➢ **Sleep** with a Sleepshield, a grounded, steel mesh screen mounted on your bedroom floor and the walls on either side of the bed that, according to the manufacturer, attracts EMFs and then deflects them harmlessly away.

➢ **Turn** off as much electricity as possible when going to sleep. Some appliances, like TVs, continue to draw current even when they are off. If your system permits, turn off all the breakers at night.

Appliance Arrangement:
➢ **Place** microwave, computer, or TV so electromagnetic energy does not pass through walls, exposing others.

Fuse Box:

➤ **Use** a system that attaches at the fuse box and compacts the electrons. This will reduce EMFs from the whole home and also lower your phone bill.

Other Protection:

➤ **Wear** a device to deflect EMFs such as zero point, or Q-Link or use a digital clock (the Clarus Clearwave) that emits an invisible vibration to block electromagnetic fields up to 25,000 square feet (see Resources). Check the internet for the many other extensive EMF protective devices available.

➤ **Arrange** your office and home area to reduce exposure to EMFs from the sides/backs of electric appliances and computers. To avoid creating an EMF field in an adjoining room where others may be, and especially bedrooms, place all major electrical appliances, such as computers, TVs, refrigerators etc against outside walls.

➤ **Wear** plastic eyeglass frames, without wires as metal ones can serve as an antenna to focus the radio and cellular phone waves directly into your brain.

➤ **Use** crystals to harmonize your energetic field.

Crystals and EMF Protection

According to Bojan Schianetz, Australia's health expert (renewyoujourney.com), crystals are powerful tools to harmonize EMFs. Suggestions:

➤ *Place a Unakite or Rose Quartz on or near your television or computer screen.*

➤ *Use Amazonite, Fluorite, Yellow Kunzite, Smoky Quartz or Black Tourmaline to neutralize the radiation of microwaves.*

➤ *If you are working a lot on your computer, wear Amazonite, Fluorite, Herkimer Diamond, Jasper (Brown), Kunzite (Yellow), Lepidolite, Malachite, Smoky Quartz Elestial, Sodalite, Tourmaline (Black) or Turquoise during computer use.*

He cautions not to wear more than two crystals at any one time if you have little experience with their use.

> ➤ **Take** nutritional supplements

- ○ **Antioxidants SOD, catalase, glutathione, and Coq10**: naturally occurring in the body, these antioxidants are shown to decrease from microwave radiation.
- ○ **Melatonin**: a powerful antioxidant noted to prevent DNA breaks in brain cells and kidney damage from cell phones.
- ○ **Zinc**: protects the eye from oxidative damage and helps preserve the levels of antioxidants in the blood.
- ○ **Gingko Biloba**: a powerful antioxidant herb that prevents oxidative damage in the brain, eye and kidney and supports the body's production of SOD, catalase and glutathione.
- ○ **Bilberry extract**: preserves vision and reduces oxidative damage to the eyes.

Quick Review

➢ **Televisions,** computer monitors, cell phones, high tension wires, industrial radar, ordinary sixty-cycle electric current, fluorescent lights, microwave beams, electric blankets, hair dryers, and other electrical appliances all emit electromagnetic radiation.

➢ **Though** most radiation has been assumed too low in frequency to harm us, cumulative exposure may give us doses beyond safe. This creates a constant source of stress, altering body polarity, and magnifying our body's self-protective "fight or flight" response. The result can be a variety of mental and physical symptoms that, because each one could have multiple other triggers, don't get associated with EMF.

➢ **To** protect yourself from EMF pollution, you can take a number of steps.
   1. Measure EMF levels with a gauss meter. According to the US Environmental Protection Agency, 2.5 milligauss is safe for the surrounding background EMF field.
   2. Avoid exposure from electric blankets, clock radios, microwaves, hair dryers and so forth.
   3. Take protective action when working at your computer, watching TV, or talking on your cell phone.
   4. Wear a protective device like a zero point or Q-Link.
   5. Turn off your electricity, and especially while you are sleeping.

Resources

Suggested Books

- *EMF Book: What You Should Know About Electromagnetic Fields, Electromagnetic Radiation & Your Health* by Mark Pinsky (Warner, 1995).
- *Cross Currents: The Promise of Electromedicine, the Perils of Electropollution* by Robert O. Becker (Jeremy P. Tarcher, 1991).

Products

Computer Screens: Safe Technologies Corporation, 1950 NE 208 Terrace, Miami, FL 33179; tel: 800-638-9121 or 305-933-2026.

ZeroPoint Global.com: Fashionable, protective devices such as gemstone necklaces.

Clearwave Professional and Q-Link Pendant: Clarus, 800-4-CLARUS; clarus.com

Sleepshield: Bio Design, P.O. Box 1742, Easley, SC 29642; tel: 864-859-4900.

Electronic Smog Busters: Feng Shui Warehouse, P.O. Box 6689, San Diego, CA 92166; tel: 800-399-1599 or 619-523-2158

EMF Blues.com: Protective devices for your cell phone to your computer.

Conclusion

Being Your Own Detective

Now that you've explored the myriad of conditions that can mimic anxiety and panic, it's now time to put it together. Check off the anxiety mimickers and anxiety symptoms/causes in the next pages that apply to you.

ANXIETY MIMICKERS

*"C"indicates chapter
Write on the line: **Y**-yes; **P**-possibly;

PHYSICAL DISORDERS	Immune system
	__ Allergies – C1
Digestive	__ Chronic fatigue - C5
__Candida overgrowth – *C1	__ Amino acid deficiencies – C1
__Caffeine jitters – C1	__ Enzyme deficiencies – C1
__Food sensitivities – C1	**Metabolic Diseases**
__Leaky gut syndrome – C1	__ Hypocalcemia - C1
__Sugar seesaw – C1	__ Niacin deficiency – C1
Nutrition	__ Cobalamin deficiency – C1
__ Celiac Disease – C1	__Wilson's disease – C1
__ Lactose intolerance – C1	**Infectious Diseases**
__ Acidity – C1	__ Chronic fatigue – C5
__ Vitamin deficiencies – C1	__ Mononucleosis – C2
__ Mineral deficiencies – C1	__ Hepatitis – C2
Endocrine Disorders	__ Lyme disease – C2
__ Thyroid Disorders – C2	__ Strep throat – C2
__ Hyperthyroidism – C2	__ Encephalitis – C2
__ Hashimoto's Thyroiditis – C2	**Cancer**
__ Diabetes mellitus – C2	__ Brain tumor – C2
__ Cushing's syndrome – C2	**Cardiovascular Disorders**
__ Pheochromocytoma – C2	__ Mitral Valve Prolapse – C2
__ Carcinoid syndrome – C2	__ Hypertension – C2
__ Panhypopituitarism – C2	__ Arteriosclerosis – C2
__ Adrenal exhaustion – C2	__ Bacterial Endocarditis – 2
__ Hypoglycemia – C1	__ Cardiac Arrhythmias – C2
Musculoskeletal	__ Tachycardia – C2
__ Fibromyalgia – C5	__ Myocardial Infarction
	Female hormones
	__ PMS – C4
	__ Menopause – C4

CNS DISORDERS

___Post-Concussion
   Syndrome– C6
___ Seizures – C6
___ Brain Tumor – C6
___ Chiari Malformation –
   C6
___ Hyperventilation – C7
___ Cranial misalignment –
   C8
___ Head trauma – C6

DRUG RELATED DISORDERS

___Drug Side Effects – C3
___ Psychiatric – C3
___ Non-psychiatric – C3
___ Over-the-counter drugs
   – C3
___ Drug Withdrawal – C3
   ___ Anti-Depressants
   ___ Benzodiazepines
   ___ Amphetamines
   ___ Narcotics
   ___ Nicotine
   ___ Caffeine

SENSORY PROCESSING DISORDERS

___ Underresponsivity – C9
   ___ Passive/Languid
   ___ Active/Bold
___ Sensory defensiveness – C9
___ Sensory discrimination – C9
___ Sensorimotor issues – C9
___ Balance issues – C10
___ Photosensitivity – C11
___ SAD – C11

ENVIRONMENTAL TOXINS

___ Chemical sensitivity – C12
___ MCS/Gulf War Syndrome –
   C12
___ Mercury poisoning – C12
___ Lead poisoning – C12
___ CO/MUSES syndrome – C12
___ Autism – C12
___ EMF exposure – C13

Anxiety Symptoms/Causes Checklists

Write on the line: 1 – severe; 2 – moderate; 3 – somewhat.

PHYSICAL

SYMPTOMS

__Allergies

__Respiratory problems

  __Short of breath

  __Fast & shallow
    breathing

__GI problems:

  __Diarrhea

  __Constipation

  __Nausea

  __Vomiting

  __Gas

  __Bloat

  __Heartburn

__Weight problems

  __Binge eating or
    drinking

__Food cravings

__Water retention

__Sinus congestion

__Excess mucous

__Body odor

__Chronic fatigue

__Aches and pains

__Headaches, head
pressure, migraines

__Cardiovascular

  __Fast heartbeat

  __Irregular h.b.

  __Palpitations

__Other

CAUSES

__Diet

__Toxicity

__Medications

__Surgery

__Injury

__Illness

__Infection

__Stress

PSYCHOLOGICAL

SYMPTOMS

__Anxiety
__Panic
__Mood problems
  __Depression
  __Mania
__Irritability
__Nervousness
__Tension
__Emotionality
__Aggression

__Violence
__Compulsions
__Obsessions
__Substance Abuse
  __Alcohol
  __Street drugs
__Repeated nightmares
__Depersonalization
__Hallucinations

CAUSES

__Non-empathic parenting
__Dysfunctional family
__Neglect
__Physical abuse
__Sexual abuse
__Sensitive constitution
__Trauma

__Loss
__Disabilities
__Sociocultural influences
__Stress beyond coping
__Family history of mental
  disorder

ENVIRONMENTAL

SYMPTOMS

__Allergies
__Respiratory:
  __Short of breath
  __Fast & shallow
    breathing
__GI problems
  __Diarrhea
  __Constipation
  __Nausea
  __Vomiting
  __Gas

__Bloat
__Heartburn
__Weight problems
  __Binge eating or
    drinking
  __Food cravings
  __Water retention
__Sinus congestion
__Excess mucous
__Body odor
__Chronic fatigue

__Aches and pains
__Headaches, head
  pressure, migraines
__Cardiovascular:

__Fast heartbeat
__Irregular h.b.
__Palpitations
__Other

CAUSES

__Diet
__Toxicity
__Medications
__Surgery
__Injury

__Illness
__Infection
__Stress

SENSORIMOTOR

SYMPTOMS

Sensory

__Overreactive to:
  __Touch
  __Food texture
  __Smell
  __Sound
  __Sight
  __Movement
    __Roller coaster
    __Driving through
      tunnel
    __Flying in plane
    __Escalator

__Underreactive & Seeking:
  __Touch
  __Strong tastes &
    smells
  __Loud sound
  __Visually stimulating
    environments
  __Movement:
    __Roller coaster
    __Swing
    __Trampoline

Motor

__ Can't get body moving
  & easily exhausted
__ Constant motion,
  fidgeting; rocking

__ Clumsy, awkward,
  accident prone
__ Dizzy easily
__ Motion sickness
__ Poor handwriting

Emotions

__ Fearful

__ Shy

__ Feisty
__ Lethargic
__ Wild; fearless

__ Feel different,
     weird, crazy

Behavior

__Avoid eye contact
__Easily frustrated
__Impulsive
__Rigid/non-adaptable
__Obsessive/compulsive
__Demanding

__Short-tempered
__Difficulty in transitions
   or changes
__Disorganized
__Lose things easily
__Get lost easily

Thinking

__Head fog
__Poor focus &
   concentration

__Poor short-term memory
__Confusion
__Disorientation

CAUSES

__Prematurity
__Birth trauma
__Illness

__Head trauma
__Abuse
__Genetic predisposition

Getting a Diagnosis and Treatment

Now that you've identified specific problem areas that could be triggering your anxiety or panic, you need an accurate diagnosis of your symptoms with the appropriate health care professional who will fully explore all possible conditions affecting your *body* first, and then, if appropriate, your *mind*.

If available in your area, check out a *biopsychiatrist,* a psychiatrist who believes that all diagnoses of a mental disorder should begin with ruling out non-psychiatric conditions. This person will begin your evaluation with a thorough medical history, including information on your past and present use of medication, alcohol, and illegal drugs.

Next, he or she will conduct a series of medical, neurological, and endocrinological exams, followed by diagnostic tests. These will determine if a medical condition is triggering your anxiety symptoms such as hyperthryroidism or mitral valve prolapse, or something neurological, such as seizures or post-concussion syndrome.

If you are unable to get an evaluation with a biopsychiatrist, get a thorough physical exam. If nothing shows up on medical tests, and your symptoms appear to fit a profile of a medical condition, like hypoglycemia, insist on further testing for the particular dysfunction and consider a second medical opinion. Standard blood tests often don't detect conditions until they've become serious disease. If nothing shows up it doesn't mean nothing is there!

If you are a woman, be sure and get your hormone levels checked as hormonal fluctuation premenstrually, during pregnancy, and during menopause can trigger anxiety and in some cases panic.

In addition, you will need to check:

- **Diet** if you suffer any symptoms of yeast overgrowth, food sensitivities, sugar imbalance, or vitamin or mineral deficiency (consult a holistic doctor or nutritionist)
- **Musculoskeletal system** if you have poor posture or any symptoms indicating skull misalignment, such as headache, dizziness, and lack of facial synchrony (consult a chiropractor or NCR or biocranial practitioner)
- **Sensory processing** if you have any of the symptoms of sensory processing disorder (consult a pediatric occupational therapist or set up your own sensory diet)
- **Vestibular functioning** if you have poor balance and coordination and have panic attacks and phobias (consult an ENT, an audiologist, or an occupational therapist trained in sensory integration)
- **Breathing** if you hyperventilate and suffer panic attack (consult a holistic physician or body-oriented psychologist)
- **Chemical toxicity** if you are chemically sensitive or have been exposed to environmental toxins (consult a holistic or environmental physician)

If you discover that an anxiety mimicker has been driving your anxiety or panic and treat it, you may not necessarily need psychological intervention unless you find it helpful. If you choose to go the holistic treatment route, practitioners such as a naturopath, a holistic chiropractor or a doctor of Chinese Medicine will routinely look at nutritional factors and exposure to environmental toxins for causes of dis-ease or disease. And they look for and treat energy blockages that, in the new/old science of vibrational medicine (new to the West, old to the East), often account for many of the problems investigated in this book. Though all this unraveling may sound overwhelming, nothing can change until you know what is wrong and what you can about it! You've taken the first step on that journey.

* * * * * * * * *

Index

Z

Made in the USA
San Bernardino, CA
10 October 2017